THE
TECHNIQUES
OF
URBAN
ECONOMIC
ANALYSIS

Edited By
RALPH W. PFOUTS

CHANDLER-DAVIS

PUBLISHING COMPANY

THE TECHNIQUES OF URBAN ECONOMIC ANALYSIS

Copyright 1960, by Chandler-Davis Publishing Company.
Printed in the United States of America by Parkway Press, Inc.

HT321
.P4

Library of Congress Catalog Card Number 59-11409

For all business matters, address communications to Business
Office, Chandler-Davis Publishing Co., Post Office Box 36,
West Trenton, New Jersey.

THE TECHNIQUES OF URBAN ECONOMIC ANALYSIS

TABLE OF CONTENTS

EDITOR'S PROLOGUE

During the inter-war period a theory of urban growth and development that was named the economic base theory arose and was accepted by city planners and administrators, urban geographers, Chamber of Commerce officials and other professional groups interested in urban development. This theory may be characterized briefly by saying that it divides urban economic activity into two categories: exporting industry that brings money into the community from the outside world and non-exporting industries whose goods and services are sold within the community. The exporting industries are referred to as basic industries and the non-exporting industries are called service industries. It is also contended in discussions of the theory that the exporting or basic industries provide the sources of urban growth; they are "city building" industries.

The theory gained impetus during the decade of the thirties through the development of base-service ratios and other techniques for applying the theory to actual urban economics. These techniques paved the way for a large number of base studies in various communities. Consequently the theory appeared to be established both as theory of urban growth and the source of valuable planning techniques.

The acceptance of some theory of urban growth is understandable because planners, administrators and others have a strong need for an explanation of urban growth. Such a theory or explanation is needed by planners and administrators to understand and assimilate the phenomena of urban change that constantly surrounds them. They need a theory to point the way to adequate analysis and cataloguing of economic forces in their communities.

In addition the planner and the administrator need a theory that has predictive or forecasting power. The concept of a plan for the future necessarily implies the existence of a prediction on which the plan was founded. Predictions made without a theoretical basis merely rely on an intuition that may or may not be adequate.

Within the past few years the economic base

theory has come to the attention of a small number of economists who have, so far as I know, unanimously rejected it as a theory of urban growth. These economists agree that, with the possible exception of small communities, the economic base theory is an inadequate explanation of urban development. Their objections center on the flow of goods and services within the community; they argue that the magnitudes of such flows are too great to be ignored, as they are in the economic base theory, in any sizable community. To point up their argument in an extreme case, consider the meaning of the application of the theory to the United States. The theory in this application would argue that the national economy could grow only through increasing exports—that domestic trade is only service industry and is not "nation-building" industry. Clearly the larger the economic region under consideration, the less is the charm of the economic base theory.

In discussions, planners have often suggested that even if the strictures of the dissident economists are accepted, the basic-service concept should be retained as a useful planning device. At first glance this seems to the individual of concillatory temperment to be a reasonable solution to the problem at issue. Admit the economists are right about the theoretical aspects because they will then fall silent and no longer annoy the planners with talk of multipliers, consumption functions, etc. Allow the planners intellectual license to use the basic-service classification because they will then be satisfied with turning out base studies and the economists don't care what the planners do anyway.

But all thoughtful parties to the agreement are likely to have lingering doubts about the seemingly happy compromise. Has the issue really been decided on its merits? If the theory itself is not meaningful then a base study of a community is simply a type of economic inventory with an associated dichotomy (the basic-service classification) that has no special meaning for economic growth. In other words the base study reduces to a listing, and while listings are often necessary, they are not theories or guides to constructive thought.

Similarly, can the basic-service concept be used for prediction if its validity is in doubt? Certainly, it would seem that if one rejects the economic base theory as a theory of urban development one has no right to use it as a fundamental in the direction of urban development.

As a consequence, it seems clear that there is a theoretical issue here that is of primary importance to city planners, municipal administrators, Chamber of Commerce officials and all students of urban subjects. The theoretical issue gains an urgency from the fact of its immediate application to problems of planning and administration. The era of prodigious growth that American cities have experienced in the postwar years adds to the urgency of the need for a theory of urban growth that is valid and workable. Even if the economic base theory is fundamentally correct, a re-thinking of it and a hearing of objections to it or proposed modifications of it seems desirable at a time when a sound theory is crucial.

It is *not* the purpose of this book to decide the issue outlined above; rather, a purpose of the book is to present statements of the economic base theory and statements in support of the economic base theory as well as statements against the economic base theory, but no editorial decision will be handed down.

The dissident economists, who have recently opposed the economic base theory, are not merely destructive; they have an apparatus of thought that they would substitute for the economic base theory. This apparatus is derived from the modern theory of international and inter-regional trade and makes use of economic concepts, such as the multiplier, that have become well established in recent times. In other words the economists' suggestions represent an application of accepted economic theories and constructions to the urban economy.

Up to this time, the greatest and most serious weakness in the economists' case is the absence of a large number of actual studies in which their theories are applied to existing communities. A few such studies have been made and one of the best of these is reprinted in this book. In large part the absence of empirical work can be explained by the fact that relatively few economists have given their attention to urban economics and most of these have done so only within the last few years. Time may remedy the lack of empirical work.

In the field of urban economics, our dissident economists have met another group of economists who are adapting a different branch of economic methodology to urban studies. These latter are the group who apply the input-output or inter-industry methods to urban economics. The input-output approach is not viewed as necessarily conflicting with the economic base theory. In a strict sense this approach does not provide a theory of urban development, but rather a methodology for measuring and examining the structure of the urban economy. Indeed it seems conceivable that input-output methods could be used as planning devices without being accompanied by a theory of urban growth. In any case papers dealing with the input-output methods have been included in the present volume.

The purpose of this book is to present in an organized fashion some of the recent writings on the economics of urban development. As the foregoing remarks indicate, various viewpoints are presented but no *ex cathedra* decisions on the correctness of the viewpoints are offered. Speaking as an economist, rather than as editor of this book, I have my own viewpoint which is recorded below. But in justice to other contributors and to thoughtful presentations, I have strenuously attempted to maintain the necessary intellectual schizophrenia. Perhaps the reader will feel capable of making his own decisions on the various points at issue, but he should be satisfied if he finds that he is better informed and sees the issues more clearly, even if he does not feel capable of deciding the issues.

I. THE ECONOMIC BASE THEORY AND ITS IMPLICATIONS

The basic-service concept emerged shortly after the first world war. Its development to its present status preceeded at an accelerating pace for twenty-five or thirty years. In the first paper in our collection, Richard B. Andrews, a respected scholar, traces the development of the economic base concept.

Richard B. Andrews—Mechanics of the Urban Economic Base: Historical Development of the Base Concept

Mechanics of the Urban Economic Base:
Historical Development of the Base Concept*

In the language of the urban land economist and city planner the term "economic base" has within recent years become a familiar one. There is a fairly general concensus that the economic base refers to those activities of an urban community which export goods and services to points outside the economic confines of the community or which market their goods and services to persons who come from outside the community's economic boundaries. From a trade-flow viewpoint these base enterprises through their export function earn a dollar inflow for the community from the surrounding region, the nation at large, and even from other nations. In yet another sense the base activities can be considered the wage earners of the community family. Without them, or if they decline in earning power, the economic health of the community suffers accordingly.

That economic section of the community which the base directly supports is often referred to as "service activity." Service activities include enterprises whose principal function is that of providing for the needs of persons within the community's economic limits. They are also distinguished from the base in the fact that they are, principally, importers or, if they do not import, do not export their finished goods or services. In a limited sense they can be considered the spenders of the community wages earned by the base activities. Yet they are clearly necessary to the successful operation of the base in that they care for most of the service needs of the base itself and of the base employees. The dependency of service activity upon base activity is evident in the fact that employment and profitability in service activities is highly sensitive to changes in the base, rising and falling with it.

---

* See Acknowledgements

As with nations, one economic objective of the community seems to be either to keep its trade in balance or to obtain a favorable export balance. If a community's trade balance becomes negative for a considerable period or if the exporting functions decline in activity, reallocations of the local economy as between base and service employment ratios are sure to take place and an eventual downward adjustment in total community population is almost certain to result.

Since this base-service-community relationship is, in an economic sense, a relatively obvious one there is no particular point in trying to trace and list its first formal recordings. It is however, of more importance to trace the historical evolution of the thinking and conditions which have tended to formalize and systematize thought around this concept within relatively recent years. It can fairly be said that the most significant stages in the evolution of the idea of the economic base as a theoretical concept have taken place within the past thirty years concurrent with the gradually increasing impetus of development of the city planning movement in this country. Up until the Twenties the city planning movement in the United States was not greatly concerned with economics. However, the late Twenties and, of course, the Thirties witnessed a heavy use of this discipline in the planning process as urbanization increased and the complex, delicate balances of an interdependent economy became apparent. Nor is it by any means coincidental that the development of urban land economics as an independent field and the rise of economics as a tool in city planning went *pari passu* through this period.

The modern history of the development of the economic base concept and the evolution of its techniques of application can be rather briefly told.

One of the most complete early statements of the concept appeared in connection with the planning efforts of New York City in its *Regional Survey of New York and its Environs* published in 1928, and in particular in the monograph put out by

Robert Haig with Roswell C. McCrea as his consultant. In the Survey the statement was made that:

". . . the multiplicity of . . . productive occupations may roughly be divided into those which can be called *primary* . . . manufacturing goods for general use (i.e., not confined to use within the community itself) and those occupations which may be called, *auxiliary,* such as are devoted directly or indirectly to the service and convenience of the people engaged in the primary occupations."[1]

However, the novelty of the idea and the, at that time, slight degree of understanding of its significance can be noted in another passage which states:

"The project of an economic and industrial survey was ambitious in scope and novel in character. No general agreement existed as to the facts which were essential and pertinent for an analysis of the operation of economic forces under conditions of collective action such as those contemplated by a regional plan . . . . It was necessary to break new ground."[2]

Frederick Nussbaum, an historian, writing five years after the publication of the Regional Survey made a simplified yet well expressed statement describing the base and its service complement when he said:

"The principal, constituent elements of the town were those who are able by power or wealth to command a means of subsistence from elsewhere, a king who can tax, a landlord to whom dues are paid, a merchant who makes profits outside the town, a student who is supported by his parents. These are 'town builders'. After them come what we call the 'town fillers', those who serve the needs of the 'town builders': the shoe-

---

[1] Robert M. Haig, *Major Economic Factors in Metropolitan Growth and Arrangement;* Vol. I of *Regional Survey of New York and Environs* (Extract of a letter from Mr. Frederick Law Olmsted to Mr. John M. Glenn dated February 21, 1921) (New York: 1928), p. 43.

[2] *Ibid.,* p. 114.

maker who makes the king's shoes, the jeweler who depends on the purchases of the merchant's wife, the landlady from whom the student rents his room".[3]

The more pragamatic beginnings made by the *Regional Survey* in 1928 were extended to a higher plane of development in the housing market studies made under the Federal Housing Administration in connection with the development and execution of its mortgage risk rating system in the late Thirties. Under the guidance of Ernest M. Fisher, the Division of Economics and Statistics of the FHA employed the talents of economist Homer Hoyt. In the course of his work with the Division, Mr. Hoyt devised a quick survey technique that would reveal the salient facts and relationships of the economy of a community which could, in turn, be converted into an indicator of local housing market demand.[4] It was in 1936 that Hoyt developed the essential outlines of the economic base idea as we now know it. At that time, on the basis of admittedly limited experience and data, he conceived of the basic and service elements of cities as having an employment ratio of 1:1. As Hoyt himself was soon to point out, this ratio actually varied from city to city.

As a result of his work with the FHA accompanied by independent research, Hoyt's thinking on the nature of urban structure and the economic base quickly matured. Consequently, in 1939 Hoyt, in cooperation with Arthur M. Weimer of the University of Indiana, brought out the text *Principles of Urban Real Estate*.[5] Here for the first time in the literature ap-

[3] F. L. Nussbaum, *A History of the Economic Institutions of Modern Europe* (New York: F. S. Crofts & Company, 1933), p. 36.

[4] Federal Housing Administration, *Basic Data on Northern New Jersey Housing Market*, July 1937; *Hartford, Connecticut Housing Market Analysis*, March 1938; *Akron, Ohio Housing Market Analysis*, November 1938; *Indianapolis, Indiana Housing Market Analysis*, August 1939; and Form No. 2096 (Rev. Dec. 15, 1936) *Economic Background Rating Form*.

[5] Arthur M. Weimer and Homer Hoyt, *Principles of Urban Real Estate*, (New York: The Ronald Press Company, 1939).

peared a complete statement of the theory of the economic base. This statement included much material that was new outside of technical reports. For example, it introduced in formal fashion the idea of a mathematical relation between basic employment and service employment. It suggested, though it did not specifically state at that time, a ratio relationship between basic employment and total population. Identification and weighting of various elements of the base was also presented as a mathematical analysis technique. Hoyt considered the economic base idea to be a tool that might be employed in analyzing the economic background of cities with the objective of forecasting the future of the entire city. He applied a four-stage technique in this analytical process which assumed the following outline:

(1) Calculation of total basic employment in the community and, particularly, the amount of basic employment in *each* basic activity. This last was in itself a new and more precise approach inasmuch as, up to that time, cities had been all too loosely characterized as "factory towns," "college towns," "commercial centers," and the like.

(2) Estimation of the proportion of basic employment to service employment. As mentioned above Hoyt assumed this ratio to be 1:1 but later determined that actual calculations and estimates had to be made for individual cities.

(3) Estimation of the future trend in each segment of the base as indicated by analysis of the demand for its product or service locational factors, productive efficiency, etc.

(4) Calculation of total employment and total future population on the basis of future trends in basic employment.

The calculation of total future population was implicit in Hoyt's first formal statement but became explicit in later statements and in applications of the four-stage technique such as those made for the Chicago Plan Commission and the New York Regional Plan Association in 1944.

Just prior to the publication of Weimer and Hoyt's text there appeared two studies which are worthy of note in connection with the evolution of the economic base concept. The first of these, "Oskaloosa (Iowa) versus The United States," was a lengthy report based on a survey made by staff members of *Fortune* Magazine.[6] It adopted the balance-of-trade approach in analyzing a small Iowa county seat. In the process of tracing the dollar volumes of imports and exports it performed an admirable job in distinguishing the community's "growth" and "service" factors. In this connection it also attempted, with some success, the measuring of rents, profits, and other forms of unearned income as a part of the base and of the import-export flow. This report was definitely a pioneering effort in the sense that it applied foreign trade principles to the analysis of an urban economy and in the fact that it threw much light on the nature of the export or basic phase of that type of economy. The practicability of the technique as a general analytical approach, particularly in large urban areas, was and still is open to question.

Also appearing in 1938 was Glenn McLaughlin's *Growth of American Manufacturing Areas.*[7] Whereas McLaughlin did not use terminology that had up to that time been associated with discussions of the economic base he did emphasize relationships within urban economies which were vital to an understanding of the base. For example, he was greatly concerned with the association between changes in metropolitan-area industrial activity and expansion or contraction in local area population. He also invested much analytical effort in an examination of centrifugal and centripetal forces affecting plant location within an area and on the factors which caused the composition of local economies to change in character.

Following the relatively fertile period of thinking on the concept of the economic base which characterized the latter part of

[6] "Oskaloosa versus the United States," *Fortune,* April 1938.

[7] Glenn E. McLaughlin, *Growth of American Manufacturing Areas* (University of Pittsburgh, 1938).

the Thirties there began a period of review, evaluation, and testing in which we still find ourselves. The historical development of the "base" idea as it entered the Forties followed a trend which is, undoubtedly, characteristic of most new lines of thinking. There appeared many, though far from a flood of planning reports and articles which refined the original base concept in its specific aspects and added significantly to the techniques by which the idea might be explored and applied.

It was also true that, after a lapse of more than a decade, local planning agencies began to follow the lead of the Regional Plan Survey and the Federal Housing Administration in applying the base concept directly to the planning process.[8]

The concluding remarks of this survey will not pretend to present a comprehensive bibliography of the studies which relate to thinking on economic base theory and practice but rather will touch upon those highlights from 1940 to 1952 that seem significant.

It should, of course, be mentioned that the FHA and later the National Housing Agency continued into the Forties the previously-mentioned housing market analyses which employed economic base studies as an integral part of their presentation.

An example of the trend toward refinement can be found in Hoyt's more precise presentation of the process of making an economic rating of cities with emphasis on the prospects of future employment.[9] A further refinement of this same variety was introduced by Hoyt into the Regional Plan Association's review study of the economy of the New York Area.[10] In this study a technique was introduced by which it was possible to

---

[8] The Federal Reserve Banks also adopted the technique as a part of their economic analysis and forecasting system.

[9] Homer Hoyt, "Economic Background of Cities," *Journal of Land & Public Utility Economics,* May 1941, pp. 188-195. (This was the first formal statement of base theory to appear in a technical journal).

[10] The Regional Plan Association, Incorporated, *The Economic Status of the New York Metropolitan Region in* 1944 (New York: 1944).

identify which portion of an industry in the community could be considered basic and which service by relating local employment and population proportions to national employment and population data. This report presented many other refinements of an equally important nature. Appearing in the same year (1944), a study of Detroit's economic base made by its plan commission was further proof of the skill with which the idea of the base was being handled and the practicability of applying it to local planning situations.[11]

Further signs of the times appeared in the planning journals one of whose editors commented: "Analysis of the urban economic base is increasingly attracting attention. Actually we are in the beginning stages of development of needed technique . . . ."[12]

Despite the strides that had been taken in the organization of thinking relative to the concept of the urban base and the mechanics of the urban economy generally, one planner was prompted to state that:

"One of the most important but neglected elements of the economy of a community is the functional organization and inter-relationships of the various activities and industries within the area. Exploration of economic linkages and interdependence among the commodity producing industries of the area, among trade and service enterprises and between commodity production, distribution and services would doubtless show many gaps waiting to be filled."[13]

During 1946 much constructive thinking was coming from the Cincinnati City Planning Commission, and, specifically, from

[11] Detroit City Plan Commission, *Economic Base of Detroit* (Detroit, Michigan: 1944).

[12] Editor's note, *Journal of the American Institute of Planners,* Summer 1945, p. 10.

[13] Van Beuren Stanberry, "Planning for the City Secure," *Journal of American Institute of Planners,* Summer 1945, p. 10.

the pen of Victor Roterus. One specialized contribution to this "school" was a correlation technique, a variation of Hoyt's 1944 technique, whereby local employment data are correlated and projected in relation to national employment. These estimates are then translated into local labor force and finally population.[14] The Cincinnati Commission report refined the base identification technique of the New York (1944) report and among a series of general observations pointed out that urban growth (base) employment was not the only impetus to growth of an urban area since "growth is also induced through increasing real incomes."[15]

Through the six-year period 1947-1952, several other studies emerged which tended to document theory, extend technique, and expand application of the concept.[16]

Two particularly interesting applications of base theory were made by Hoyt during this period. One of these centered around a survey made in the Brockton Massachusetts area.[17] In his

---

[14] Victor Roterus, "The Economic Background for Local Planning," *Planning* 1946, Proceedings of the Annual Meeting of the American Society of Planning Officials in New York" May 6-8, 1946, Chicago, 1946, p. 86.

[15] Cincinnati City Planning Commission, *Economy of the Area* (Cincinnati, Ohio: 1946), p. 23.

[16] W. D. Knight, *Subsidization of Industry in Forty Selected Cities in Wisconsin,* 1930-1946, Vol. I, No. 2, Wisconsin Commerce Studies. Bureau of Business Research and Service, School of Commerce, University of Wisconsin, Madison 1947; Homer Hoyt, "Economic and Housing Survey of the Orlando, Florida, Metropolitan Region," *Journal of Land & Public Utility Economics,* May 1947; W. E. Hoadley, Jr. and C. G. Wright, *Employment, Production, and Income in the Chicago Industrial Area* (Research Department, Federal Reserve Bank of Chicago, 1948); Edgar M. Hoover, *The Location of Economic Activity* (New York: McGraw-Hill Book Company, 1948); Federal Reserve Bank, Kansas City, Missouri, *The Economy of Albuquerque,* New Mexico, 1949; Chicago Plan Commission, *Chicago Industrial Development, Recent Trends* (Industrial Study 2, April 1952).

[17] Homer Hoyt, *A Report on the Economic Base of the Brockton, Massachusetts Area* (Brockton, Massachusetts: January 1949).

drafting of this report Hoyt introduced a picturization with supporting tables, of the money flow of the Brockton Study Area. The breakdowns and relationships of income and expenditures were comparable to those made in the Oskaloosa Study of 1938 referred to earlier. Hoyt, however, introduced color indicators showing the effect on total income and expenditures that might be anticipated from a let alone policy as against a policy of planned stimulation of certain portions of the base.

In another survey which was focused on Arlington County, Virginia, Hoyt again employed base technique as a planning tool.[18] This study is notable in the fact that it presents a highly comprehensive and detailed application of the economic base concept and technique to the problem of estimating the amount of land required for each type of land use on the basis of the calculated need for expansion of the industrial space, the requirements for new homes and apartments, etc.

A very recent contribution in the field of technique has been made by Professor John Alexander.[19] He has devised a system of base and service activity identification which works through a questionnaire issued to individual enterprises of the community. Their reported proportions of export activity are then applied (particularly in the case of retail establishments) to their total employment figure in order that it can be broken down into its base and service components.

The revised edition of Weimer and Hoyt's text published in 1948 pretty well caught together the loose ends of thinking on the base of the previous decade and gave the field a consolidated

---

[18] Homer Hoyt Associates, *Economic Survey of the Land Uses of Arlington County ,Virginia* (September 1951).

[19] John W. Alexander, *The Economic Life of Oskhosh, Part I* (Madison: University of Wisconsin, University Extension Division, 1952).

point from which to continue.[20]   However, it was Ratcliff's text
of the following year which performed the long-delayed task
of emphasizing in greater detail the strategic position of the
economic base as the "coloring" factor of an entire urban economy in all its aspects, economic, social, and institutional.[21]

That this sphere of land economics was gaining increasing
recognition as one demanding not only close technical attention but also deep consideration from the standpoint of theory
as well became apparent with the appearance of two papers in
the annual proceedings of the American Economic Association.[22]   Both papers tended to emphasize the broader territorial
aspects of the local economic base and its position in an economic system.   In short, these studies contributed long-needed
perspective to a concept which had been in danger of becoming
entirely too narrow in its scope and which, in all fairness, has
been said to be "artifical" in its tendency to cut urban economies from "context," so to speak, for the purpose of test-tube
analysis.

In conclusion, it seems fitting to point out that, in the case of
urban base theory, we have operated far too long on a set of
ideas which appear valid but which, despite substantial conceptual omissions and difficulties of application, seem to be accepted all too blithely as gospel by many researchers and active

---

[20] Hoyt changed the usage of the term "weighting" in this text.   In the 1939
edition weighting of the elements of the base was accomplished by measuring
the proportion of total employment in the community claimed by the base element then doubling this proportion to account for the service employment total
directly tied to that portion of the base.   However, in the 1948 edition, in line
with procedures developed in the New York study of 1944, he refers to weighting as the process of adjusting the numerical employment order of a group of
base enterprises by the percentage of total payrolls for which each one accounts.

[21] Richard U. Ratcliff, *Urban Land Economics*, (New York: McGraw-Hill
Book Company, Inc., 1949).

[22] Rutledge Vining, "The Region as an Economic Entity and Certain Variations to be Observed in the Study of Systems of Regions," *American Economic
Review*, Papers and Proceedings of the American Economic Association, May
1949, pp. 89-104; and Phillip Neff, "Interregional Cyclical Differentials: Causes,
Measurements, and Significance," pp. 105-119.

city planners. While the tendency of research effort in the past fifteen years has been in the direction of perfecting technique, obtaining more precise statisical data on base elements, and applying theory (and this is as it should be), it seems to this author that concurrent with this activity there must also take place more fundamental thinking on and questioning of the reality and utility of base theory as presently conceived.

In the field of technique itself there exist serious blind spots. For example, there does not seem to be any accepted technique of delimiting the economic community. Yet this is crucial if we are going to talk in terms of exports from and service within a community. This leads in turn to the difficulties of base identification and measurement. Are we to talk about the base in terms of numbers of employees, value of product, volume of wages paid, or some combination of these? What are the implications of using some of these measurements singly as is done at present? Is our classification of basic activities clear and meaningful? This author thinks that it is not.

Aside from technique there arises a more important question concerning the dynamics of base and service components in a community. What exactly are the changes to be expected from employment or wage total declines in the base? Do they actually have the direct proportional effects on service employment, total community employment and population that we think they have? This is a particularly dark area of the jungle.

Again in the field of dynamics what do we know of the linking of base activities aside from some of the more obvious linkages in the base fields of trade and manufacturing? The answer is, relatively little. And yet if base theory is to become an even more meaningful concept-tool for the city planner, the land economist must make a more forthright effort to clear away the underbrush that hides the true features of this idea. An attempt will be made in future articles to make a preliminary examination of some of these preplexing questions.

The economic base theory was made applicable to planning problems through the development of base-service ratios and other techniques. A pioneer in this work was Homer Hoyt, co-author of our next selection. Hoyt's work for the FHA during the 1930's pointed the way to present techniques of base analysis. His later work developed the techniques to virtually their present state.

The present selection, taken from a textbook on Real Estate, starts with the viewpoint of the real estate business, but it presents a rather complete statement of the methods of economic base analysis.

Arthur M. Weimer and Homer Hoyt—Economic Base Analysis

Economic Base Analysis*

IMPORTANCE OF FUTURE CITY CHANGES

Since the value of every parcel of urban real estate will be affected by its surroundings—by the location factors which have a bearing on it—the prediction of future changes likely to affect these location factors is essential to long-range business decisions and to governmental programs. If you are planning to buy a house, your decision will be influenced in no small measure by the future prospects of the neighborhood in which it is located and by the economic outlook for the city. Similarly, investors in real properties, mortgage lenders, planning officials, public utility operators, subdividers and builders, apartment house developers and many other people concerned with real estate programs and with land values must, of necessity, undertake to forecast probable future changes in location factors.

This does not mean that we shall undertake to learn the techniques of "crystal-gazing." Obviously, no one can be certain of the future trend of events. Our only guide is a study of past developments in order to determine probable future trends. Granted that a wide margin of error may be involved, both business and government officials as well as private investors in and consumers of residential, commercial, and industrial real estate have no alternative but to make predictions in regard to future city, neighborhood, and district changes. By analyzing the more important location forces affecting specific pieces of real estate, it should be possible for us to reach at least tentative conclusions in regard to future developments.

FUTURE DEVELOPMENT OF CITIES

The future growth of all of our cities will depend . . . on the size of our total population and the proportion of this total that can be maintained in cities. Estimates of the size of our future population in this country have been revised upward as a re-

* See Acknowledgements

sult of the high birth rate in the postwar years. While it was predicted in 1941 that a maximum population would be reached in the decade of the 1980's of around 153 million, we have already exceeded this total. In 1950 the Census Bureau estimated that the 1960 population would be approximately 169 million. Recently this estimate has been revised upward. By 1975 the population of the United States may reach 200 million, an addition equal to three times the present population of Canada.

The country currently is growing at a rate equal to the addition of a Miami or Providence every month. The impact of the rising trend of population is already being felt by the schools and by industries specializing in supplying goods and services for children.

As we pointed out earlier, the future distribution of our population between rural and urban areas will depend largely on the productivity of agriculture. Current trends indicate that we may expect agricultural productivity to remain at high levels and probably to advance somewhat. Improved techniques of production and farm management, more productive machinery, higher grades of livestock, and improvements resulting from the development of hybrid seeds are all evidences of this trend. Thus it seems probable that in the years ahead an even greater proportion of our people may be supported in cities than is now the case.

Future city growth, however, will not be uniform for all regions of the country or for all sizes of cities. In the northern areas of the country over two thirds of the people now live in cities, while in the South only about one third are urban dwellers, and in the Mountain areas the proportion is only slightly larger. It should be noted also that in the half century since 1900 there has been a tendency for the larger cities to grow rapidly and for the smaller cities to remain stationary or to lose population.

We should note also that certain other factors are likely to modify the future course of urban development. (1) Fewer people may choose to live in cities; rural or semirural areas may be preferred as places to live, especially if air transportation develops rapidly and if the fear of atomic bomb attacks increases. (2) Decentralization of industry may develop to a more marked extent. Past trends would not argue for great industrial decentralization, but the possibility cannot be completedly discounted. (3) The city birth rate is much lower than that of rural regions, and a considerable migration from farms to cities must take place even if present urban populations are to be maintained. (4) Migration from abroad, one of the main sources of urban growth prior to World War I, is now limited sharply by law, and such restrictions seem likely to be continued. (5) Cities are spreading out over wider and wider areas. It may be that the line of demarcation between town and country will be almost completedly eliminated within a few decades.

THE FUTURE GROWTH OF SPECIFIC CITIES

Regardless of general developments, some cities will grow and others will diminish in economic importance whether the country as a whole experiences further urbanization or not. In each case the extent of growth will depend on "basic" employment and income. Greatest expansion may be expected during periods of local business prosperity. In Chicago, for example, annual population estimates show that highest annual rates of population growth occurred during such periods of business expansion as 1845 to 1855, 1862 to 1872, 1879 to 1892, 1920 to 1927, and in the years after World War II.

Every city is either gaining, declining, or standing still with respect to its ability to maintain existing levels of employment and incomes. Hence, careful forecasting of the future growth of any city involves an analysis and interpretation of the present trends which are likely to affect its urban growth sources of employment and income.

The value of any given group of urban real estate resources and the intensity with which those resources are used depend on their convenience of access to a stream of income flowing from the factories, offices, stores, mines, and other sources of employment in the region. If there is a serious long-run decline in the number of persons gainfully employed in a city, even if the loss amounts to only 10 percent, a vacant margin of structures will appear which by their competition will weaken the rents and values of all properties. Almost complete cessation of new building, except for certain replacements of existing structures, may be expected. Under such circumstances the opportunities for the development of new business enterprises will be limited, the intensity with which specific properties are used will decline, all property values will be undermined, and the security of mortgages on existing structures will be endangered.

Careful analysis should help to forecast the possibility of such developments. Obviously no one can be certain of the changes in the basic sources of employment that are likely to develop, but reasonable estimates of future probable developments can be made. In order to make a careful analysis of the present character and potential future of the basic sources of employment and income in a specific city, it is necessary to (1) determine the basic sources of employment and the relative importance of each in the economic life of the city and (2) analyze each as a basis for estimating future probable advancement or decline.

RELATIVE IMPORTANCE OF BASIC SOURCES OF INCOME

The basic sources of employment and income in an urban economy are many and varied, but for convenience of analysis they may be combined into the following primary groups: (1) manufacturing, (2) extractive industry, (3) wholesale and retail trade, (4) finance and banking, and (5) special sources of income such as political, educational, institutional, resort, or amusement activities. The stream of income brought into the city by people who receive pensions, rents, royalties, and interest from elsewhere should also be considered a part of the urban growth income. Few cities are supported by any one of these income sources alone; nearly all rely on a combination of various types.

Chicago, Detroit, Dayton, Hartford, Cleveland, Milwaukee, and Baltimore are predominantly industrial cities, while Los Angeles, New Orleans, Minneapolis, Kansas City, Omaha, and Portland are predominantly commercial centers. Miami and Atlantic City are chiefly tourist resorts. Washington is supported almost entirely by the activities of the federal government. In St. Louis, Boston, and Philadelphia there is a fairly equal division of employment and income between trade and industry. In Springfield, Illinois, and in Oklahoma City there is an extraordinary diversity of support from manufacturing, extractive industry, trade, and state institutions. Ann Arbor, Michigan, is primarily an educational center.

The first step in determining the economic potentialities of a city is to estimate the relative importance of each of the various sources of urban growth employment and income. Information concerning total employment, as well as the number employed in each of the main types of economic activity, can be secured from such sources as the Bureau of the Census, state employment services and their local branches, and chambers of commerce. Where more detailed information is desirable, assistance may be secured from the personnel departments of principal firms, and local labor unions. Information concerning payrolls is often available from census reports, local or state taxing authorities, and similar sources. From one or a combination of these sources, total employment can be obtained and the percent of the total engaged in each of the major types of economic activity outlined above can be computed.

Utilizing the technique above, a study recently prepared for the city of Evansville, Indiana, classified total employment into the following groups:[1]

TABLE 1

DISTRIBUTION OF EMPLOYED PERSONS BY INDUSTRY GROUP
FOR THE EVANSVILLE METROPOLITAN AREA, 1950

Industry Group	Total Employment
Manufacturing	24,858
Retail Trade	10,793
Wholesale Trade	2,637
Professional Service	5,177
Personal Service	3,749
Transportation	3,465
Communications and Utilities	1,307
Mining	443
Construction	3,177
Finance	1,714
Public Administration	1,618
Business and Repair Service	659
Entertainment and Recreation	659
Industry not reported	570
Total	61,472

Several practical difficulties are involved in determining whether a specific employment and income source is in the urban growth or urban service category. For example, a manufacturer may market a small percentage of his product within the city and the remainder in other parts of the country or in world markets. A merchant may have some customers who are local people and others who live elsewhere. In such cases the relative importance of urban growth and urban service employment for each major type of economic activity must be estimated.

There have been different techniques devised to provide estimates of this type. One recent study allocates total employ-

---

[1] George Pinnell, *Analysis of the Economic Base of Evansville, Indiana.* Doctoral dissertation, Indiana University, 1954.

ment between "basic" and "service" on the basis of an analysis of the sales of individual firms. "Thus, if X company sells 50 percent of its product outside the area, it is assumed that 50 percent of its employment is basic [growth] and the remaining 50 percent local service."[2]

While this method of selecting the basic sources of income and of determining their relative importance in the economic life of the city will give accurate results, it may be simplified for some types of analyses as follows:[3]

1. From the sources mentioned earlier determine the size of the total labor force and the number of persons engaged in the principal types of employment.

2. Determine the number engaged in manufacturing, excluding those firms whose production is intended predominantly for the local market. Part of the total production of local manufacturing firms who market their product nationally will be consumed by the local public and for very large cities that portion of employment and income should be extracted from the urban growth classification. In the Evansville study the following procedure was used: A ratio was established between local income or purchasing power and national income or purchasing power.[4] In 1953 Evansville received approximately one tenth of 1 percent of the total national income. Therefore, for a product manufactured locally and marketed on a national basis it was assumed that one tenth of 1 percent of

[2] *Working Denver,* an economic analysis by the Denver Planning Office, 1953, p. 26.

[3] *A Report Upon Scope and Objectives and the Social and Economic Background of Dayton, Ohio.* Prepared for the City Plan Board by Harland Bartholomew and Associates, and Homer Hoyt Associates. Dayton, Ohio, April, 1952. *The Status of the New York Metropolitan Region in* 1944, prepared by Homer Hoyt for Regional Plan Association, Inc., New York, 1944. Also, Detroit City Plan Commission, *Economic Base of Detroit,* Detroit Department of Purchases and Supplies, 1944.

[4] From income data contained, for example, in the "Survey of Buying Power," published annually by *Sales Management* magazine.

the total employment and income from such industries should be extracted from the urban growth category.

3. Determine the number engaged in extractive industry obviously intended for the nonlocal market.

4. Determine the number receiving income and employment from such special sources as political, educational, institutional, resort, or amusement activities.

5. A rough approximation of other urban growth sources of employment can be determined by alternative methods. One method used in the Evansville study proceeded as follows: It was assumed that the local population would consume its proportionate share of the national production of goods and services based on population or income or both. For example, if, in 1950, 57 persons per thousand population were required to provide retail services nationally, then the same ratio applied to Evansville would mean employment in retail trade of 9,144. Since employment in Evansville in 1950 in retail trade was 10,793, the difference (1,649) was assumed to be basic employment. Much the same result may be obtained by utilizing the method outlined in paragraph 2 above. For example, since Evansville in 1950 had slightly more than one tenth of 1 percent of the total national income, it was assumed that it would have one tenth of 1 percent of the total employees in the nation employed in retail trade. Employment above that figure was considered basic. Either formula should be varied with each type of economic activity to allow for differences between local and national tastes and preferences.

6. Total the figures arrived at in paragraphs 2 to 5 above and compute the percentage of this total which each type of urban growth employment represents. These percentages will indicate the relative importance of manufacturing, extractive industry, trading, and other types of activity in the economic development of a city, as shown below.

7. Where the funds are available for an intensive survey of

the economic base, the proportion of basic or urban growth employment to total employment can be most accurately determined by interviewing each individual large firm and by taking samples of the smaller firms to ascertain the proportion of business derived from shipment of goods outside the city or the performance of services for persons living beyond the city's

TABLE 2

DISTRIBUTION OF URBAN GROWTH AND URBAN SERVICE
EMPLOYMENT IN EVANSVILLE BY INDUSTRY, 1950

Industry Group	Urban Growth Employment		Urban Service Employment	
	Number	Percent	Number	Percent
Manufacturing	24,700	83.5	148	.5
Retail Trade	1,600	5.4	9,193	28.9
Wholesale Trade	500	1.7	2,137	6.7
Professional Services	500	1.7	4,677	14.7
Personal Services	500	1.7	3,249	10.2
Transportation	700	2.3	2,565	8.1
Communications and Utilities	200	.7	1,207	3.8
Extractive Industry	375	1.3	68	.2
All other	500	1.7	8,553	26.9
Totals	29,575	100.0	31,797	100.0

borders. This was the method employed by John W. Alexander in his study of Madison, Wisconsin.[5] In this study it was found that governmental agencies accounted for 39 percent of basic employment in Madison, manufacturing for 35 percent, and services and trade for 25 percent. In most studies of the economic base, however, it is not possible to carry out such detailed analyses. In such cases the techniques outlined in the preceding paragraphs may be used to advantage.

When determining the relative importance of various sources of urban growth employment and income, allowance must be made for the fact that wage levels vary between firms and between industries. For example, in 1949, employment in retail

---

[5] John W. Alexander, "An Economic Base Study of Madison, Wisconsin," *Wisconsin Commerce Papers*, Vol. I, No. 4, University of Wisconsin, School of Commerce, Bureau of Business Research and Service, Madison, 1953.

trade in Albuquerque, New Mexico accounted for over 21 percent of the total labor force but less than a sixth of the total payrolls. On the other hand, wage levels in transportation, communications, and public utilities were high enough to account for almost 15 percent of the total payrolls but made up less than 11 percent of total employment. The following table presents the data in more detail:[6]

TABLE 3
RELATIVE IMPORTANCE OF SOURCES OF EMPLOYMENT AND INCOME IN ALBUQUERQUE, NEW MEXICO, 1949

Sources of Employment	Percentage of Total	
	Total Employees	Payrolls
Manufacturing	6.4	8.1
Extractive Industry	.3	.2
Construction	13.1	13.0
Transportation, Communication, and Public Utilities	10.8	14.9
Wholesale Trade	4.7	6.7
Retail Trade	21.5	17.3
Services	12.1	8.8
Government	17.4	24.6
Finance, Insurance, and Real Estate	3.7	4.3
Other	10.0	2.1

Regardless of the method used to determine the relative importance of various types of employment, the main point to remember is that we are trying to find the basic economic supports of the city, the urban growth sources of employment, and to determine their relative importance. These will play the predominant part in shaping the city's economic future. If there is reason to believe that the relative importance of the basic sources of income will be altered sharply in contrast to past developments, this condition should be reflected in the weights assigned to each major source.

---

[6] Adapted from *The Economy of Albuquerque, New Mexico,* Federal Reserve Bank, Kansas City, Missouri, and Bureau of Business Research, University of New Mexico, 1949, p. 21.

THE RATIO BETWEEN BASIC EMPLOYMENT TO TOTAL EMPLOYMENT

The ratio between urban growth or basic employment and service employment is not constant but varies between different cities. As the following table, compiled by Edward L. Ullman shows, the ratio between urban growth or basic and service employment has varied from 1 to 0.8, for smaller cities, to 1 to 2.1 for the New York metropolitan area.

TABLE 4

ESTIMATES OF BASIC-SERVICE EMPLOYMENT RATIOS BY SIZE OF CITY

City, Date, and Source	Population	Urban Growth or Basic Employees	to Service Employees
Auburn, Washington (1953, Simms)	6,500	1	.8
Oskaloosa, Iowa (1937, *Fortune* Mag.)	10,000	1	.8
Medford, Oregon (1952, Erwin)	20,000	1	.8
Oshkosh, Wisconsin (1950, Alexander)	42,000	1	.6
Albuquerque, N. M. (1948, K. C. Fed. Res. Board)	100,000	1	.9
Brockton Area, Mass. (1948, Hoyt)	120,000	1	.8
Wichita, Kansas (Average 1940-50, K. C. Fed. Res. Board)	200,000	1	1.4
Denver Metro. Area (1951, Denver City Plan Comm.)	564,000	1	1.56
Cincinnati Metro. Area (1940, Roterus, Cin. Plan Comm.)	787,000	1	1.7
Washington, D. C., 1947 (Natl. Cap. Park & Plan)	1,000,000	1	1.1
Detroit Metro. Area (1940, Detroit Plan Comm.)	2,377,000	1	1.1
New Jersey (1948, Hoyt)	4,800,000	1	1.1
New York Metro. Area (1940, Regional Plan Assoc.)	12,000,000	1	2.1
Evansville, Indiana Metro. Area* (1953, Pinnell, Indiana University)	160,000	1	1.2

* Added by authors.

CHANGES IN RATIO BETWEEN URBAN GROWTH OR BASIC AND SERVICE EMPLOYMENT IN THE SAME METROPOLITAN AREA

The ratio between basic employment to service employment in the same city does not necessarily remain constant. In the

Washington, D. C., metropolitan area, the service industries tend to be undermanned in time of war or military preparation. Thus the ratio between urban growth or basic and service employment which was 1 to 1.54 in 1940 dropped to 1 to 1.08 in 1951 during the defense preparations following the outbreak of the Korean War.

ANALYZING URBAN GROWTH SOURCES OF INCOME

By breaking down the employment of a city into its "urban growth" sources of income we can concentrate our attention on those types of economic activity which may be expected to have greatest influence on the future growth of the city. However, cyclical and seasonal variations in employment and income should be considered as well as general trends. Real estate values in a city where employment fluctuates widely between periods of depression and prosperity are not likely to be as stable as the values of properties located in a city where economic activity is less erratic. The extent to which a city is subject to such fluctuations in employment is indicated by the ratio of the number of persons employed at the bottom of a depression period to the number employed at the height of prosperity.

Seasonal variations in employment are also important, since the value of real estate in cities where employment is highly seasonal in character is seldom as stable as in those where economic activity shows little fluctuation from one season to another (assuming other things equal).

In order to forecast carefully the employment and income trends of a city, each of the major sources of employment must be studied in detail. In the analysis of each source of employment, it is important to note not only the future trend of the number of people who may be employed in various types of economic activity, but also the *level of wages and other incomes* and the meaning of these in terms of real income and purchasing power.

ANALYSIS OF MANUFACTURING EMPLOYMENT
AND INCOME

In forecasting the trend of manufacturing activities in a city as a source of future urban growth employment and income, each type of industry should be studied in some detail. Attention should be given to such factors as the nature of the products manufactured by each firm, the location of raw materials, principal markets, trends of demand for the products, and the competitive position of each of the establishments. Such factors as the competence of management, the character of the labor supply, and special local advantages or disadvantages should be considered. In addition, tax burdens, the attitudes of local community leaders toward each firm, and the trends of local government policies generally merit consideration.

Special attention should be given to competitive advantage of the location, diversification of industry, competitive position of the firm, and cyclical fluctuations.

From the standpoint of future effects on real estate values it is important to determine whether the industries located in a city will remain, advance in importance, decline, or move to another location. Among the factors that tie an industry to a city are large plants, heavy fixed capital investments in new and modern machinery, the availability of a large body of skilled labor, favorable freight rates, convenient access to raw materials, proximity to markets, favorable attitudes of local community leaders, and low taxes. In addition, it is important to determine whether any new industries are likely to move into a city. The above factors will also have a bearing on such probable developments.

There is always an element of danger if a city has great concentration of industrial activity along one specific line. If half of the workers in a city are employed in a single establishment, the whole structure of real estate values may collapse if that establishment moves away. If there are many establishments in the same industry, the risks are less, but the city may suffer severely because of a decrease in the demand for the product or the rise of a competing product. In addition, single-industry towns are more likely to fall under the dominance of a relatively few businessmen or labor leaders, with the result that real estate values may suffer from shortsighted managerial policies or from prolonged strikes and industrial disturbances.

The relationship of industrial plants in the city being analyzed to the industry as a whole and to competitive plants in other locations is a matter of basic importance. If a factory is located poorly, managed inefficiently, uses obsolete equipment, or lacks satisfactory outlets, it will tend to lose out in competition with other manufacturers unless these conditions are typical of the entire industry. Under the latter conditions, the introduction of laborsaving machinery may lead to less total employment, but may put the plant in a much stronger competitive position, with the result that it may play a greater part in the future economic life of the city.

As we pointed out above, cyclical fluctuations of employment and incomes are of vital importance to real estate values. In analyzing industrial employment, the potential effect of cyclical fluctuations should be determined for each firm involved.

ANALYZING INCOME AND EMPLOYMENT FROM TRADE

The prospects for future employment and income from trade in any city depend chiefly on the following:

1. The extent to which the city is expanding its trade area at the expense of competing cities or losing out in competition with such cities.
2. The growth or decline of resources and purchasing power in the trading area.

3. The potential growth or decline of population in the trading area.

Diversification of types of trading activities and firms is not so important a consideration as in the case of industry, since we seldom find cities in which one or two stores serve all of the needs of a trade area. Similarly, cyclical fluctuations in trading activities are not likely to be so marked as in the case of industry, although such fluctuations will occur. To the extent that wide variations are anticipated, proper allowances should be made in estimating future devolopments.

ANALYZING INCOME AND EMPLOYMENT FROM EXTRACTIVE INDUSTRIES

A forecast of employments and incomes which are dependent upon mines, oil wells, or timber resources requires an analysis of the probable future life of the natural resources involved and of the extent to which these resources can be utilized at prevailing or anticipated price and cost levels. Competition of the products of such extractive industries with other products of the same type should be considered, as well as the possibility for the development of substitute products.

ANALYZING INCOME AND EMPLOYMENT FROM OTHER SOURCES

For several decades employment in governmental agencies has tended to expand. Incomes of government workers have advanced. Since the seats of governments, such as state capitals or county seats, are relatively fixed, the possibilities of changes of location of such governmental activities are remote. However, cities with a large number of federal agencies may lose or gain income as the activities of such agencies are expanded or diminished or as changes of location are made.

Educational institutions are usually fixed in location and are not likely to move to other places unless exceptional conditions arise. Normally employment in such institutions is relatively static, with great expansion or decline occurring only gradually.

During recent decades there has been a marked expansion of educational activity, and this general trend was strengthened by higher income levels, population growth and by GI educational benefits.

Employment and incomes derived from resort and amusement activities are subject to unusual fluctuations. People must live in industrial or commercial cities even during depression periods, but it is not essential that they take winter and summer vacations in resort areas when their incomes have been reduced. Hence, future probable cyclical variations of business activity are the principal key to the analysis of the future economic advance or decline of resort cities. To the extent that a resort enjoys a prestige reputation or is endowed with exceptional natural advantages, of course, it will tend to be affected less by business recessions than will other resort centers.

In a number of towns and cities, and notably in "country towns," retired people represent an important source of income. The extent and stability of such income depend on the sources from which it is drawn. As more and more people qualify for pensions or build up retirement funds, incomes of this type will play an increasingly important part in the economic fortunes of many cities.

THE ECONOMIC BASE AND THE LOCAL MARKET

Up to this point we have been concerned chiefly with urban growth sources of income and employment in terms of their potential effects on real estate values. However, another factor remains which may necessitate modification of our earlier analyses, especially in the case of smaller cities. This is the factor of *long-run marketability, or the salability of real estate over a period of years.*

As a general rule, larger cities provide a more stable market for real estate than smaller towns. For example, if a plant employing 1,000 men moves from a small city, the local real estate market will suffer an immediate decline. The same occurrence in a large city might scarcely be noticed in terms of the salability of real properties. While the size of a city is not the only factor affecting the long-run marketability of properties located there, it is probably the most important single consideration. The general level of income, the kinds of economic activities represented, and the types of people living there should all be considered.

Other things being equal, it should never be necessary to modify an analysis of the economic potentialities of a city on account of its size if it contains more than 100,000 inhabitants. Cities with populations ranging from 50,000 to 100,000 represent a more limited market for real estate, and some modification of the original analysis may be necessary because of the limitation of the market. Long-run market factors become highly important considerations in the case of cities and towns with populations of less than 30,000.

While an analysis of a small city may indicate economic advance over a five-year-or ten-year period, such an advance is never likely to be steady and continuous. Any recession period will make it difficult to sell real properties even at low prices. Because of the special risks arising from these long-range market factors, it is usually necessary to modify any conclusion reached from an analysis of the future trends of urban growth sources of employment and income.

METHOD OF CALCULATING FUTURE POPULATION BY ANALYSIS OF ECONOMIC BASE

Economic base analysis provides a method for estimating future population trends and the potential demand for various types of land uses in any city. The steps may be summarized thus:

1. By the methods already indicated, ascertain the number of urban growth or basic employees in each industry or trade.

2. Subtract the number of urban growth or basic employees

in each industry or trade in order to determine the number of service employees.

3. Calculate the ratio between basic and service employment.

4. Calculate the percentage of the total employment to the total population of the metropolitan area being studied as of the last available census. This percentage usually ranges from 41 to 47 percent.

5. By interviewing the managers of principal basic industries, or by taking into account past trends, make an estimate of the probable future total number of basic employees.

6. Estimate future total employment of the metropolitan area by applying the ratio of basic employment to total employment now existing or by adjusting this ratio for changed conditions.

7. Estimate future population of the entire metropolitan area by applying the percentage of employment to population that prevailed in 1950 or on the basis of some other selected percentage if this seems warranted.

8. To estimate potential need for housing divide the estimated population increase by the average family size, taking into account trends in the birth rates.

9. To estimate the growth of any segment of the metropolitan area, allocate a percentage of the total growth to the particular segment on the basis of new highways, new sewer and water extensions, new industries, vacant land suitable for residential use, trends of growth, and prestige of the area.

10. To calculate the amount of land needed for new residential growth, estimate the proportion of added families that will live in apartments, row houses, detached single-family houses, and small estates and the areas required for each type of residence.

11. To estimate the amount of land required for new commercial centers, calculate the square feet of floor area required in department stores, variety stores, supermarkets, apparel stores, and all other types of stores to handle the volume of

sales created by the added population, and also allow a 4-to-1 ratio between parking and selling area.

12. To estimate the amount of industrial space required for new growth, ascertain the number of square feet of factory and yard space now required for each employee in each type of industry. On the basis of the total increase of employment expected in each industry, calculate the amount of floor area or yard space required by multiplying the number of added employees by the average space now used by each employee in modern factories.

The next eight articles are reprinted from Richard Andrews' noteworthy series of articles on the economic base that appeared in *Land Economics*. In these papers Andrews deals with several of the central and knotty problems of base analysis. The problems include terminology, classification of base types, base measurement and identification, the base ratios, and the base concept and the planning process.

Andrews does not appear as an advocate of the base theory. His attitude is judicial and he criticizes the base theory at several points. Nonetheless he must place considerable confidence in the base theory or he would not have dealt with it so extensively.

Richard B. Andrews—Mechanics of the Urban Economic Base: The Problem of Terminology

Mechanics of the Urban Economic Base:
The Problem of Terminology*

The relatively rapid rate at which the American economy has shifted from a rural agricultural to an urban commercial-manufacturing axis is a widely recognized fact. When this fact is combined with the associated fact that there is now a very high percentage of the country's population living under urban conditions it becomes apparent that the urban land economist is faced with a definite responsibility.[1] This responsibility takes the form of developing as promptly as possible a better understanding of the internal workings, or economic mechanics of our urban communities. The emphasis must be largely economic for the reason that our urban culture has economic motives and forces as its principal explanation of creation, growth, and decline.

Partly as a result of the relative recency of investigation into the field of what might be termed "urban economic mechanics" there have arisen two conditions which are typical to the developmental stage of any new field of thought. These conditions center around (1), the fairly wide number of terms in vogue that refer to the same thing or situation within the urban economic structure and (2), the lack of agreement on the meaning of single terms.

It has been only within the past twenty-five to thirty years, however, that definite steps have been taken by urban land economists to rationalize the internal economic functioning of the city. We are now at the point where we are aware of rough relationships between what we sometimes call "basic enter-

* See Acknowledgements

[1] Under a new definition of "urban" the 1950 census reported 64 percent of the population in this category and an additional 7 percent in places of less than 2,500 persons. *Table 5a—Population in Groups of Places Classified According to Size: 1950. Number of Inhabitants, United States Summary; United States Census of Population*: 1950, Bureau of the Census, United States Department of Commerce, Washington, D. C. 1952.

prises" and "service enterprises" of a community and between the employment sum of these two and total community population. But concerning the dynamics of these elements we know relatively little.[2]

If social scientists are to make satisfactory progress with the statement and analysis of a problem situation, they must proceed in a scientific manner and do their best to come to an agreement on terms so that there will be some comparability of lines of reasoning and conclusions. Failure to act in this manner has often been the basis for justified criticism of social science procedures.

It is, therefore, the objective of this brief article to present a summary statement of the evolution of the terms which have come into use in discussions of the mechanics and make-up of the urban economy and to highlight what appear to be the principal points of confusion.

Principal attention is given in the paragraphs that follow to the development and meaning of the term "economic base" which in a current specialized sense refers to the export activities of a community that bring in its *net* earnings and enable it to continue as an independent economic entity. Consideration is also given to the terminology surrounding the economic complement of the base, the "service enterprises," whose activities are completely local and involve no export beyond the predetermined limits of the economic community. The base and service elements are, in the opinion of current theory, the principal parts of the economic machine. Finally, attention

---

[2] Most of the precision work of a theoretical nature which relates to the economics of urbanization has been performed in the general problem field of the location of economic activity. This external approach has been most competently handled by Alfred Weber, E. M. Hoover, and others. The city planner, is, of course, that technician who on the firing line contending with the internal problems of city growth and adjustment has seen, though often imperfectly, the multiple relations of his local economic structure to the housekeeping problems of planning such as zoning, traffic control, parking, annexation, and the like.

will be given to the apparent confusion that exists between the terms "economic survey" and "economic base study."

Again let it be emphasized that this review of terminology seems necessary because of the fact that while some of the terms referring to the base and service elements are synonymous others are inclusive of additional concepts. In a few cases the same term has an entirely different meaning when used by two authors. So it is, in part, for purposes of clarification, and it is hoped, increased precision that the following paragraphs are presented.

DEVELOPMENT OF TERMINOLOGY

In the *Regional Survey of New York and Its Environs* the statement was made that:

". . . the multiplicity of . . . productive occupations may roughly be divided into those which can be called primary . . . manufacturing goods for general use (i.e., not confined to use within the community itself), and those occupations which may be called *auxiliary,* such as are devoted directly or indirectly to the service and convenience of the people engaged in the primary occupations."[3]

Here there is, clearly, no reference made to the "economic base" in precisely those terms yet the ideas apply, from the standpoint of terminology, to what is considered by many today to be the base, i.e., primary occupations, and the economic complement to the base, i.e., auxiliary occupations.

Weimer and Hoyt in their text *Principles of Urban Real Estate* present a series of terms which refer to the base concept.

". . . a city must be able to command a stream of income from beyond its borders if it is to be founded at all. In other words, some division of labor between city and country or between one

[3] Robert M. Haig, *Major Economic Factors in Metropolitan Growth and Arrangement,* Vol. I (monograph) of *Regional Survey of New York and Environs* New York: 1928, p. 43.

city and others is essential to urban development. Since the existence and growth of a city seem to depend especially on these outside sources of income, they have been referred to as 'basic employment supports' or as 'urban growth employment.' In contrast to the basic sources of income, there are 'secondary' or 'non-basic' 'urban service' employments, that is, sources of income derived from serving the needs of those who command incomes from beyond the borders of the city."[4]

Hoyt's statement added substantially to the range of synonyms for the idea of the base and its economic reciprocal. Yet there were other terms, such as those contributed by Nussbaum who described basic enterprises as "town builders" and those enterprises which served the local community alone as "town fillers."[5] An extension of these terms could be found in the thinking of the Regional Survey of New York which made reference to ". . . those (activities) that create populous districts and those that follow population . . . ."[6]

In yet another treatise the term "economic base" is defined as the "supporting activities" of the community or those activities that emphasize production of exportable goods and services.[7] From this line of reasoning has evolved yet another term which pinpoints the concept of the base, namely, "export industries" or enterprises. Vining aptly states this latter concept when he says:

"A community seems to be organized around its "export" industry, this being the source of the flows which this community injects into the larger independent system and which acts

[4] Arthur M. Weimer and Homer Hoyt, *Principles of Urban Real Estate* (New York: The Ronald Press Company, 1948) pp. 85-86.

[5] F. L. Nussbaum, *A History of the Economic Institutions of Modern Europe* (New York: F. S. Crofts and Company, 1933), p. 36.

[6] Haig, *op. cit.,* p. 13.

[7] Federal Reserve Bank of Kansas City, Missouri, *The Economy of Albuquerque, New Mexico,* 1949, p. 21.

as a balance for the flows diverted from the larger system and channeled into this community."[8]

Vining goes on to introduce other terms which by his standard of definition apply to a broader geographical concept than the community but which are, nonetheless, applicable to a description of this more restricted economy.

"Within a primary regional unit [approximately the familiar primary trade area] . . . a part of the employment produces products and services sold only or primarily to the inhabitants of this region. This employment is called the "residentiary" or passive employment . . . . The rest of the employment produces primarily for export to other regions. This employment is called the "primary" or "active" employment . . . ."[9]

Up to this point the main fault that can be found with terminology surrounding the subject is that it is over-heavy in alternate terms. However, the meanings of these terms admittedly remain uniform and clear. A degree of confusion, however, creeps in with a rather broad rendering of the base concept presented in the Municipal Yearbook which states that:

"Economic base or function . . . whether it is manufacturing, retail trade, wholesale trade, mining, government . . . [is] that [which] furnishes the major volume of employment in the city."[10]

In this statement the emphasis of meaning as it applies to the base has been shifted from the idea of export activity to the idea of the base as major employer in the community. Aside from the shift in terms a question arises as to whether or not it is a fact that the base or even a combination of base elements

[8] Rutledge Vining, "The Region as an Economic Entity and Certain Variations to be observed in the Study of Systems of Regions," *American Economic Review,* May 1949, *Papers and Proceedings of the Sixty-first Annual Meeting of the American Economic Association,* Dec. 1948, p. 90.

[9] *Ibid.,* p. 93.

[10] Grace K. Ohlson, "Economic Classification of Cities," *The Municipal Yearbook* (Chicago: International City Managers' Association. 1950), p. 29.

would furnish the major volume of employment if they were to be defined in terms of export activity. If primacy of employment is actually meant to be the condition which distinguishes the base then, truly, a new way of looking at the base has been introduced.

That the meaning of the term "ecomonic base" is not uniform in all quarters is further apparent in a statement made at an urban problems conference sponsored by the Chamber of Commerce of the United States. Here it was said:

"The two senses in which we think of the economic base of the community are these: First, the tax or income base on which the tax revenue for any community is predicated, on which it relies for the funds to provide the public services and the other facilities that the community needs. Second, its broader application to the fundamental sources of income that may be available to the citizens in any particular community, from which they derive their livelihood and on which the community's activity as a whole depends. I am thinking particularly of such industries as mining, agriculture, fishing, construction, manufacturing, and wholesale and retail trade."[11]

Here the base appears in different dress as the total income earnings of the community available as a tax base. The other meaning stated by Smith is somewhat closer to the traditional view but vague in its use of the expression "fundamental sources of income."

Another aspect of semantics which is likely to cause trouble is the fact that there is terminology in the field of general economics which closely parallels some of the key terms used in referring to the structure of the urban economy. This provides a basis for confusion that would beset, particularly, economists other than land economists reading materials on the economic

[11] Larry Smith, *The Economic Base of the Community, Business Action for Better Cities* (Chamber of Commerce of the United States, Washington, D. C., 1952), p. 44.

base. A short statement by Colin Clark is here introduced which concisely highlights this point as he outlines the standard, broad classification of industrial activities. The similarity of these terms with some of the terms used to describe urban industrial economies and the possibility of consequent confusion because of differing meanings is readily apparent:

"Primary industry includes agricultural, pastoral, forest, fishing, and hunting industries. Secondary industry includes manufacture, electric power production, mining, building, and construction. Tertiary industry is defined by difference as all other economic activities."[12]

THE ECONOMIC BASE STUDY AND THE ECONOMIC SURVEY

It is appropriate next to call attention to the fact that there does not seem to be complete agreement at the present time on the meaning of the term "economic base study." The essence of the question is whether a base study concentrates its attention on the basic exporting enterprises of a community *and* their service complements, on the basic enterprises alone, or on the full scope of the local economy in all its manifold aspects. A statement of the latter point of view is well put by Ratcliff when he says:

"In general, the process of appraising the economic base of a community is a matter of gathering all available facts of economic significance, analyzing past experience and present status, and basing the forecast on an extension of recent trends as modified by those factors of change which can be discerned. More specifically, this procedure involves a prediction of the nature, volume, and stability of employment and income in the community, and a forecast of the characteristics of the population. As a first step, there should be an inventory of local eco-

---

[12] Colin Clark, *The Economics of* 1960 (London: McMillan & Co. Ltd., 1942), p. 22.

nomic resources—the geographic advantages of the community, the manpower resources, and the productive activities now being carried on. . . . . The primary . . . activities should be identified . . . .

"The analysis of the economic base of a community requires both a cross-section description and the identification and evaluation of the forces of change."[13]

Some reports labelled as "economic base studies" are as broad in their coverage as those Ratcliff describes.[14] However, they do not always make a careful identification of and devote intensive analysis to the "city building" or basic elements of the economies in question. This leads the present writer to the conclusion that in the minds of some planners and economists the term "economic base" refers to the *entire* economy of the community which serves as a *base* for the continued functioning and existence of that community. There are, on the other hand, those who think of the economic base as constituting the "city-building," "urban-growth" factors or "export industries" which serve as the base or main support of the *rest* of the local economy—in short, a base and economic superstructure type of approach. There is, therefore, some ground for believing that an economic base study may be a more limited type of venture and can be viewed as a *part* of a broader economic survey.

For the sake of keeping terminology clear and unequivocal there might be some point in labelling broad-scale description (and, preferably, analysis) of a community's economy as an "economic survey." Such a survey, as presently issued, might or might not include a careful and precise job on the city-building activities of the community. However, if it did include

---

[13] Richard U. Ratcliff, *Urban Land Economics* (New York: McGraw Hill Book Co., 1949), p. 42.

[14] Philadelphia City Planning Commission, *Economic Base Study,* Planning Study No. 2, 1949.

such an analysis it might, in turn, be appropriate to include it in the title thus, "Economic Survey and Base Study of . . . ." Moreover, separate studies of the base alone should certainly carry a precise title and not the broadcast sort of labelling now indulged in.[15]

A few titles taken at random may better demonstrate the confusion on this point. For example, *The Economy of the Sacramento Area,*[16] and *The Economic Survey of Allegany County, Maryland*[17] include no discussion whatsoever of the specialized concept of the economic base as it has thus far been presented. On the other hand, there is a very competent study, *"The Economy of Albuquerque, New Mexico"* which not only uses the specialized concept of the economic base but makes some very valuable contributions to the theoretical content of that concept.[18] And again, on the other side, as was noted in the case of the excellent Philadelphia study, the exact title, "Economic Base Study," was employed though not in the specialized sense. But in the case of the Hoyt study, *The Economic Base of the Brockton, Massachusetts Area,* we again encounter the specialized use of the term.[19]

---

[15] It should not be concluded from anything that has been said by this writer concerning economic surveys and economic base studies that he believes the one to be "better" than the other. Obviously, the broad urban economic survey whether it includes the specialized base approach or not is a must for the planner and economist. Without the comprehensive approach as a background many wrong conclusions might be drawn from a "pure" base study. These two terms are, therefore, simply labels for the minimum data required for an understanding of any urban economy. While it might be desirable for all "economic surveys" to have as an assumed part an economic base study, the term "base study" would undoubtedly have to be retained for narrower gauged surveys which were pointed at only that portion of the metropolitan economic structure.

[16] Sacramento Chamber of Commerce, *The Economy of the Sacramento Area* . . . , Sacramento, California, 1951.

[17] University of Maryland, *An Economic Survey of Allegany County, Maryland,* Bureau of Business & Economic Research, Vol. 1, No. 1., 1947.

[18] Federal Reserve Bank, Kansas City, Missouri, *op. cit.*

[19] Homer Hoyt, *A Report on the Economic Base of the Brockton, Massachusetts Area,* 1949.

CONCLUSIONS

Whereas this entire situation may not appear to be a matter of any profound seriousness to many persons it is unfortunate in that it is, of course, symptomatic of a lack of general agreement on terminology in the field and is certainly indicative of some degree of confusion to the outsider and beginning student. Moreover, such confusion is certain to retard the rate of research progress in this particular area of thought.

It is natural that terminology is far from set in the field of urban land economics inasmuch as it is a field that is relatively new to economics while the concept of the economic base is of even more recent origin. Consequently, the idea of the base and its attendant terms have not yet become a standard part of the vocabulary of general urban economy studies. It must also be pointed out that the concept of the economic base represents a special approach to the description and analysis of urban economies. It is a new, though far from untried, analytical technique. Therefore, as is true of all ideas that are still in a semi-raw state, it is not surprising to find the term "economic base" being employed in equally reputable reports with meanings that are quite distinct one from the other.

In the hope that agreement on, and simplification of terms can evolve more quickly in the field this writer here presents his view of term usage as a basis for argument. It appears that the specialized use of the term "economic base" has earned a sufficiently wide acceptance in respectable quarters to have gained the status of legal tender. It is further recommended that in general description the terms "basic industry" and "basic enterprise" be discarded since they do not seem to carry the proper connotation that would embrace, for example, such base forms as education, government, and religion. Moreover, they do not describe accurately the economy of the commuters' community, investment export, etc. Hence it seems proper to adopt either the term "basic activity" or "export activity." Of these two the former seems the better. In these circumstances the complement of the base would then be referred to as "service activity." Finally, from what has been said in the course of this article there should be no doubt as to the advisability of referring to the base, in an economic sense, as an export activity rather than, for example, as the principal employer of a community.

The urgency of the situation surrounding the tidying up of the terminology of urban economic mechanics stems from the conditions of intensified urbanization mentioned at the beginning of this article. It also relates to the impaired efficiency of land economists in explaining urban economies and assisting in the rectification of their economic difficulties when they work with terminological tools that tend to be blunt in their imprecision and, consequently, inadequate to the difficult work to be done.

Richard B. Andrews—Mechanics of the Urban Economic Base: A Classification of Base Types

Mechanics of the Urban Economic Base:
A Classification of Base Types*

Within the past twenty-five to thirty years the concept of the economic base as applied to cities has grown in familiarity and has been employed with increasing frequency and success in attacks on problems in city planning.

The urban economic base, as currently conceived, refers to those activities of a community which involve the export of goods or services to firms or individuals who live and gain their incomes from locations outside the economic limits of the community in question. The trade effect of this activity is such that a net inflow of dollars is created for the subject community which either balances or more than compensates for the spendings of the community for goods and services which are not locally produced and therefore must be imported or are wholly produced and consumed locally. The planner's concern with these economic relationships arises in the fact that total population tends to rise and fall with overall shifts in the employment size, wage weight, and net earnings of the base. Moreover, qualitative change in the base, in the sense of change in the kinds of activities carried on, is likely to have a very definite, though possibly not immediate, effect on the pattern of land use demand (quanitative and qualitative) in the community.

The fact that the urban economic base concept in its present form is relatively new in part explains the associated fact that in many respects theoretical aspects of the concept are either inconsistent or are inadequate in their role of explaining the functioning of this sector of the urban economy.

In the opinion of this writer, one of the more important inadequacies of the base concept is to be found in the classification of the base activity types that may be identified in the modern urban community. Inadequacy of classification can be

* See Acknowledgements

of practical significance to the city planner in that it can greatly complicate his work and, at worst, dilute the accuracy of his decisions. Up to now classification has been more nearly a listing of different urban economic functions arranged by activity type that may stand in a basic relation to their communities. Unfortunately, a few types, such as manufacturing, are thought of rather automatically as basic in nature whereas the truth of the matter is that they can be either basic or service.

Hoyt presents a concise listing of urban base activity types in which he distinguishes the fundamental employment and income sources that might be found in the modern city. He includes:[1] (1) manufacturing, (2) trade, (3) extractive industries, (4) governmental activity, (5) educational institutions, (6) resort and amusement centers, and (7) retirement.

If, as is now commonly argued, the essential economic characteristic of base activity is exportation there does not as yet appear to exist an adequate classification of the different forms which this process assumes. It appears preferable, therefore, to classify the various varieties of bases under headings which appropriately distinguish the peculiar nature of the export activity involved.

Again, it is assumed that a classification presented in this form will highlight for the city planner the fact that planning for one classification of basic activities may be quite different from the planning that would be done for another due to the peculiar economic actions of the bases of that class. At present there is a tendency to plan for each variety of base rather than for broad classes. Whereas this is necessary up to a certain point, broad classifying would tend to simplify the work of the planner in that he could generalize more of his policies around broad categories. In many instances, however, it might be unrealistic to plan for a pure class since there often occur activity

---

[1] Arthur Weimer and Homer Hoyt, *Principles of Urban Real Estate* (New York: The Ronald Press Co. 1939), pp. 49-52.

linkings not only within but between classes. Clearly, not enough is known of the economic actions peculiar to each base classification so that a planner might yet proceed on the basis of tested cases but the classification will give him a simplified, organized basis for procedure while a body of knowledge continues to accumulate. At the same time classification will give the researcher a more coherent, organized point of departure not only for assisting in building a body of knowledge but also for testing more adequately the theoretical reasoning of base theory and filling in the gaps which appear within it.

Since urban base activity assumes the export of some good or service beyond the economic boundaries of the community, thus producing a net inflow of income, classification of base activities might logically proceed according to the different patterns assumed by export activity. These export patterns appear to be arranged in two general groups. The first might be a classification strictly according to the genre of export: (A) export of goods, (B) export of services, and (C) export of capital. But from the standpoint of the city planner it would seem appropriate to introduce a heavier geographic emphasis into the economic picture indicating the two principal space relationships of consumer and producer, thus: Export Patterns of Goods, Services, and Capital; (Class A) Movement of G-S-C to Consumer-Producer, and (Class B) Movement of Consumer-Purchaser to G-S-C. Let us briefly review the makeup of each of these classes with the objective of clarifying the argument as to content and relationship of factors.

CLASS A BASIC ACTIVITIES: MOVEMENT OF G-S-C TO CONSUMER-PURCHASER

(1) *Movement of Goods to Consumer-Purchaser.* Those basic activities of a community which are engaged in the export of merchandise beyond the borders of the economic area in which they are located are, perhaps, most familiar to the average observer and most easily identifiable as "basic." The goods which are exported may be either consumer or capital goods

and in a raw, semi-processed, or finished state.

The merchandise is physically exported on order to the customer who lives or operates beyond the limits of the community in question. An example of this type of relationship might be a shoe factory in a small city, a farm implement assembly plant in a city of the farm belt, a steel plant in Gary, Indiana, or the mail order firms of Chicago.

(2) *Movement of Services to Consumer-Purchaser.* Certain basic activities of urban areas operate by exporting their services in some form beyond the economic boundaries of the community. Situations of this variety are exemplified by insurance sales and servicing, legal aid, correspondence education, financial market services, research centers, also state and, in most cases, county legislation.

A unique and actually distinct phase of service export to the consumer-purchaser is found in the case in which the creator or seller of the service personally takes the service outside the economic area in order to dispose of it. Commuter communities are the best demonstration of this relationship. Here the executive, office worker, or factory hand journeys from his own small community to the central city to market his skills in both the basic and service activities of the larger settlement. This classification is clearly based on special geographic-economic distinctions that may have to be made within a larger base area. For example, we may say that Yonkers, New York is *within* the base area of the City of New York and hence may not have much export activity. But in itself as a separate urban node and planning entity it exists through its ability to export services to Manhattan—a relationship that is not diluted by the fact that the "true" source of basic activity appears to lie in Manhattan. In this special situation Manhattan must be looked upon as the market for Yonker's services. In the same sense the nation at large is the market for many of the goods and services produced in Manhattan.

(3) *Movement of Capital to Consumer-Purchaser.* Custom-

arily the idea of base activity is exclusively associated with the export of goods and services. However, it is clear that if the export concept of the base is to be pushed to its logical conclusions it must also embrace activities of capital export which yield a net inflow of earnings to the community.

In this category, therefore, must be placed familar investment activities which earn a return from outside the area in the form of interest on bonds, dividends on insurance and stocks, net rents and mortgage interest from real estate. In accordance with the customer relationship followed in the classification here under discussion it is assumed that capital is exported under the initiative of the local individual or firm of the community or has been extended on request to the consumer via long distance communication rather than in the form of a face-to-face transaction.

Of a slightly different nature would be returns in the form of pensions and social security payments. A part of these payments would, of course, merely be a return of capital to the claimant. However, other portions would represent interest earned on pension deposits and matching shares paid by employers not operating within the base area.

Yet another community bookkeeping transaction which might be included in the concept of capital export is that in which tax payments exported to the state or federal government are more than balanced by an inflow of school, highway, hospital, airport, relief, river and harbor aids. Most communities would not show a net gain from this source but there are a few that could because of low tax payments traceable either to low average incomes, to heavy exemptions, or to a low volume of trade on which a sales tax might be based.

It is unlikely that in any particular instance capital export would be the most important element of a community's economic base. On the other hand, it will be a tangible element in nearly every community and in some may approach significant proportions. For example, the common garden variety of rural trading center usually has a heavy seasoning of retired farmers and tradesmen who live on the proceeds of outside investment. Then, of course, there are the specialized retirement communities of Florida and California where the economic weight of capital export income is even heavier.

CLASS B BASIC ACTIVITIES:
MOVEMENT OF CONSUMER TO G-S-C

Economic movements of Class B activities can be identified in a briefer fashion than these just covered due, not to lesser importance, but to a certain duplication of conditions.

(1) *Movement of Consumer to Goods.* This relationship has reference to the familiar situation in which the consumer enters the base area, purchases, and carries away the merchandise he desires. The most obvious example of this type of base-consumer relationship is, of course, the retail trading center.

(2) *Movement of Consumer to Services.* In most urban areas this is the commonest technique for the export marketing of services. It is one in which the consumer enters the area where the basic activity is located and, for the most part, consumes the services on the spot. The impact of such a relationship upon not only the planning policies of the community but also upon the volume of attendant or auxiliary purchases will vary with the time spent by the consumer in the area. The time element involved will vary from the one day or its fraction devoted to obtaining medical or other personal services to such extremes as the long-term tourist vacationer or full-time university student.

(3) *Movement of Consumer to Capital.* In this circumstance the principal distinction from the other export relation of capital is that the initiative for export comes from outside the area and the negotiation is on a face-to-face basis. The situation is the one familiarly found in which the commercial bank or other local financial institution arranges a business, real estate, or personal loan at the direct request of an individual

(or firm) from outside the area who appears at the institution office to participate in the transaction.

Service Activity Classification

Although the main objective of this paper is that of classifying economic base types and indicating the significance of classification, increased perspective of this aspect of the urban economy is gained by an introductory look at a possible classification of the economic complement to the base—service activities.

As the discussion thus far has emphasized, the basic activities of a community are involved in export transactions.[2] Service activities have a negative sort of identification in that their end transactions are all local, they do not export. These local transactions are with the population of the community in general, with basic activities, and with other service activities.[3] For the sake of maintaining the consistency of classification on the basis of trade flows it seems proper to think of service activities as constituting two general types.

The first service activity type, which may be called Class 1, is that which imports goods, services, and capital for local processing and distribution, or just distribution. This classification would include, for example, the dry goods merchant as an importer of finished goods, the stock broker as the importer of stock quotations (services) on which ultimate security purchases may be based, and the insurance company correspondent who imports capital for real estate loans. Importation by service activities could also include raw materials imports by fabricators such as bakeries, printing firms, and building contractors. Restaurants would, perhaps, represent a slightly different sort of raw material processor. Many other gradations within this

---

[2] Basic activities do, of course, make direct imports of goods and services but their finished product is exported.

[3] Again it is recognized that there are few pure types (either base or service) and that a great many so-called service activities do some exporting.

type could no doubt be identified.

A second general classification of service activities, Class 2, includes those whose goods fabrication, service production, and capital origination and distribution is entirely local, involving no direct importation of any great significance. Here pure types may include sand and gravel extraction, truck gardening, the practice of law and medicine, barbering, and local lending and investment of funds.[4] Included in this same class but of a slightly different variety would be those local firms which are almost entirely dependent for their goods on local large-scale base enterprises. For example, there are the local meat markets that draw heavily for fresh and packaged meats on a local packing plant which is principally in the export business. The same relationship might exist between small local independent groceries and a large-scale grocery wholesale house. Here again we see a demonstration of the previously mentioned fact that there are few pure basic or service types. Whereas the packing plant and grocery wholesale house are predominantly basic they may play a definite service role in the community.

This discussion also brings up the question of linked activities. We say, for instance, that the automobile-starter factory which sells its product to the automobile manufacturer in the same community is linked industry. If the line of argument thus far presented is followed rigidly, we would classify the starter factory as a service activity which does not export. However, it is felt that from a more realistic point of view the starter factory should be considered basic in that there exists only an organizational line between the starter and automobile manufacturers both of whom are engaged in the final steps of putting together a finished exportable product. Identification of

---

[4] In most of the cases mentioned there is involved mechanical equipment that must be imported but the raw materials and the heaviest part of the investment leading to the finished product is of local origin. Also persons living on retirement incomes gained from local investments would be considered as a part of the service element of the local economy.

sub-linkings as basic enterprise could be said to extend through all stages of a particular manufacturing process found within a community. These stages are frequently separated only by the distinctions of horizontal organization. However, in order for these sub-links to gain identification as basic, nearly all of their output would have to go to higher links and ultimately into the exported product. It is unlikely that there would be many links of one industry within a single community due to an absence of complete monopoly of locational advantages but it is likely that the number of links involved may very well be in direct ratio to community size, scale of operating units of the enterprise, and the like.

CONCLUSIONS

To summarize, the purpose of classification is, in very general terms, that of clarification of the conception under consideration by a simplified, logical ordering of the various forms of that conception. It is a necessary first step, along with organization of terminology, in the scientific approach to any problem or field of inquiry. Successful and meaningful classification that will act as a reliable guide to research and field action must, moreover, have as its mold the strategic factor of identification, which in this case is export activity.

It is the hypothesis of the approach presented here that each of the two major base classifications described in preceding paragraphs has a pattern of social, economic, and geographic needs and action that varies only slightly from one subtype to another. The city planner might, therefore, order his master plan and day-to-day actions in such a way that they will conform with the peculiarities of the base class or classes found in his community.

While the form of base classification recommended in this paper has not been tested it does suggest some rather broad possibilities of application in the field of urban planning. The examples of application that come to the writer's mind are not completely satisfactory but will at least give more concrete form to the general ideas discussed thus far.

If, for example, the city planner finds that the basic activities of his community are strongly oriented toward Class A (Movement of Goods, Services, and Capital to the Consumer) and linked base enterprises, he should be prompted to devote much attention to conditions of transport and communication within the base area and between the base area and the areas to which exports move. Specifically, this would suggest concern for rail yards, siding systems, warehouses, truck routes and terminals, carrier registration systems, insurance rates, commercial air transport facilities and rate control. In the field of communications, questions of telephone, telegraph, and cable rates should hold a position of great importance in his plans.

A question arises here concerning the relationship of the economic base's complement—service activity—to the subject of classification and resulting problem fields for the planner. At this stage of hypothesis development it can be said that service activities of Class 1 (*import* of goods, services, and capital) seem closely associated with Class A base enterprises in that their needs and actions in relation to the movement of goods and services and to communications are very similar. Class 2 service activities (*local origination* of goods and services) do not, in the present opinion of this writer, seem to have a generalized planning focus such as that noted for Class 1. Their needs and actions are apparently those of producers who, in a negative sense, can be said to have relatively limited requirements for storage space, transport and long distance communication. Class 2 activities which obtain their goods from local base enterprises are, of course, greatly concerned from a planning viewpoint with programs designed for their supply sources.

It appears to this author that Class B base activities (Movement of the Consumer to Goods, Services, and Capital) provide more complicated situations for the planner than those found under Class A. The essence of the problem is simply that communities with a dominant Class B base are called upon to handle the customer in person as well as the goods and services being marketed. Here, of course, the complexity of the problem is in direct proportion to the length of time that the consumer is in the community purchasing (and perhaps consuming on the spot) his goods or services. The extremes of this situation range, as noted earlier, from the Saturday night out-of-town shopper in the retail trade center to the university student who is a "customer-resident" of the community for nine months of the year. The demands on the city planner are clearly increased as a result of this situation. Class B base communities involve far greater concentration on housing supply and distribution, and on zoning that will adjust to these housing needs and to the supplementary commercial demands of long-term consumers. Peak load problems of traffic and parking are much more likely with Class B, not to mention more detailed contingent problems of building codes, fire and police protection, recreational area allocations, and even public school planning.

Capital export operations are not likely to cause the city planner difficulty in either Class A or Class B situations. The greatest likelihood of trouble, however, again arises with Class B when, as in our larger cities, capital export operations combined with other financial service-export activities are concentrated in financial districts.

Finally, the city planner should be aware of these broader patterns of the base and their planning ramifications for the sake of preparing himself against the approach of problems of change. A shift in the dominant character of a community's base from Class A to Class B, though gradual, would suggest the preliminary drafting of rather sweeping changes in policy that would not necessarily be apparent if a more piecemeal approach to the community's economic makeup were employed. Shifts from B to A might be equally revolutionary, depending upon the case under consideration.

An approach such as the one described above should reduce the volume of analysis that would otherwise go into a study of each base activity of the area and lend organizational unity to what could be a diffuse patchwork of urban economic activities. Classification does not, of course, eliminate the necessity of progressive studies of individual base activities which show a changing relationship to their raw materials, markets, productive factors, to other base activities, and the service activities of the economic area. The city planner is, moreover, concerned with the qualitative character of each of his base activities and appreciates the specific planning needs of manufacturing, commercial, and institutional activities and their individual and combined influence over general community needs.

However, our argument contends that general understanding by the planner of the planning significance of the two principal base classifications is important not only from the standpoint of simplification but also from the point of view that an overall improvement in planning efficiency is to be gained. The system of classification suggested tends to give an uncluttered view of the urban economy which may well bring to the planners' attention core relationships and cumulative effects that he had not previously appreciated in drafting long-term policy. In short, classification can be a means of creating a better adaptation of present plans to present and future urban needs.

This entire problem of ordering and reorganization will take another tack in the next article of the series when the question of base measurement is discussed.

Richard B. Andrews—Mechanics of the Urban Economic Base: The Problem of Base Measurement

Mechanics of the Urban Economic Base:
The Problem of Base Measurement*

The urban economic base is represented by those activities of a community which are engaged in the export of goods, services, and capital to other communities, regions, and nations beyond the boundaries of what may be defined as the community in a particular case. Within the economy of the community there may also be identified activities which are classified as service rather than basic. Service activities in their pure form do not engage in export but sell their produce or capital to local basic enterprises, employees of the base, other service activities and their employees, and to persons of the community who may be unemployed or receiving local public assistance.[1] This set of relationships summarizes the meaning of the term "urban economic base" and its economic complement, service activity.

If the base of a community is to be analyzed and the results of such an investigation are to be applied by the city planner certain preliminary decisions must be made concerning the ways in which base phenomena are to be measured. It is the contention of this writer that the way in which the base is measured has an important bearing on ultimate interpretations and applications of data collected. Moreover, measure is an inseparable part of the associated process of identification of the base. In the process of identification the city planner or researcher has not only the broad problem of separating basic or export activity from service activity, but he also has the associated technical problem of quantifying these phenomena. Therefore, one of the most challenging problems that must be faced by the planner at this point in his work is that of choosing a unit or units of measure.

It is the intention here to evaluate briefly the more common

---

* See Acknowledgements

[1] Persons on retirement incomes are in most cases considered as being a part of the base.

units of measure that have been employed in studies of the economic base and attempt to indicate what their shortcomings are in terms of what they do and do not measure. The article will also try to give a clearer comprehension of the scope of the measurement problem and of the interrelation of different units of measure, facts not always apparent in straight base studies. This suggests, therefore, that final answers are not forthcoming from the discussion; it is not a procedural guide but, more nearly, an indication of what further work needs to be done to bring the use of the unit of base measurement to a state of greater precision and broader significance.

Thus far in the development of the urban economic base concept there have been employed, or in some cases only suggested six different units of measure. These units are (1) jobs, (2) payrolls, (3) value added, (4) value of production, (5) physical production, and (6) dollar income and expenditure accounts for the community.

EMPLOYMENT AS A UNIT OF MEASURE

The job or employment as a unit of measure has been the device most widely used thus far. It has many rather obvious advantages. Moreover, the job unit is a universally experienced thing; and employment, in a general sense, is one of the major concerns of any economic system whether it be national, regional, or local. Information in this form is usually readily available although detail breakdowns by firm or occupation may frequently be difficult to obtain in large urban centers. From a local planning point of view the job unit is to a very large extent equivalent to the family group, though less so than in the past due to the employment of wives. The family group moving as a unit within the community and the region is an important measure, in turn, of innumerable planning decisions. In a similar sense the changing degree of availability of jobs is a basic determinant of the changing volume of local family groups in terms of in-and-out migrations, marriages, and divorces.

However, employment as a unit of measure is not a device of perfection. An instance of this fact is cited in the following extract from the very limited literature on this whole problem: "A picture of the economy in terms of number of persons employed is not without defects. For example, output per worker may increase tremendously in a decade and there may be differential changes in the output per worker in different activities."[2] Here is introduced the idea that questions of physical production and total value of production may have a position of importance as units of measure. A rise in productivity may, moreover, be associated with an increase in the rate and total wage assigned to the individual job.

There is a definite dilemma here for the planner in that he is well aware of the fact that basic activities are important to his community by virtue of the fact that they export goods and services and earn, in the process, a return for the community. In the general case just cited rising productivity could well mean heavier exports and hence, possibly, a greater volume of net returns to the community. Yet this very important development in the base of the community might not be reflected in a unit of base measurement confined to employment. It is, of course, very likely that a situation such as the one described would lead to an increase in total number of jobs in the community. This would be the product of sympathetic growth on the part of service activities with a change in the base. Specifically, higher wage rates, over-time work, greater productivity, and heavier profits in the base would lead to heavier spending for service activities and the necessity for expansion of service activities simply to handle the increased physical production moving out of the community.[3] Clearly the economic dynamics of

[2] F. L. Kidner and P. Neff, *An Economic Survey of the Los Angeles Area*, (Los Angeles, California: Haynes Foundation, 1945), p. 5.

[3] More detailed discussion will be devoted to this question of base-service interaction and total employment in later articles.

the community would in this case, not be explained by simply looking at base employment data.

Another difficulty of detail which is encountered in the use of employment for base measurement is that of the counting of seasonal and part-time employment. It is, of course, not reasonable to count this type of employment "straight" since the balance of the base is counted on a full-year basis. In attacking this problem there appears thus far to be but one general approach. Seasonal employment may be converted to full-time equivalents in terms of man-hour totals. The same treatment may be given part-time employment. In cases of this type it can be seen in what ways another unit of measure such as payrolls might obviate what is a rather bothersome and rough process of conversion.

An associated problem is that of the basic enterprise with widely fluctuating monthly employment during the year. Obviously this problem can be taken care of by some averaging device. However, it leaves a question in the mind of the investigator concerning the advisability of finding and using some other measure that does not require such adjustments.

PAYROLLS AS A MEASURE

Other inadequacies of employment as a measure of base activity appear as alternative situations are considered. Payrolls are here a case in point. Hoyt rendered a clear view of payroll weight and its possible influence on the conclusions that are to be drawn from base employment data when he compared employment and payrolls in his New York study.[4]

Here is demonstrated the rather striking change in perspective that occurs with a change in the basis of measurement. If the planner were to work with employment data exclusively he might establish an entirely different line of priority in attacking

---

[4] Arthur M. Weimer and Homer Hoyt, *Principles of Urban Real Estate* (New York: The Ronald Press Co.: 1948), p. 109.

his problems than if he viewed his economy in terms of payrolls. This line of thinking also suggests that he, in turn, might

RELATIVE WEIGHTS OF SOURCES OF EMPLOYMENT AND INCOME IN THE NEW YORK REGION, 1940

Source of Employment	Number Employed	Percentage of Total	
		Number Employed	Payrolls
Manufacturing	900,000	60.0	48.2
Banking, Finance, and Administrative Offices	220,000	14.7	23.1
Wholesale Trade	190,000	12.7	18.4
Transportation	150,000	10.0	8.4
Hotels and Amusements	40,000	2.6	1.9
Total	1,500,000	100.0	100.0

reach a third priority arrangement and different general conclusions concerning his local economy by looking at the combined results of the two approaches. This line of thought might be summed up in the proposition that one job at $10,000 per year has the same economic weight as two jobs at $5,000. The implications which lie in this relationship for local service spending, service employment, property tax collection potential and quality of public services are profound. And yet if this line of reasoning is carried to an extreme its strength diminishes rapidly. For can the planner properly say that ten positions in the community each paying $50,000 are the economic equivalent of one hundred $5,000 positions? There are, certainly, considerations to be weighed in the case of each variety of measurement. It is obvious that there exists great planning significance in the mere *number* of jobs. Number of jobs represents an indicator of economic opportunity. It is in turn a measure of potential population to be supported whereas payroll weight or annual remuneration may be more nearly a clue to the standard of living to be expected once a job has been obtained. Measurement on the basis of payroll totals by basic enterprise has, therefore, to be considered in terms of the distribution of income within the particular enterprise and within the community. As suggested in one of the examples above, heavy concentrations of salaries toward the upper end of the scale in an industry can suggest a greater rate of saving and consequently less expenditure in proportion to dollars earned in the lower income levels where the expenditure rate is not only higher but in greater volume. It is also likely that, although the actual total of dollars expended by the higher bracket earners will be greater per capita than in the case of lower-bracket earners, there also may be a marked tendency in large metropolitan areas for the higher salary groups to spend a lesser percentage of total income locally, in their home satellite cities, and more in the central city.

This entire line of reasoning suggests that, in addition to total payroll by basic activity, there may well be a closely associated unit of measure, namely median or average income of the employee in the basic activity. With a measure of this variety, however, it is clear that the planner may be getting a bit far afield. Salary medians by basic activity would in themselves give no indication of quantitative weight which would be essential if an accurate picture of the local economy were to be gained. It is probably advisable therefore to employ central tendencies of salaries and wages as base measuring devices only as an adjunct to payroll as a measure. If so used they might give a condensed indication of the qualitative aspects of a particular activity payroll without entangling the planner each time in the laborious review of a complete salary distribution scale.

Payroll data, moreover, if employed as a measure of base activity are open to the highly significant price change adjustment. This, of course, suggests that base data are to be used by the planner on a progressive basis rather than in the form of a single inventory. With time change introduced the use of payroll data may become more difficult. Under inflationary and deflationary pressures the payroll totals of various base enterprises are certain to change. Part of the planner's task is that of adjusting his new payroll data upward or downward in order that they may be rendered comparable to the data of his base year. The difficulties of adjustments of this nature are almost too well known to warrant repetition. Therefore, a simple indication of some of these problems will suffice.

For many cities no individual retail price index is available that might be used for payroll adjustment once volume of employee comparability with the base year had been established. Consequently, adjustment data from neighboring cities that may not be comparable in character have to be employed. However, if a generally reliable adjustment can be made it will show at least two important facts concerning the urban economy under analysis. On the one hand the adjustment will show the change, positive or negative, in the total payroll weight of the basic enterprises. This is a type of change, which, as indicated earlier, could take place without change in total community employment. The other application of the adjustment process is similar to the first. In this instance price adjustment is used more in a qualitative sense to show the net change from the base year of particular basic enterprises that go to make up the community total. This second application would also, of course, show any changes in payroll rank. However, it is perhaps obvious that payroll rank of basic enterprises would be determinable without price adjustment.

Aside from difficulties of price adjustment, annual payroll data are subject to other conditions that may lead to inaccuracies. For example, extensive cuts in reported payroll totals might develop in a single year as the result of a strike. If the base measurement were taken in that particular year, it would show the strike-bound enterprise at a disadvantage. Even though the planner would be aware of this situation he would have difficulty adjusting it with any great degree of accuracy. The same line of reasoning might be applied to enterprises of the base which accumulated heavy overtime in the year selected for review by the planner. Again, payroll adjustments could be made but a question remains as to their precision. Employment as a measure is open to some of these same criticisms but is less affected than annual payrolls due in part to the fact that it does not represent a cumulation of units overtime.

One final observation on payroll data or employment as exclusive measures of base activity circulates around the following idea. Employment, occupation, and payroll data do not accurately reflect that portion of the community's activity which is centered on capital export. These same measures would be found equally lacking in this respect if applied to service rather than base capital activities.

VALUE ADDED AND VALUE OF PRODUCTION

Value added and value of production as units of measure have not found great favor among those faced with the task of investigating urban economies. Such a view is stated in a Los Angeles study which points out that "these considerations led to the view that measurements of, for example, value added by manufacture, distort the description since they are beclouded by complex price movements, while measurements made in terms of number of wage earners are beclouded by technological changes."[5]

It appears that this type of measure would also encounter practical difficulties where base activities were involved which had intangible inputs and value products, i.e., educational institutions and medical centers. Whereas value added and value of production may possess dubious utility as general base measurement devices, they have a definite contribution to make from a qualitative point of view. That is to say, they can render added perspective to analysis of the manufacturing aspects of the base. This point of view is suggested by the Chicago Plan Commission in one of its reports which states:

"It is of value to compare the rankings of the Area's indus-

---

[5] Kidner and Neff, *An Economic Survey of the Los Angeles Area*, p. 5.

tries based on employment with their positions measured by value added by manufacture . . . . In general, some of the non-durable goods industries, such as food, printing and publishing, chemicals, and petroleum and coal products create a higher value in the process of manufacture than would be expected on the basis of their proportion of the Area's production workers."[6]

Sales volume represents another possibility in the general field of value of product measurement. Dollar sales volume might be applied to trade in general that was classifiable as basic. But here again there would be the inherent difficulties of price adjustment, complex price movement, and restricted applicability insofar as other parts of the base might be concerned. The residual virtue, as in the other cases cited, would be that of contributing added perspective to one variety of basic activity.

It must be emphasized, nonetheless, that sales data are highly important as a unit of measure for purposes of identification. These data are most commonly used in the identification process of segregating basic from service activity within an enterprise. In this process they are converted into another measure which is, as a rule, employment. Briefly, the process is one in which the proportion of export sales of a firm or industry is distinguished from the proportion of local area sales. These proportions are then applied to the employment totals of the firm or industry to accomplish a sales-to-employment conversion. The weakness of this procedure lies mainly in the fact that, as with other approaches, it does not cover all situations. For example, it is deficient in its ability to measure capital export and commuter activity.

PHYSICAL PRODUCTION

Physical production has, to the knowledge of this writer, never been employed as a unit of measure in base analysis. Its

6 The Chicago Plan Commission, *Industrial and Commercial Background for Planning Chicago* (Chicago, Illinois: no date), p. 9.

practical drawbacks are rather obvious. As with value-added and production-value, physical production cannot account for non-physical output. Consequently, it is more adaptable to the manufacturing elements of the base than to any other and is in that respect a valuable supplementary measure of activity. In fact the principal use of this type of measure may well be found in analyzing the comparative positions of base activities engaged in manufacturing. However, even here product heterogeneity might well present serious difficulties.

There might be some basis for arguing that a physical production measure could be applied to such a seemingly inappropriate activity as a university. Here the parallel with factory production is not entirely absent. The university produces a fairly homogeneous product line at a relatively uniform price. The number of educations sold might, consequently, follow trends independent of university employment and adjusted payroll.

Despite the limitations of physical production as a general unit of measure it appears to have some special virtues that tend to counterbalance one of the drawbacks of employment and payrolls as measures. Specifically, physical production can, in the field of manufacturing, indicate the quantitative impact of technological change leading to greater output which may not be accompanied by an increase in employment or in payrolls.[7] Here the implications of such change for the community are great not only in terms of the economics of handling more physical goods but also in terms of increased profits, potential plant expansion, and the attraction of other manufacturers to the community.

COMMUNITY INCOME AND EXPENDITURE

Dollar income, outgo, and internal circulation measurements for an entire community are far more inclusive than any of the

---

[7] In fact a decrease in employment and payrolls would be possible in these circumstances.

units of measure thus far discussed.[8] This approach embraces all monetary transactions of the community both basic and service. In a sense this approach, if combined with employment data, would represent the most complete (also complex) and, perhaps, satisfactory statistical view of the urban economy available to the city planner. A particular advantage of this approach is that it could identify the capital exports of the community so often neglected in base studies in the absence of a satisfactory measurement unit. It is certain, however, that this type of community trade analysis would be out of the question for cities of any great size. This would be true not only because of the immense diversity of materials sources but also because of the utter impossibility of getting at some of the data which if actually assembled would represent a maze of internal transactions. This type of accounting would be expensive initially for the large city and, to be meaningful, would have to be incurred as a regular planning budget item somewhat reduced from the initial expenditure. Even for the small city the expense of such a measuring technique would be close to prohibitive.[9]

CONCLUSIONS

In conclusion, it is appropriate to emphasize the fact that general measurement data on the urban base have two principal applications. The first of these is measurement of the base with the idea of distinguishing it in quantitative terms from the service elements of the urban economy and establishing relative quantitive positions for the basic elements. This is, actually, part of the process of base identification. The other objective is that of using base measurement data to explain an urban economy more fully and to indicate how it can be expected to work in varying situations. It is on this latter score that measurement technique appears most inadequate. For while a

---

[8] "Oskaloosa versus the United States," *Fortune,* April, 1938.

[9] The Oskaloosa, Iowa study was underwritten by *Fortune* magazine.

particular unit of measure may work admirably as a means of identification it can fail to meet its other objective almost completely. This situation may, of course, beg the question in the minds of many as to whether a unit of measure can be expected to assist more than just the process of identification. In the opinion of this author, once identification has been established with one unit of measure, many other units must be introduced that will give some indication of the relationship of the parts of the base one to the other and the relationship of the total base and each of its parts to the terms other than those of the unit of measurement used as the basis of identification. The introduction of these other units of measure will thus give a more complete and meaningful picture of the static urban economy as of one moment in time. Moreover, these measures will also provide the vitally necessary basis for understanding, explaining, and planning for the local urban economy in motion.

As was suggested earlier in connection with the New York and Chicago studies the thing that supplementary units of measure provide in addition to qualitative perspective is a series of quantitative weight scales that can give the planner a better idea of the comparative rank orders of the basic activities of his community. Weighting is, consequently, a specific employment of measure that is intended to aid the planner in making more precise, and, at the same time, more comprehensive decisions. One criticism that comes to mind at this point is that weighting appears to have been used on a far too restrictive basis thus far in urban economic base studies. One or perhaps two weighting factors may be employed in a study and, in some instances, none at all. A concluding thought on the general subject of weighting and measure centers about the idea that there are probably other significant measuring concepts that are still unformulated but even in their undigested condition could be introduced into the field for experimental use. Such a concept is that of comparative base activity stability. If an enterprise is given a heavy employment and/or payroll weight in a particular year but proves highly sensitive to changing business conditions and has uncertain markets or new materials sources there would be ample ground for giving it a negative stability rating. A firm with a less impressive employment or payroll record in the survey year but a good stability record might have a positive rating or greater stability weight in the local base rankings than its otherwise more impressive companion.

Another weighting factor approach which has rich possibilities of adding perspective to economic base judgments involves the volume of local purchases of goods and services made by the base enterprise itself rather than by its employees. There appear to be some basic enterprises, as for example a large university, which make very heavy purchase demands on the goods and services of the communities in which they are located. This is in contrast to other basic enterprises which, though larger in terms of employment, have relatively light local demands. This general idea is well stated by Hoover when he points out: "Plainly an industry that pays out most of its costs locally, for payrolls or for materials in fairly elastic local supply, and that furnishes a product suitable for further processing at that point has a relatively high leverage."[10]

Finally, it might be re-emphasized that the problem of units of base activity measurement remains a very real and vital one. From a practical point of view one must perhaps conclude that, for the present, units of measure are in large part dictated by the types of statistical materials that are available as well as by a comparison of relative performance characteristics of these measures. But this state of expediency, which is common to many fields of investigation in the social sciences, should not discourage the planner from attempting to spell out in his own mind the kind or kinds of measurement units that would best serve his needs. It is only in this way that he can ultimately

---

[10] Edgar M. Hoover, *The Location of Economic Activity*. (New York: McGraw-Hill Book Company, 1948), p. 153.

foster the regular collection of data in the form that he most desires.

At the present time it appears that the measurement unit most appropriate to the process of identification may well be the widely used employment measure. However ,this is not a satisfactory universal measure due to its almost complete inapplicability to capital export. Its inadequacies in other directions have already been reviewed. Moreover, as was emphasized above, general measure as a procedure is not solely a part of the machinery of identification but is, as well, a fundamental in base analysis. It is this latter role, which involves a wide range of weighting in its static and dynamic aspects, that must be more fully appreciated and cultivated by both planner and researcher if they expect to obtain the full three dimensional picture of their urban economy in the present and all four dimensional implications over time.

Summarized, the above discussion boils down to a few recommendations for the city planner and researcher worker in urban land economics:

(1) In the process of judging an urban economy use *all* the measuring techniques feasible at the time. The single unit of measure used for identification alone is usually inadequate for general qualitative analysis though it is traditionally so employed. There is a direct proportional relationship between the adequacy of one's perspective on an urban economy and the number of measures of the base used.

(2) Carry on research which will indicate more clearly what the relationship of each of the various units of measure is to the base, to the general urban economy, and to other units of measure.

(3) If the local limitations on statistical materials necessary to an adequate measurement program are great the planner should outline his data needs and take steps toward their ultimate fulfillment.

(4) City planners should make preliminary field tests of unfamiliar measuring devices such as stability and volume of local purchases by basic activities in order that the difficulties of application can be identified and research steps be taken to mitigate these difficulties.

The complexities of the base measurement problem do, at times, appear disheartening. There seems to be no easy yet adequate solution to the difficulties involved. However, much is to be gained by stating the problem and by appraising the degrees of its resistance to attack in varying circumstances. An ensuing article on base identification will add perspective on the problem of measure with further clues to the selection and application of measurement devices.

Richard B. Andrews—Mechanics of the Urban Economic Base: General Problems of Base Identification

Mechanics of the Urban Economic Base:
General Problems of Base Identification*

The urban economic base for purposes of this discussion can be defined along lines followed in earlier articles of the series. Briefly described the base is that part of an urban economy which is composed of activities whose principal function is that of exporting goods, services, or capital beyond the economic boundaries of the community. The economic complement of the base is made up of service activities. Service activities of the community are primarily engaged in internal trade which involves sales of goods, personal services, and capital to local base enterprises, employees of the base, other service enterprises, employees of service enterprises, and unemployed persons within the community.

In the process of analyzing the economic base of a specific urban area there arise certain technical problems which include not only the selection and application of units of measure but also the process of base identification. Identification of the base is essentially simple as a working plan but rather difficult in application.

Identification, in a broad sense, is made as soon as the base is defined. If we think of the base as representing the export activities of an urban area then the problem seems to be simply that of identifying and listing such export organizations. However, it is at this point that a unit of measure is introduced. Clearly the exporters must be quantified in some way other than by a mere statement of number of exporters. If the unit of measure for purposes of identification is employment then this measure is applied to the exporters and their relative employment standing in the community is established. A statement of the relation of base employment to service employment, total employment, and population is thus made possible. However, application of this procedure is vastly complicated by the

* See Acknowledgements

fact that there are relatively few "pure" activities which can be said to be entirely basic or entirely service. It is, therefore, the segregation of basic and service elements from what we may call typically "mixed" activities that represents one of the principal general problems in the identification process.

There is also an associated difficulty, much narrower in scope than the problem of mixed enterprises, which arises as a result of limitations of the unit of measure. Reference is made here to the fact that the standard employment measure has difficulty in identifying such fields as capital export activity in a suitable manner.

Finally, it must be emphasized that an integral part of the process of identification is the setting of economic boundaries for the community. Without a clear definition of these boundaries it becomes difficult to identify basic activities with any degree of precision. For if exportation is to be distinguished it must be in terms of movement of goods, services and capital outward across the line which separates the urban community from its market. This particular aspect of identification will be discussed in a subsequent article on technique.

IDENTIFICATION TECHNIQUES

There are currently in use several general techniques whereby the basic economic activities of a community may be segregated and measured. The paragraphs that follow will summarize some of the more prominent of these techniques and indicate what their principal virtues and shortcomings are. An attempt will be made to estimate which of the techniques shows the greatest promise and would therefore warrant the greatest concentration of effort directed toward procedural refinement and, perhaps, conceptual extension. Particular attention will be paid to the common problems that arise in the application of familiar identification techniques. These common or general problems are to be distinguished from special identification problems which are not found to an important degree in all cities.

The discussion is not concerned with detail problems of obtaining raw employment data where this unit of measure is used. It is assumed that the usual sources for this particular unit are available, i.e., direct data collection from federal, state, and urban governmental agencies.

RESIDUAL METHOD

The residual method of identification is a technique devised by Homer Hoyt, but no longer used by him in his later studies. Operating as a rough rule of thumb, it was employed prior to 1940 when a detailed breakdown of employment by type of industry was unavailable.[1] Briefly stated the residual method may be described as follows:

All known basic enterprises are measured in terms of the number of their employees. As long as a heavy proportion of the activities of these enterprises was in the export field and only a minor proportion identified with local trade the entire enterprise was considered basic.[2] A 1:1 ratio between basic and service employment was assumed by Hoyt in his earlier studies. From those activities which were not predominantly basic were subtracted the number of employees typically assumed to be necessary for the performance of the service functions of the community. The size of this deduction was computed from the 1:1 ratio. The residual following this deduction for service purposes was allocated to the base side of the local economy since it was assumed that the service requirements of the community had been completely cared for by the previous computation. In this manner the mixed enterprises—those not clearly basic—were broken down into their base and service components.

---

[1] Arthur M. Weimer and Homer Hoyt, *Principles of Urban Real Estate* (New York: The Ronald Press Company, 1939), pp. 44-45. For most recent method, *see*: Weimer and Hoyt, *Principles of Real Estate,* 3rd edition (The Ronald Press Company, 1954), ch. 18, pp. 332-345.

[2] This idea seemed to be implicit in Hoyt's reasoning in his first studies.

At the present time this technique should no longer be used as a complete breakdown of employment, for every urban region is available. Hoyt changed his views on the immutability of the 1 to 1 ratio and changed the entire technique of identification in his New York study.[3] It may be to the point, however, to criticize the technique which is now obsolete, since it has a certain persuasiveness traceable in part to the relative ease of its application.

The assumed ratio was the core weakness of the technique. As will be emphasized in later articles, one of the principal objectives of investigating the economy of a community is to discover what the base-to-service ratio is.[4] Consequently, to estimate the ratio is to assume away what should be one of the important findings of base research. Of course in the circumstances under which Hoyt was working with the Federal Housing Administration in the Thirties survey speed was important, complete data on employment by type of industry was not provided until the census of 1940, and a rule of thumb such as the ratio provided was an expediter. With far more complete statistical data on employment now available, and with more improved techniques for analyzing basic and service employment, this early pioneer method is merely a museum piece.

It is no longer necessary to make the assumption that certain activities are 100 percent "base types" and can, therefore, be classed automatically as basic. Manufacturing is an example. However, certain portions of such enterprises may be engaged in service activity; a situation which, apparently, this technique does not assume away but simply does not regard as important.

We must conclude, therefore, that the residual method had many limitations and employed assumptions which would not

---

[3] Homer Hoyt, *Economic Status of the New York Metropolitan Region in 1944* (New York: Regional Plan Association, Incorporated, 1944).

[4] The ratio between basic and service employment is found to vary from 1 to 0.6, to 1 to 2.1. Weimer and Hoyt, *Principles of Real Estate,* 3rd edition, (New York: The Ronald Press Company, 1954), p. 352.

produce the most accurate results. Since this method has been abandoned by its originator, interest in it would now be only historical.

MACROCOSMIC METHOD

Base identification by the macrocosmic method is of fairly recent origin as a technique.[5] It is used, principally, in large urban areas where more detailed techniques would be costly and time-consuming. What this approach does, in essence, is to make a comparison of the employment pattern of the area under study with that of the nation at large. As one research team expressed the idea:

". . . manufacturing currently employs 40 percent of all gainfully employed persons in the Chicago area, whereas the national percentage is 27 . . . . It may be inferred, therefore, that the goods produced by these 13 percent 'extra' workers are probably destined for export markets."[6]

It is not assumed, of course, that each urban area conforms strictly to the national pattern of production and consumption. But it is felt that relationships such as the one described will indicate the rough magnitude of local employment as compared to a national norm. Situations will occur with great frequency in which all or part of an industry within a community may be below the national average and yet that industry may be a heavy exporter. This calls to mind as an example the highly specialized production of machine tools in a small city. The likelihood is great that none of the machine tools will be consumed

---

[5] The term "macrocosmic" is here introduced by the author in view of the absence of a single descriptive name or term in the literature.

[6] W. E. Hoadley, Jr., and C. G. Wright, *Employment, Production and Income in the Chicago Industrial Area* (Chicago: Research Department, Federal Reserve Bank of Chicago, 1948), p. 3. The authors are of course, emphasizing the idea that all industrial activity devotes a certain proportion of its energies to serving local needs. This proportion is here assumed to be the same for the local urban community as it is for the national community. Anything in excess of this proportion is considered export activity.

locally. Yet under the macrocosmic method a substantial proportion of the employment total of the firm would be classified as service rather than basic. In his studies Hoyt assumed that all capital goods industries such as machine tools were basic. Roterus made an attempt to estimate the proportion of output of a capital goods industry that was consumed locally but found it involved very elaborate and difficult compilations. There may be adequate ground for the criticism that as the size of the city under study declines the reliability of the macrocosmic method also declines. The basis for this thought is to be found in the example cited above. It suggests that plant employment size within an industry as among a group of communities may not necessarily vary widely whereas the population distribution of the communities under consideration may be very wide. This line of reasoning further suggests that as communities decline in size the proportionate volume of local purchases of the goods being produced will also decline. Consequently, a heavier proportion of employees would be attributable to the export or basic phase of the industry in the case of the small community than in the case of the large one. In addition to this quantitative question consideration there is a qualitative question of which users of the macrocosmic method are well aware. This question is again one which is suggested in the example of the machine tool plant. Specifically, locally produced goods or services may not be demanded locally for many reasons which would include the traditional deterents of price and taste, a high degree of specialization, or the simple fact that the good or service produced is part of a production chain which is to be continued in another community. On the other hand it is well recognized that the production of consumer necessities, such as certain forms of finished food products, would engender fairly large local trade.

Recognition of some of these situations is apparent in the adjustments which are made for variations in urban consumption and savings habits as against those of the nation as a whole.[7]   This type of qualification, however, raises a question as to whether there may not be, in addition, some significant variations among urban areas in consumption and savings habits traceable to variations in the character of their economic bases and social patterns.

Among the many involved adjustments which must be made when the macrocosmic method is employed are those emphasized by the short but deep section on technique found in the Cincinnati study of 1946.[8]   Here Victor Roterus and his staff point out that "the formula for determining the urban-serving employment must be varied with each activity because urban consumption differs in many cases from national (urban-rural) consumption."[9]   The report correctly stresses, moreover, the fact that macrocosmic conversion assumes that a community draws as heavily as possible on local production to satisfy its demands before turning to outside sources.   This assumption simply does not hold in many instances.[10]

A minor criticism of the macrocosmic method which was also mentioned in connection with the residual technique is the question which arises concerning the inclusiveness of the approach. In other words macrocosmic conversion is no more effective for identification purposes than the residual approach when it comes to problems of capital export, retirement incomes, commuter activity and the like.   There is also the observation to be made that occupational and industrial classifications of the U. S. Census may not always be sufficiently fine in particular cases to give the precision that may be desired, especially in situations where firms contain mixtures of activities which must be separately counted in order to be used in the technique.

---

[7] Hoyt, Regional Plan Association, Inc., *op. cit.*

[8] Cincinnati City Planning Commission, *Economy of the Area* (Cincinnati: City Planning Commission, December 1946), p. 23.

[9] *Ibid.,* p. 23.

[10] *Ibid.,* p. 24.

This writer is left with the feeling that, whereas some such approach as that of the macrocosmic is almost a necessity in very large metropolitan areas, it leaves wide margins of error traceable in the main to the numerous potential variables involved. There is certainly a substantial question as to whether or not the variables (if recognized) can be weighed and compensated with satisfactory precision. Finally, it is not altogether clear from the writings inspected by this author whether or not ample testing of the macrocosmic method has been carried out. Apparently single industries within a community have been tested.[11] However, there is the very real likelihood that the testing has not been extended at one time to several communities. Consequently, the unwary investigator who attempts to identify the basic and service elements of his community and uncritically applies the macrocosmic technique may obtain inaccurate results. What is needed is an investigation of the technique *per se,* one which tests it in different sizes and types of communities. It might be possible to start this type of investigation economically by using several small cities where the macrocosmic method could be applied and then checked by actual counts that employ other methods of identification that are impractical for large metropolitan areas.

SALES-EMPLOYMENT CONVERSION

Among the identification techniques which are applied with varying degrees of success to small cities the sales-employment conversion method is the one deserving most attention. As was indicated in the preceding article on units of measure this method employs the two "standard" measures (employment and payrolls) for identification purposes. Its objective is simply that of determining the proportional shares of sales made by an enterprise inside and outside the economic community however it may be defined. These proportions are then applied to

---

[11] *Ibid.*

what might be called the "working" unit of measure, let us say employment, and a basic-service distribution of the measurement factors results.

The commonest means of applying this technique is through the questionnaire and interview. The questionnaire approach is simple in concept but often complex in execution. It has been employed principally as a means of segregating basic from service employment in the retail fields. It has not been used quite as extensively for segregation purposes in the field of personal and professional services. Both the questionnaire and interview techniques of executing sales-employment conversion are to be thought of as field approaches *contra* the deductive residual and macrocosmic. Because of their more direct approach and the fact that they usually are employing fresher data they are to be preferred to the deductive techniques. However, there are problems of size of universe, speed of data collection, and cost to be considered in the application of any identification technique. It is because of these conditions that in many instances the process which is less desirable in terms of precision must be employed.

In execution the questionnaire and interview techniques may be used separately or in combination depending on the conditions under which the investigation is to be made. A simplified interview approach involves obtaining from responsible management an estimate of the percentage of business which is carried on by the enterprise outside of the boundaries of the economic community or the percentage of sales to shoppers, tourists, and similar groups who come from outside the community. These proportional estimates are then applied to whichever unit of measure is used in the identification process, here *employment*. The basic and service elements can then be quantified (or converted from sales to employment) for the particular enterprise and eventually cumulated into industry, basic and service, enterprise classifications. In the event that management is not certain concerning the export and service aspects of its enterprise other approaches must be employed to obtain the data or to check on management's statements.

It is at this point that the customer questionnaire may be introduced. The objective is, of course, that of determining the residence or business location of the on-the-spot purchaser. Such questionnaires are usually distributed directly to the customer when he is at the place of business under analysis and can easily include questions on patronage of other places of business and local buying habits in general.

Mailing lists are of doubtful value as a customer data source in this connection because they may either be purchased lists or include only charge customers of the enterprise being studied.

Delivery and mailing records provide another general variety of sales-source check. However, these records are not kept by all enterprises and if they are maintained they alone are not adequate indicators of export trade, particularly in the retail field where cash and carry is still strong as a buying technique.

However, in the case of enterprises the bulk of whose transactions are with customers at a distance as against an on-the-spot-purchase basis the problem of segregation of base and service enterprise data may be somewhat simpler, providing the data are made available to the investigator. The principles of sales-employment conversion are, of course, applied here as well. Greater accuracy of results may be obtained if customer account records are made available. This type of segregation can be applied with even fewer complications to the operations of the mail order house and hotel.

However, for the retail merchandise firms of a city and the dispensers of business, personal, and professional services the practical problems of segregation are formidable. Partly by way of review some of the more outstanding difficulties may be pointed out.

The customer questionnaire has, to this writer, always appeared a difficult device with which to work. Even assuming a good percentage of responses there remain knotty questions concerning the representative character of the sample in terms of all types of customers. The meat of this last point is that it cannot always be assumed that customer responses are evenly distributed by type and hence by location.

Another problem in applying the questionnaire and interview technique arises in the fact that the number of small operators in the merchandise, personal and professional service field within one community is often very large. The baffling scope of a complete coverage operation consequently forces the use of some sampling device. As a result the investigator may have to accept the sample of a sample. This problem will, of course, increase in seriousness progressively with city size.

Finally, it should be re-emphasized that where management is requested to estimate export activity it is at a disadvantage since it is forced to think in terms of an economic community boundary which may be entirely unfamiliar in terms of patronage breakdowns. As a consequence, estimates are not likely to be accurate.

From what has been said it is apparent that, whereas the character of data collected by questionnaire and interview is to be preferred to that made available by more round-about processes, it is also guilty of significant flaws. The presence of defects in an investigatory process suggests certain compensatory actions. On the one hand, weaknesses in a procedure may be lessened in seriousness or, at best, completely removed by concentrated analysis of the causes and balancing cures. In any event, conclusions drawn from data based on procedures with recognized blemishes must be treated carefully and adequate allowances made. If the flaws appear insuperable under the system of data collection used and if there are encountered, at the same time, great difficulties in judging what compensation should be made for such inadequacies, then there is ample ground for believing that a new technique must be found.

Specifically, the interview and questionnaire methods are too closely bound to the rather unwelcome but often unavoidable process of estimating. The inadequacies of this process stemming from errors in human judgment and simple lack of supporting data are too well known to warrant further comment. One must conclude, therefore, that, whereas there are no doubt many improvements yet to be made in this approach, there remains the fundamental weakness of the source material. Consequently, there appears to be an urgent need for the development of new identification techniques in the field of segregation particularly as they apply to wholesaling and retailing of merchandise and other business, personal, and professional services.

SAMPLING

Sampling is not a technique for general base identification segregation. It is, rather, a statistical device which is implicit in such techniques as sales-employment conversion involving use of the questionnaire and interview approach.

There may also be a sampling decision to be made as to which "representative" enterprises shall be studied within the various industrial classifications of a community. Then, when the selection has been made, there arises the possibility of the application of sampling within the individual enterprises.

From another point of view the sampling device is a compromise between residual techniques and the more desirable form, complete coverage by questionnaire and interview. It almost goes without saying that the accuracy of this device is dependent of the individual reliability of the sampling system employed.

Whereas sampling holds great hopes as a means of improving the precision and increasing the simplicity of the identification process, it must be remembered that the really important factor in this picture is the reliability of the data being sampled. As was indicated in previous discussion of this matter the data in too many cases are imprecise. Hence the task seems to be one of improving the data gathered at the enterprise level. This may be brought about by the development of new and more intensive techniques of analyzing enterprise records and/or by devising questionnaires that get at the ultimate facts desired by indirect means that reduce the use of personal estimates. Procedures such as these will be expensive and time-consuming. However, these difficulties may in turn be reduced by the intelligent use of sampling devices.

DOLLAR-FLOW MEASUREMENT

Up to this point the discussion has not concerned itself with the question of the identification of capital export. As was mentioned in the article on measure, the unit of measure employed in the process of base identification is not universal in that is can identify all types of base activity within the community.[12] Thus far, identification has been analyzed in terms of employment and sales as the units of measure. Capital export has been ignored for the technical reason that there is, as yet, no generally practicable means of identifying it. The Oskaloosa study which presented a rather complete dollar-flow picture for that small Iowa community was able to make such an identification.[13] However, this technique due to its complexity would be impractical for general application particularly in the case of large cities.

In the opinion of this writer the broad outlines of capital export as a problem in measure and identification take the following form.

Capital is exported from a community by specialists and non-specialists. The specialist may be thought of as the familiar financial firm whose business is concentrated on the making of loans both local and "foreign." In the case of the specialist there is no peculiar type of measure and identification problem

---

[12] Richard B. Andrews, "Mechanics of the Urban Economy Base: The Problem of Base Measurement," *Land Economics*, February 1954.

[13] "Oskaloosa versus the United States," *Fortune*, April 1938. Homer Hoyt in his *The Economic Base of the Brockton, Massachusetts, Area* (1949) gives attention to property returns as a part of a community income and expenditure analysis. However, he does not examine the intricacies of capital export *per se*.

other than those described in connection with the standard approaches discussed earlier. A relatively simple case is that of the large metropolitan commercial bank where a base-service division of employment and payrolls could be established on the basis of geographical distribution of loans. Here, of course, a concurrent determinant of base-service segregation would be the geographical dispersion of depositors some of whom would also be the consumers of loans. Clearly, therefore, the commercial bank presents a dual type of function, loan and deposit service, the parts of which would have to be successfully reconciled in order to yield an accurate segregation of base and service activity. This type of reconciliation has apparently never been attempted but may well find a solution in a geographical allocation of profits as between local and extra-area borrowers and depositors.

It is, however, the non-specialist exporter of capital who presents one of the most difficult problems within the field of identification, one that may never have a satisfactory solution.

The non-specialists include business firms and individuals with surplus funds available for outside investment. Also classed as non-specialists are individuals whose pension and insurance transactions involve, in the community aggregate, an important capital export volume and hence an important influx of interest payments and matching funds. How these types of capital export are to be located, measured, and then integrated with other base data remains a challenging and yet unconquered segment of the identification problem.

CONCLUSIONS

One leaves the subject of general identification technique problems of the urban base with a limited sense of frustration brought about by the sheer size and complexity of the task of introducing greater precision and coverage into a subject field which throws up impressive barriers of a variety so common in the social sciences. It is this writer's belief that up until the present such significant problems as measure and identification have been treated all too summarily. The main fault of approach lies in the fact that all the work which appears to have been done in these technique-problem fields has been performed as a part of a larger work project. For example, an economic base study is executed within a particular community. In the course of the study the inadequacies of measure and identification techniques are appreciated anew. The research staff involved reviews the thinking on the subject and makes some change for the better in identification approach. In a sense these are measures of expedience. Time and money are at a premium and there are many other problems with which to contend. It is not surprising, therefore, that we inch ahead, and sometimes backward, in this vital sector of the urban base technique field. It is impossible to avoid the somewhat sententious ending of articles such as this by saying that what is needed is more research. But that is precisely the need in this case. However, the research must be devoted exclusively and intensively to the one subject and not combined in general studies of the base.

Unfortunately the complexities of the base identification process have been merely sketched in this discussion of *general* problems. It must, therefore, be the business of the next article to discuss the detailed special headaches of the identification field. Here will be touched upon such subjects as commuter identification, "significant" base activities, and the variety of base activities derived from certain types of on-the-spot purchase processes.

Richard B. Andrews—Mechanics of the Urban Economic Base: Special Problems of Base Identification

Mechanics of the Urban Economic Base:
Special Problems of Base Identification*

The urban economic base concept can be thought of as the means of describing and explaining the roots of individual urban economies and, for that matter, the economic trunk and branches that are nourished by these roots. One might continue with appropriate figures of speech by saying that the base is the germ cell from which develops the rest of the urban body, it is the gene aggregate which determines the character, social as well as economic, of a particular community. However, in a more direct economic sense the base is represented by those activities of a community which export goods, services, or capital to persons or firms whose source of payment is beyond the predetermined boundaries of the economic community. These are the activities which through a favorable trade balance with other cities, regions, and nations enable the community to continue its existence and to pay for the necessities of living and production which it must import. It is patent, therefore, that changes in the prosperity of the base will have important repercussions in local employment and consequently in population.

Actually the economic machinery of the urban community is made up of two complementary gears, one the base activities, the other service activities. The service activities do not export but are engaged in caring for local demands for goods, personal services, and capital. Local demands stem from the base itself and its employees, from service establishments and their employees, and from the rest of the population not directly identified in an employment sense with either base or service activities. The character and employment size of service activities are directly sympathetic to changes in base activities.

The technical process of identifying the economic base involves listing and tabulation according to some unit of measure

* See Acknowledgements

of those activities which export beyond the boundaries of the economic community. Common difficulties arise in segregating base and service activities within a single enterprise or industry. These difficulties and the current techniques employed to solve them were discussed in the preceding article.[1]

There are, however, a few situations found in many but not all communities that do not respond to the standard identification techniques and it is toward an examination of these special problems that this article is directed.

THE COMMUTER

Unlike the case of the mixed enterprise (base *and* service) there usually exists relative to a body of commuters from a community no question as to their identity. They are clearly of the local base in that they are exporting their services to another community or area. Consequently, the problem in this case resolves itself into determining a suitable means of counting the commuters. This is, of course, a problem situation which usually arises in making a base analysis of a satellite community rather than a central city.

The means of approaching this counting problem are not very numerous. In some instances a count may be taken of monthly commutation tickets sold by interurban transport lines. This type of count has the advantage of a clear identification of destination which is of importance if several economic area boundary lines are involved. However, this type of tally clearly misses the commuter by automobile who is of increasing importance in the commutation field and yet cannot be counted in as easy a manner as the patron of public transport lines. Here sampling techniques are of assistance and if the community is small, a direct questionnaire is likely to yield good results.[2]

[1] Richard B. Andrews, "Mechanics of the Urban Economic Base: General Problems of Base Identification," *Land Economics*, May 1954.

[2] Homer Hoyt, *The Economic Base of the Brockton, Massachusetts Area* (Brockton, Mass.: 1949); *Economic Survey of the Land Uses of Evanston, Illinois* (Larchmont, New York: 1949).

Another approach which may prove useful if the data are available is a check of central city industry payroll data sheets or personnel records to determine location of the employees' residence. This would be an efficient means of commuter identification if several satellite cities were making base studies at about the same time and were interested in pooling their research resources. The technique would, however, fail to catch inter-satellite commutation which might be of significance in some areas.

Another data source possibility arises in the event that a state-collected, locally-distributed income tax exists. If tax returns are accessible to the investigator the place of employment of satellite residents may be identified and the commuter segregated from other employed persons. Sampling of returns would simplify this otherwise arduous approach.

However, there is a technical difficulty that may arise for communities in making a negative allowance for commutation rather than the usual positive adjustment to the base. Here is suggested the situation in which commuters move from the central city to the satellite city or between satellite cities. Base calculations for the satellite city into which commuters are moving will have to be adjusted for these movements; otherwise the ratio of base to service (assuming an employment measure) and base to population will be thrown out of line. In other words, base employment may well register at an unusually high level in relation to service employment or local population. Of course, in the case of the central city itself the commuter zone may well represent the local economic area therefore cancelling out negative commuter adjustments for the central city. But for the satellite community the problem of negative adjustment is a real and continuing one.

There exists substantial uncertainty as to how this situation should be handled. When a portion of the labor force identified with the base of an area is non-resident, identification is complicated by questions of not only base-service-population ratios but also by questions as to the tendency of this "foreign" labor force to spend a part of its earnings in the community where it finds employment.

UNIVERSITY COMMUNITIES

Yet another detail problem in the field of identification arises with the community in which a university is located. The traditional technique of identification-segregation here has been that of determining the proportion of students in the total university enrollment coming from outside the economic area and applying this proportion to the unit of measure used to indicate base and service-activity shares for the university.[3] This approach appears to have given fairly logical results. However, there is another aspect of identification in connection with the university that is far more complex. The university student is, of course, an on-the-spot consumer of the service which he purchases, namely, education. Since his consumption period is lengthy he has need of many goods and services such as food, shelter, entertainment, clothing, and numerous personal services. It has been observed logically that the employment created or the gross value of goods purchased by and services rendered to the students are, actually, exports since the out-of-area students are temporary, tourist-like residents of the community.[4] Consequently, enterprises catering to students are to be considered in whole or in part base-associates of the university which in this case is the key base unit.[5] This same line of reasoning may be applied with variations to other on-the-spot-consumption patterns which are associated with tourist activity, medical centers, conventions, large-scale athletic events, state legislative and temporary administrative bodies. With each of these activities

---

[3] Homer Hoyt, *Economic Survey of the Land Uses of Evanston, Illinois.*

[4] Federal Reserve Bank, Kansas City, Missouri, *The Economy of Albuquerque,* New Mexico, 1949.

[5] In the opinion of this writer the recent Census classification of out-of-area university students as a part of the local population does not alter their true (export) economic relationship to the community.

adjustments must be made for the shorter consumption-time periods involved and, therefore, different qualitative patterns of goods and service consumption as compared to the university student. If the goods and services exported to consumers of this type are to be calculated into the economic base of the community there arises the question of how this is to be done. Actually, there is thus far in the literature no completely satisfactory means of accomplishing this necessary part of the identification process. It is a process almost completely dependent on estimates usually made by the investigator and not as yet, by the enterprises under investigation.[6] When employment is used as the unit of measure, in the case of universities, an attempt is made to convert student purchases into an employment equivalent. This is done by assigning an average school-year expenditure to each student. The expenditures of out-of-area students are converted into an average retail wage which is then assigned to a basic employee in retail trade.[7] The principal attraction of this approach is its logic. But the execution leaves so much margin for error that a question naturally arises concerning the advisability of searching for other techniques while attempts continue to perfect the one at hand. One immediate step that should be taken on this latter score involves the gathering of more precise data on student expeditures. We particularly need not only more complete coverage of students making these expenditures but also a better idea concerning the range and frequency of the spendings they make within the community.

No mention has been made in this brief summary of the confusion that is added by the fact that many students from

---

[6] Homer Hoyt, *Economic Survey of the Land Uses of Evanston, Illinois*, p. 18. Also, an unpublished preliminary study done by this writer on the economic base of Madison, Wisconsin, 1947 and 1948, for the Bureau of Business Research & Service, School of Commerce, University of Wisconsin.

[7] Federal Reserve Bank of Kansas City, Missouri, *The Economy of Albuquerque* (New Mexico: 1949).

outside the area are also employed on a part-time basis within the community. Negative adjustment should, undoubtedly, be made for such part-time employment as was done in the case of commuters working in the community who came from outside the boundaries of the economic area.

TOURISTS

The tourist has much the same relation to the economy of a locality as the out-of-town university student. He is an on-the-spot consumer of goods and services which the community has available to exchange for capital brought in from outside. Tourists differ from students principally in the length of their stay in the area. Because they stay a shorter time the range of their purchases may be far narrower than that of the student. On the other hand, their total contribution to export trade can in many circumstances be as great or greater than that of students where both are factors in a community's economy.

In the case of enterprises which cater to travelers the identification process is not a highly difficult one. Filling stations, motels, hotels, souvenir shops, scenic trip enterprises, and restaurants outside of the central business district usually have no difficulty in making a fairly accurate statement of the proportion of their local as against their export trade. It would be well, however, for the investigator to spot-check these operations in large communities where the chances are great of local trade drifting in, in proportions larger than the enterprise operator realizes. And, of course, there is the usual human variability in judging a situation on which no formal records are kept.

The real difficulties of tourist identification arise in cases where the tourist patronage of the department store in a large community is involved or, for that matter, patronage of personal service establishments. Whereas the dispensers of personal services such as doctors, lawyers, dentists, and beauty parlor operators may, because of relatively low customer volume, be able to distinguish their tourist trade the larger operators such as department stores, and especially moving picture theaters, will have great difficulty with identification segregation. In the latter cases estimates have been, to date, about the only sources of information. The inadequacy of estimates in these cases only points the need for an intensive search for more precise techniques.

The question may be asked at this point: why is it necessary to identify the tourist segment of local trade? Is it not enough to bulk all export trade together? A more inclusive approach certainly reduces the scope of the identification problem by the removal of one troublesome item. And yet a little thought on the matter seems to indicate that in the case of on-the-spot-purchase activity such as tourist trade a careful identification is necessary. For if tourist trade on analysis proves important to the community this implies closer attention to those community planning programs which will protect and stimulate it.

The complexities which are encountered in tourist trade identification cause us to consider the feasibility of using some such technique as that currently employed in university student identification. This suggests that we ascribe an average expenditure per visit to each tourist and then convert these expenditures into appropriate equivalents of the unit of measure employed.

An average tourist expenditure for a particular year could be calculated from sample questionnaires. However, the bitter aspect of the whole approach appears in the difficulty of counting tourists. The frustrating nature of this procedure is well described in a recent study.[8] The fact that problems of this sort would be magnified many times in major metropolitan tourist areas such as New York, Los Angeles, and Chicago only tend to sober the technique research worker.

However, it is encouraging to observe the possibilities that exist for increased precision in identification procedures as they

---

[8] Denver Planning Office, *Working Denver* (Denver, Colorado: 1953) pp. 82-87.

relate to tourist trade. One of the most careful and detailed studies on this subject which at the same time concentrates heavily on technique is R. P. Wolff's book on the Miami resort area.[9] In this publication the author has adopted for his analysis a "tourist-day" concept apparently devised by the Miami City Department of Finance. Visitors to the Miami area are estimated on the basis of three indicators: use of electricity, garbage disposal, and gasoline consumption. Employing monthly data for these indicators a four-year average by month was computed. Percentage increases over September were calculated for the months of December through April, the winter tourist season. The increases computed for the month of the "season" were converted into population equivalents to determine the tourist addition. Numerous adjustments were, of course, necessary to refine these data. The tourist day computation was made by multiplying the population gain for the month by the days in the month. This calculation assumes greater economic pertinence when the tourist days are in turn multiplied by the estimated daily expenditure of the tourist. Spot studies in the area indicated the rough distribution of this dollar so that appropriate allocation to local industries might be made. The basic assumption running through the technique is that tourist trade is not essentially a separate business or industry but, rather, an increase in normal activities. In order to obtain a measure of added tourist activity, therefore, comparisons have to be made with those of a "normal" town.[10]

This approach and other details of the Wolff technique can well provide a stimulating springboard to higher levels of tourist-identification procedure. At the same time the approach shows the general possibilities that exist for attacking identification problems which at first contact seem insuperable.

---

[9] R. P. Wolff, *Miami. Economic Pattern of a Resort Area* (Coral Gables, Florida: University of Miami, 1945).

[10] *Ibid.,* p. 35.

However, by way of negative criticism it should be pointed out that the Wolff approach is not a total solution to the tourist-identification problem. The indicators employed to compute the tourist day while suitable in a major resort area such as Miami might not be sufficiently sensitive to reveal tourist volume in an area or community where tourist trade is a factor but not a major one in the composition of the base. Difficulties are also likely in those cases where there is no "season" due to climate but rather a relatively steady flow of tourists throughout all months of the year.

LOCAL GOVERNMENT EMPLOYEES

There does not seem to be complete agreement on the means of base-service segregation of state or county government employment totals within an urban area. One point of view maintains that this segregation may be obtained by determining first the total population of the civil division or administrative district involved such as the county or the state. A proportion is then established between this population total and the population of the urban economic area under analysis. This proportion is then applied to a unit of measure, as in the sales-employment conversion technique, to determine the base and service shares. It is here assumed that the county or state activity is a service enterprise to the locality only up to the share which its (the locality's) population holds to the whole governmental service area.[11] While many flaws can be noted in this approach it appears to this writer to be generally satisfactory.

On the other hand, in a study made by the Denver Planning Office conversion was based on total state service employment rather than just the state employment in Denver as related to

11 Federal employment other than clearly local cases such as the postal service can be split by the same technique. Preliminary work done by the author on a base study of Madison, Wisconsin for the Bureau of Business Research and Service, School of Commerce, University of Wisconsin, 1948.

population totals. As a result it was determined that all state employment in Denver (the capital city) was service rather than a split between basic and local service activity.[12] This conclusion does not seem quite consistent to this writer.

SIGNIFICANT ENTERPRISE APPROACH

Because of the rather considerable difficulties involved in the process of identification there may be possibilities of simplification. One such approach, which has been only informally suggested, is that of attempting the identification of the "significant" basic enterprises of the community rather than the complete base. This approach assumes that the significant enterprises would be concentrated in but a few firms and organizations. If this were the case the volume of interviewing and questionnaire tabulation would be reduced. At the same time the wide-scale estimating that currently appears almost a necessity with the numerous small firms of the large city might be eliminated.

This type of base identification also has the advantage of concentrating the city planners' area of analysis and perhaps increasing the quality of his decision relative to the community's economy. An improvement in decision quality might well result from the fact that the planner would have more complete data on the sections of the base surveyed than would be likely under the comprehensive approach. In yet another sense the significant basic-activity approach would enable the planner to pinpoint and hence simplify the annual or periodic check-ups which he might think necessary in his urban area. Pending preliminary research on the point this writer believes that

---

[12] Denver Planning Office, *Working Denver* (Denver, Colorado: City and County of Denver, 1953), pp. 136-137. For example, if in Denver were found 75 percent of all state employees and, at the same time, Denver's share of total Colorado population was also about 75 percent then all Denver state employees would be classified as "local-service" rather than basic. Should not 75 percent rather than 100 percent of the state employees in Denver be considered basic?

where linkage and complementary enterprise patterns exist one might further pose the hypothesis that there are certain significant basic firms or activities which, due to their key relation to the linking or complementing chains of the local economy, hold a role which might be termed "base of the economic base."

An identification technique such as the one described is of course a specialized sampling method. One difficult question that must be answered by the investigator is that surrounding the meaning of the term "significant" in each case. Significance could be expressed in terms of one or several units of measure, i.e., employment, payrolls, etc. The significant basic activities might be single firms or whole activity groups such as metalworking, research, transportation, tourist trade. Significance might be a function of size in terms of various units of measure, of strategic position in local linkage patterns, or the relation of firm size and number. This last determinant refers to situations in which the community might be dominated by one or a few very large base firms.

There are, however, several questions which must be raised relative to the utility of significant basic enterprises as a straight identification procedure. One inadequacy of the approach rests in the fact that it would be impossible to derive the highly significant ratios of *full* basic activity to service activity, to total area employment, and to population.

As a consequence of the above situation the planner may lose perspective relative to the complete community economy. This perspective is, of course, highly necessary to sound planning decisions.

There is also the risk that the investigator may take the firm as the basis of his choice of significant basic enterprises. If this is done there is the chance that many small firms will be ignored which nonetheless may, when added together, represent a highly significant industrial grouping.

Generally speaking, the significant activity approach, while it has rather intriguing specialized virtues in both the fields of identification and planning dynamics, must be used with great care. It would be wise to avoid the concept as a practical tool until more is known about it.

TRANSPORTATION AND COMMUNICATION ACTIVITIES

Other enterprises in which a divergence from the more or less standard techniques of identification is necessary are transportation and communication. The problems involved are not extremely complex but usually bothersome and often confusing.

In the transit and transportation field, transit is generally thought of as a local or service activity whereas transportation in the form of freight and passenger service beyond the economic boundaries of the community is usually considered basic in nature. However, the division is not always this simple and when so handled may result in significant inaccuracies, particularly if transport is a heavy employer.

Transit may offer difficulties of identification in that, whereas the term "transit" has a traditional local service connotation, it is always possible that certain destination points in the case of interurban travel will be beyond the economic boundaries of the community. This is a situation most likely to occur in satellite communities where the local economic area may be relatively restricted in size. In cases such as this the usual problems of segregation arise in separating local area patronage volume from extra-area patronage, then in applying these proportions on a conversion basis to the units of measure employed. One of the unresolved questions in this particular case revolves around patronage made up of commuters from the subject community to a neighboring community unit such as the central city. In the opinion of this writer such patronage should be considered in the local, transit category. By exclusion this would confine export activity to commuter patronage from other communities.

In the field of transport the writer has not encountered any

highly satisfactory techniques for handling identification segregation of rail, motor freight, and air transport activity. In
the typical case where the local operation is only a part of a very
wide regional or national service the assumption is made that
the activity is basic.[13] However, a rational technique must be
developed of rendering a more precise identification with
recognition of the fact that in some cases the proportion of
service activity in terms of the unit of measure used may be
great. One good possibility in this direction is the application
of a residual approach to an employment measure. Using this
approach computation could be made, first, of the total value or
volume of freight and of number of passengers hauled in an
average year between two division points of the transport system under analysis. A second computation could then be made
of the freight and passenger patronage contributed to the carrier by the local community in terms of out-moving and in-
moving business. This second proportion could then be applied to total divisional employment of the carrier.[14] Employment in excess of the local allocation for servicing of passenger
and freight patronage could be classified as basic.

In the field of communications a special problem arises in
connection with radio and television broadcasting stations.
Whereas this type of enterprise on an individual firm basis does
not bulk large in terms of employment several community stu-
dios may, when combined, provide a total of respectable size,
particularly in the major metropolitan centers. Again, there
appears to be no explicit statement in the literature on how identification should be handled here. Apparently estimating has
been used extensively and the assumption is implicit that
broadcasting is a service activity. If the investigator proceeds
on the guiding principles of base identification, he will ex-

---

[13] Denver Planning Office, *Working Denver* (Denver, Colorado: 1953), p. 98.
[14] Where the subject city is a division point itself the patronage and employment of two divisions could be combined along the lines described.

amine the revenue sources of the industry in question. In the case of broadcasting, revenues are derived from advertisers who in most cases are of the locality. Where the advertiser is from outside the area there is, of course, no question concerning the basic nature of the sale to him of broadcasting time. However, the typical case is that of the local advertiser, and this raises a question as to why broadcasting should be considered anything but service activity. Our thinking on the nature of the base has not resolved this question. There still remains a doubt because of the fact that broadcast advertising stimulates trade from outside the community. But in the present opinion of this writer it appears logical to think of local advertising broadcasts as service activity. For, if via a type of linkage such as is suggested with retail trade, we identify broadcasting with export we must also identify as basic the utility companies and other local enterprises which serve retail trade in the process of exporting its product. Such a conclusion is not logical.

This same line of reasoning can be applied to newspapers except for the fact that sales of the paper made outside the area will provide a small measure of basic activity not encountered in broadcasting.

LINKED ACTIVITIES

It is a self-evident fact that there exist in any urban community varying degrees of interdependence among seemingly independent enterprises and industries. Some of these relationships are in the complementary goods field such as the relation of auto sales to the sales of tires, gasoline, and accessories. Others appear in a chain of production where there is a more formal and direct supply and demand relationship. An example of this latter situation is found in the relation of the independent starter factory to the consuming automobile manufacturer in the same community—an association generally described as linking or linkage. The importance of this concept to base identification lies in the opinion that if the auto manufacturer is predominantly a basic activity the starter plant which markets its output to him must also be basic despite the fact that it does not export its product beyond the community boundaries.[15] This opinion is based on the view that only a formal organizational division exists between the two firms and that, actually, they are engaged in preparing the same final product for export. It is further assumed that, if a specific base-service split is found in the auto manufacturing plant, the same proportions will carry over to the starter factory.

Discussion of this point in the literature is thus far, very indirect and cautious. Such an attitude is understandable when the nature of linkage is considered further. The complexity of identification of basic activity in linked enterprises centers principally about the question of what shall and shall not be considered linked activity. Our example of the starter factory seems fairly clear-cut but raises questions of degree. Namely, before an enterprise can be considered linked and basic must it sell all of its output to a local factory or factories who engage predominantly in export? If the consuming factories are not predominantly basic shall the linked activity be defined as basic only up to the proportion found in the purchasing plant, as suggested in the previous paragraph? These questions are by no means as crucial as those which inquire concerning the nature of the sale made by the linked activity. If it is a tangible good (a starter) which is sold must it be part of the good (automobile) which is ultimately exported or might it simply contribute to the production of the exported item as, for example, local limestone or coal marketed and consumed in local iron smelting operations? This, in turn, raises a question concerning enterprises which market services to exporters. Cannot these also be considered linked in certain circumstances? Yet if services are admitted into a definition of the concept does this not open

[15] See Richard B. Andrews, "Mechanics of the Urban Economic Base: The Problem of Base Classification," *Land Economics,* November 1953, p. 347.

the door to defining as linked *all* enterprises which market services to an exporter such as the local utility company?

One other aspect of this problem is that of the length of local basic chains in which there may be several enterprise links. We are still very much in the dark concerning such link associations but have some satisfaction in knowing that these chains cannot usually be very long due to the small chance of a complete monopoly of locational advantages in one metropolitan area.

Unless the anachronisms of this situation can be reconciled we have upon our hands a very serious blindspot in the entire base identification procedure.

ABSENTEE OWNERSHIP

In the opinion of some students of the economic base, absentee ownership of firms that are a part of a locality's base or service activity add a perplexing aspect to the problem of identification. In this writer's opinion the difficulty is exaggerated.

Typical examples of absentee ownership that plague the base analyst are gas and light firms and chain grocery supermarkets. It is correctly observed that the profits of the firm are drained away to other localities. This aspect of the operation is the one which introduces a question concerning the status of the firm whether it is originally considered base ,service, or a mixture of the two.

For purposes of urban economic analysis it seems that the most important considerations are not the settling points of profits and the location of ultimate managerial control. In our larger cities the giant economic aggregations which make up the economic base often have a very widely disseminated ownership of stock and an absentee board of directors yet there never seems to arise a question as to their status in the local economy. It is more logical to think in terms of the volume and source of employees of a subject firm and in terms of the geographical distribution of its payroll and production processes. For the purposes of the city planner it is with these local economic impacts that his principal concern lies. He is, of course, also concerned with the policies of the firms within the local economy. If these policies are determined by absentee management an element of insecurity may be introduced.

However, returning to the problem of identification, there seems to be no question that an absentee controlled firm ought to be considered in much the same way as any other. The principal difference lies in the treatment of the profits involved. If a dollar-flow measurement device were employed the profit drain would be clearly indicated. The community receiving the profits would count them as a part of the return on its capital export activity. The subject community which had lost the profits while it still might enjoy profit plow-backs would ordinarily suffer economically by a diminution in local purchasing power, to the extent of the profits, for service activity output. On the basis of this reasoning it is probable that communities with a high percentage of absentee ownership in their economies might show a relatively weaker or smaller service activity element than economically comparable communities where local ownership was dominant.

CONCLUSIONS

It has been the purpose of this discussion to review and appraise some of the more interesting special problems in the field of base identification which do not respond to general techniques. It is evident that some of these problems such as linked activities are in a relatively chaotic state insofar as the clarity of their connection with base activity is concerned. Others such as tourist trade are somewhat further along in the process of integration into a logical and precise identification technique.

The general conclusion reached is that, as in the case of general identification procedures, we are at a stage of thought development where specialized research concentrating on one or two of these problems at a time is imperative. The shotgun approach of the general base survey is almost totally ineffective in ameliorating these dilemmas.

A final discussion of a phase of identification technique will be presented in the ensuing article which will be concerned with the crucial process of determining economic community boundaries in order that export and service activities can be segregated or identified.

Richard B. Andrews—Mechanics of the Urban Economic
Base: The Problem of Base Area Delimitation

118

Mechanics of the Urban Economic Base:
The Problem of Base Area Delimitation*

Numerous technical problems face the planning analyst in executing a study of the economic base of a particular community. Delimiting the geographical scope of his study area is one of the most important and yet, seemingly, most neglected insofar as rigorous definition is concerned.

The crucial importance of thoughtful and precise delimitation lies first of all in the fact that the economic base of a city is by definition made up of the export activities of the community. These activities involve the export of goods, services, and capital to purchasers who are outside the community or come from outside. Similarly, service activities—economic complement of the base—are customarily defined as those transactions involving goods, services, and capital which are purely local in that, in the process of exchange, they do not cross the line which separates the community from the outer economy of state, region, nation, and international markets. It is evident, therefore, that before a meaningful process of identification—which labels activities as basic or service within an urbanized area—can begin, a clear conception must exist as to the means of establishing an economic-geographic demarcation between the producing community and the beginnings of its export market. It is, moreover, impossible to speak of those indispensable data of the base study, total employment, total payrolls, number of firms, total community population, and so forth, without first having reference to the specific geographic sphere of these factors.

The need of delimitation of some kind is encountered in practically all fields of investigation. The process is peculiarly important in investigations into the nature of the urban economy

* See Acknowledgements

because of the fact that delimitation is, essentially, explicit in the phenomena to be examined. In other words, the terms "export activity" and "local trade" assume that limits have been established.

The present article emphasizes the fact that the delimitation techniques of economic base analysis are highly variant. There is nothing inherently improper in the fact that each analyst takes an individual approach to the problem. However, a substantial question arises as to whether there are right and wrong ways of going about delimitation. It will, therefore, be one objective of this discussion to examine the delimitation techniques that have apparently been used in several prominent economic base studies and to evaluate these techniques with the end in mind of determining whether they have serious flaws or substantial virtues in performing the function that is expected of them. Yet another objective in this testing of the idea-inventory will be to determine the extent to which the techniques examined have general applicability or have utility in only specialized cases.

Finally, this writer will give his views on the feasibility of a standardized delimitation technique, or techniques, to fit broad type-groups of the city. He believes that before the version of the urban economy here under discussion can become a truly efficient planning tool it must be more thoroughly tested. Part of this testing procedure is to be found in broad-scale comparisons among cities. Yet, assuming relatively similar units of measure and identification procedures, no valid comparisons can be made if area delimitation techniques are not reasonably uniform. Inter-city comparisons of strategic ratios such as the ratio of base-to-service activity, the ratio of total employment to total population, and the ratio of base activity to total population could only be made in a very loose manner if their qualitative content and hence the ratios themselves varied in part because of non-standard means of handling area delimitation.

With these remarks as an introduction the discussion will next turn to an inventory and evaluation of current approaches to the problem of area delimitation.

AREA DELIMITATION TECHNIQUES

Formal treatment of base area delimitation techniques is almost entirely absent from economic base literature. This is in a large part due to the fact that writing on the subject of the economic base is confined almost exclusively to general reports on the base of a particular community. Unfortunately, the authors of these reports do not devote much space to an explanation of technique. Too often what is said on the subject is confined to a brief footnote or over-condensed appendix remarks. As a result many of the observations made here on specific techniques will be based on deductions from report maps, and on the manner in which data are presented.

A heavy majority of the economic base studies which have been made thus far are concerned with central cities. As a result there is very little material extant which can point the way toward an area delimitation apporach for the suburb and satellite city. It will be, therefore, a further objective of this paper to suggest how the beginnings that have been made in area delimitation procedure for other than central city communities may be extended.

Since one of the principal problems is to determine the adequacy of particular delimitation techniques in establishing boundaries for an economic base area a question is naturally raised as to what the proper criteria are for such delimitation procedures. The argument here proposed is that the base area should be viewed as a producing and distributing unit of goods, services, and capital within the economic framework of its region and the nation. It is the economically integrated geographic area which includes the principal factors of production of the basic and service enterprises of the community. Land fits well into this factor approach with the possible qualification of conditions where long distance transmission of power is involved. Capital likewise accommodates to this frame of reference with the exception of capital in the form of funds borrowed from absentee lenders or invested in stock shares by persons from outside the community. Finally, labor as a production factor aids in the setting of base area boundaries through determination of the geographic range of employment pull by base and service activities. This line of reasoning may well suggest to the reader that two areas are being determined, the base and service areas. However, they are from a realistic point of view identical and therefore coterminous in respect to boundaries. Base and service activities combined represent the economic community.[1]

Emphasis must also be placed on the idea of integration and interdependence of productive activities. Interdependence within the economic community can be said to mark in a rough manner the outer limits of the economic community.

It is maintained, therefore, that delimitation factors which support the conceptions outlined in the preceding paragraphs are the proper ones from a theoretical point of view. The base area is, of course, also a social as well as an economic conception but the selection of social delimitation factors should be consonant with the guiding economic approach. If, for example, the boundaries of the base area as determined by relatively "pure" economic criteria are inside boundaries set by equally pure social criteria the economic boundaries should be the ones chosen for economic base area studies.

Criteria for the delineation of urban economic areas must, however, be stated more specifically than has been the case thus

---

[1] The apparent duality of this approach might become confusing if, for example, when using a productive factor delimitation approach the boundary of the area represented by the location of the productive factors of the basic activities was *within* the line established by the outposts of the productive factors of the service activities. The outer boundary would, with the exception of certain circumstances to be noted later, be the boundary of the economic community for both service and base identification purposes.

far. One of the earliest and yet most complete statements on the subject was made in 1922 by Professor N. S. B. Gras.[2] He looked upon criteria in terms of *tests* of metropolitan district limits. These tests assumed the following general forms:

(1) The point where systems of transportation begin to veer off toward other metropolitan centers.

(2) The radius served by the metropolitan press and other advertising media.

(3) The dependence of outlying financial institutions on the center for clearances and reserves.

(4) Whether it is the center from which the retailers in a border-line town direct their supplies.

(5) Whether the border-line town is independent or dependent upon the center for many of the following functions: (a) storage for the convenience of consumer, retailer, wholesaler, manufacturer, shipper; (b) whether the outlying producer markets directly to the local consumer or through the metropolitan machinery; (c) whether a border-line community communicates by rail, telephone, etc., through the center or independently of it; (d) where the border-line town sends its surplus products for disposal or storage; (e) whether a firm or industry which boasts its independence in some one respect, e.g., the marketing of its wares, is or is not dependent upon the center for its supplies and finances; and (f) whether the border-line town is too far away to avail itself of the central assemblage of museums, theaters, libraries, institutions of learning, and where it looks for guidance in fashions, tastes and amusements.

These tests point up rather neatly the element in delineation

---

[2] Thomas Adams, *Regional Survey of New York and Environs* Vol. II, *Population, Land Values, and Government* (New York: Committee on Regional Plan of New York and Its Environs, 1929) Part III, Chapter I, p. 201.

procedure of interdependence, both economic and social. However, some of the tests would yield an area broader than an economic base area should properly be. For example, the wholesaling function might be most accurately viewed as a part of the community base but if its outer contact points are used as community boundary markers it thereby becomes a service activity. Clearance and reserve activity would also tend to yield areas of great size. Moreover, as a criterion it would apply to only the largest cities and would therefore, not have general utility. However, most of the elements of test 5 in the preceding list would be more generally applicable. In short, it is necessary apparently to distinguish carefully between an economic-metropolitan and a regional approach.

At the time Professor Gras wrote, similar methods of procedure for defining metropolitan districts had been worked out in detail by the Civic Development Department of the United States Chamber of Commerce. In general, the indicators employed were somewhat more restrictive over the size of the geographical areas that resulted. For example, great stress was placed on areas served by telephone service from the central city; on power and light service areas; on retail store delivery; on city water supply districts; and on the commuting area.[3] Only the last could be said to be sufficiently broad in concept to attain the full scope necessary to a productive factor delineation approach. While the tests of Gras were in many cases too broad, those just mentioned with the exception of commuting are too narrow for meaningful application in a large number of cases.

THE LEGAL CITY

The economic city defined in terms of the legal boundaries of that city is undoubtedly the simplest approach to the problem under discussion. However, the inaccuracy of this approach,

---

[3] *Ibid.*, pp. 201-202.

particularly for economic base work, has been acknowledged for a very long time. Acceptance of such an approach is feasible in perhaps only two general situations. If time is short and funds for the collection of needed statistics are limited, mitigating circumstances are obviously present. There is also the extremely rare instance in which the incorporation boundaries are so extensive that they actually embrace both the economic and political city. Where suburban communities are being subjected to base analysis incorporation boundaries may frequently be appropriate base area limits particularly in those cases where the suburb is contiguous to another suburb or is an enclave.

The main concern of the current discussion, however, is with geographic-economic concepts and definitions that are far broader in scope than that ordinarily conceived in the incorporated city unit.

THE INDUSTRIAL AREA

There have developed over the years two concepts which, under the main design-impetus of the Bureau of the Census, carry in them many of the elements necessary to a sound technique of base area delineation. These concepts are the industrial area and the labor market area—sometimes referred to as the employment security area. They have been used singly and in combination with other devices to delineate base areas in many studies, notably those made in Detroit and Philadelphia.[4]

The concept of the industrial area is best described in the definition given by the Bureau of the Census:

". . . Census of Manufacturers statistics have been tabulated for the standard metropolitan areas having 40,000 or more manufacturing employees in 1947. The standard metropolitan areas replace the industrial areas shown in earlier

---

[4] Detroit City Plan Commission, *Economic Base of Detroit* (City of Detroit: 1944).

Philadelphia City Planning Commission, *Economic Base Study of the Philadelphia Area,* Planning Study No. 2 (City of Philadelphia, August 1949).

censuses. Industrial areas defined in previous years were groups of contiguous counties having large numbers of manufacturing wage earners."[5]

From the above definition the virtues and limitations of the industrial area approach for base area delineation purposes are apparent.

One feature of the industrial area concept that is quite important to the base approach is that it places geographic emphasis on a factor of production—manufacturing labor force. This approach is nonetheless highly restricted in that it is focused on only one segment of the labor force and is, by the necessities of Bureau of the Census operations, further restricted to areas of a certain minimum size.

There is, however, one observation made in the Detroit report which further highlights the economic unit character of the industrial area. The study points out:

"This area [a three county industrial area] forms an economic unit in which conditions and trends are relatively uniform . . . the Detroit area comprises a single interdependent economic unit. Trends in employment in Dearborn or Hamtramck affect Detroit's population just as much as do employment trends within the city itself."[6]

Here, succinctly highlighted, is the criterion of high interdependence and, hence, function as a single economic unit which should be a vital part of the concept of the base area.

The limits set by a straight industrial area approach (disregarding for the moment its current inclusion in the standard metropolitan area) must, however, be of a rather arbitrary quantitative nature. This situation contrasts with a more flexible conceptual approach along the lines of the labor market

[5] U. S. Bureau of the Census, *Census of Manufactures*: 1947, Volume I, General Summary (Washington, D. C.: 1948) p. 13.

[6] Detroit City Plan Commission, *Economic Base of Detroit*, p. 2.

area technique which will be discussed next. In short, the industrial area while it has utility in solving the base area delineation problem cannot stand alone as a solution because it is found wanting in relation to two criteria of a sound delineation technique. These criteria are general applicability (1) to all base phenomena and (2) to communities of all sizes and metropolitan-geographic types.

THE LABOR MARKET AREA

The United States Department of Labor's concept of the labor market and the employment security area is without doubt the most complete and rigorously worked out of its kind. As in the case of the industrial area the labor market area has been used singly and in combination with other concepts to arrive at an urban economic base area.

The labor market area as defined by the War Manpower Commission in 1945 took the following form:

"A labor market area, for purposes of classification and labor market analysis, consists of a geographical area surrounding a central city (or cities which are only a few miles apart), in which there is a concentration of urban economic activity, or urban labor demand, and in which workers can change jobs without changing their residences. The extent of this area is usually limited by local transportation and commuting facilities. A radius of 20 to 30 miles from the center of economic activity (usually equivalent to an hour or an hour and a half traveling time each way), is considered a normal maximum commuting range."[7]

A specific application of this approach is well exemplified in the study, *Economic Survey of the Terre Haute Area*:

"A study of the commuting patterns of workers employed by

[7] War Manpower Commission, Reports and Analysis Service, *Directory of Important Labor Market Areas* (U. S. Government Printing Office: Washington, D. C., May 1945) introductory statement, no page number.

various industrial firms, made by the Employment Security Division in March and April of 1950, showed that most of the workers in Terre Haute resided in Vigo County, but 2.8 percent commuted from Sullivan County, 3.6 percent from Clay, 0.7 from Parke, and 2.6 percent from Vermillion County. Only 0.5 percent crossed the Indiana-Illinois line to work in Terre Haute: persumably most of these came from communities to the southwest of Terre Haute along the main highway (U. S. 40).

"Although the results of this study do not demonstrate that Terre Haute is drawing heavily on out-of-county residents for its labor needs, it does show that there is some interdependence of these counties. Presumably additional labor requirements in Terre Haute would increase the amount of commuting, and decrease the existing degree of self-sufficiency of the local labor market. According to local information there is a sizeable movement of workers out of Terre Haute on workdays, but this is said to be mainly to coal mines and brick plants within a 15-20 mile radius."[8]

In the Philadelphia base study, population estimates are made for several types of "trading areas." These areas included, in addition to the traditional retail trading area, the industrial area and the labor market area. The industrial area employed was the Census concept which is known as the Philadelphia-Camden Industrial Area. The Philadelphia Labor Market Area is bounded by the limits of general home-to-work commuting in the industrial area. The important point to note in this connection is that the labor market area and industrial area are not coterminous. The industrial area includes a combination of eight complete counties in Pennsylvania and New Jersey, whereas the labor market area defined on the basis of a

---

[8] Indiana Economic Council *Economic Survey of the Terre Haute Area,* Part I (State of Indiana: Indianapolis, July 1951) p. 9.

"commuting area" embraces only one complete county and portions of the remaining seven.[9]

The strength of the labor market approach in economic base area delineation work lies in the fact that it is generally adaptable to all types of communities and bases while the statistical materials required are not extremely difficult to collect. There is also an appeal of precision to the labor market area technique. Reference is here made to the fact that, at least in the case of the Philadelphia study, outer limits of the labor market area are set in terms of minor civil division boundaries rather than complete counties as with the industrial area. Whereas the labor market area often deals in complete counties as it did in the Terre Haute report, it can also go down to finer geographical distinctions such as boroughs, districts, and precincts.

On the other hand the Terre Haute report raises a substantial question concerning the reliability of labor market boundaries which are defined on a less than county basis. The disturbing thought here is that in times of prosperity and boom the commuting range may well be extended to points not previously included in the base area. Conversely, depression may contract commuting well within the limits established during better times. This would seem to suggest that, whereas the county is a cruder delineation device, it can better absorb the fluctuations of national, regional, and local industrial welfare cycles and thus circumvent adjustments of base area boundaries that might otherwise be felt necessary. There is, in addition, the rather well-founded impression that the setting of boundaries for the producing economic community is not a procedure where great precision is possible and that, consequently, no serious distortions of the export relations of the community would result from the use of complete county units.

---

[9] Philadelphia City Planning Commission, *Economic Base Study of the Philadelphia Area*, p. viii.

THE COUNTY AS A BASE AREA UNIT

The county as an arbitrary measuring unit of the base area has long been employed, occasionally on an independent basis, but more often as a unit in some larger area conception such as the industrial area. Early studies which were concerned with the economic city employed the county as a unit in a broad regional approach. An approach such as this was used in *The Economic Status of the New York Metropolitan Region in* 1944. Here the New York Metropolitan Region was conceived as an area composed of twenty-two counties in three states surrounding the Port of New York. In this report great emphasis was placed on the idea of the region as an economic unit from which basic and service urban economic relationships might be computed.[10] The original delineation was made in connection with the first New York regional study which appeared in 1929.[11] At the present time there is considerable doubt as to the advisability of using a regional congeries of counties as a base area. This doubt is traceable to the fact that the region as conceived at that time is broader in scope than the economic city. This impression is demonstrated in part by the fact that the industrial area of New York is represented by only 12 of the total of 22 counties in the region. However, the industrial area contained 89.5 percent of the 1940 population and 88.7 percent of the industrial wage earners of the Region in 1939. Further substantiation of the individuality of the regional conception is found in statements made by the architects of the New York Regional Survey itself. Thomas Adams points out:

"The metropolitan district . . . is generally smaller than the area which it is necessary to consider when preparing a regional plan. The latter needs to include in addition (to the criteria of the metropolitan district): the water supply reser-

[10] The Regional Plan Association, Inc., *The Economic Status of the New York Metropolitan Region in* 1944 (New York: 1944), pp. vii-viii.

[11] T. Adams, *Regional Survey of New York and Environs* (New York: 1929).

vations of the principal cities; the contributory market garden areas; tracts of land suitable for large state or regional parks; and the land included in communities which are tributary to the metropolis . . . ."[12]

The single county as base area has been employed with great frequency in the past decade by relatively small cities such as Albuquerque, New Mexico. In this case the observation was made that from an economic point of view Albuquerque is synonymous with Bernalillo County inasmuch as 95 percent of the (county) population lives in and finds employment in the urban area.[13] The trend toward general acceptance of the county (or counties) as the base area unit gained strength between the 1940 and 1950 censuses in large part due to the fact that statistical data related to the base as well as to other problems of an urban character are rendered on a county basis. Note the county unit reporting of housing, population, manufacturing, and business. This entire line of thought gives rise to a brief examination and evaluation of the metropolitan area approach and, in particular, its Census version.

THE METROPOLITAN CONCEPT

One of the most familiar geo-economic views of the modern city and oldest in terms of ideas associated with the urban economic base is that of the metropolitan district or area. So familiar is this concept from the voluminous writings of urban sociologists, urban geographers, and the United States Census that extensive explanatory comment is unnecessary. The metropolitan area concept of the sociologist is based on social contacts of commuting, visiting, shopping, newspaper circulation, radio listening, television viewing, and patronage of central cultural activities. The geographer's concept, on the other

---

[12] T. Adams, *Regional Survey of New York and Environs,* Vol. II, p. 202.

[13] Federal Reserve Bank of Kansas City and Bureau of Business Research, University of New Mexico, *The Economy of Albuquerque, New Mexico* (Albuquerque, New Mexico: 1949) p. 2.

hand, tends to be somewhat more limited in its physical extent. For example, the 1940 Census looked upon the limits of the metropolitan district as lines determined by peripheral minor civil divisions whose population density was not less than 150 persons per square mile assuming a central city core of not less than 50,000 persons.

The current Bureau of the Census version of the metropolitan area gives every indication of being the closest approximation to the theoretical ideal concept of an economic base area that it is practically possible to attain. Excerpts direct from the Census will best give a concise description of what is to many already a familiar area delineation procedure.

". . . The general concept applied was that an area should be an integrated economic and social entity, with an attendant large volume of daily travel and communication between the central city and the outlying parts of the area . . . . The following principles were used in applying this general concept to the definition of individual areas:

(a) Each standard metropolitan area must include at least one city of 50,000 or more; the area as a whole must have a total population of at least 100,000. Areas may cross state lines.

(b) Where two cities of 50,000 or over are within 20 miles of each other, they will ordinarily be included in the same area.

(c) Each county included in a Standard Metropolitan Area must have either 10,000 non-agricultural workers or 10 percent of the non-agricultural workers in the area, or more than one half of the county's population must have been included in the 'metropolitan district' as defined by The Bureau of the Census.[14] In addition, non-agricultural workers must constitute at least two-thirds of the total employed labor force of the county.

---

[14] Contiguous minor civil divisions with a population density of 150 or more per square mile.

(d) Each peripheral county included in a Standard Metropolitan Area must be economically and socially integrated with the central counties of the area. A peripheral county has been regarded as integrated (1) if 15 percent of the workers living in the county work in the central county of the area, or (2) if 25 percent of those working in the county live in the central county of the area, or (3) if telephone calls from the county to the central county of the area average 4 or more toll call per subscriber per month. These criteria were selected largely because investigation indicated that they were the only measure of integration on which usable data might be obtained for a substantial proportion of the problem area under consideration. Preliminary field investigation indicated that comparative statistics measuring the proportion of dollars spent at retail in the central city by inhabitants of the peripheral counties or the proportion of bank deposits held in the central city by individuals and businesses in the peripheral counties, were impossible to obtain . . . .

"The requirement that each area consist of county units sometimes results in the inclusion in a standard metropolitan area of a considerable amount of territory which would not ordinarily be considered 'metropolitan,' much less 'industrial.' It is recognized that metropolitan areas could be more accurately defined in terms of minor civil divisions, but the value of areas so defined is limited by the fact that most types of economic and social data are available only on a county basis."[15]

On the positive side there is much to be said for the standard metropolitan area as an appropriate device for delineation of base areas. The definition of the metropolitan area is based on interdependent economic productive factors with the main emphasis on labor location and movement. Commutation movement is, in this version, calculated on a two-way flow

---

[15] U. S. Bureau of the Census, *Census of Population,* 1950.

basis so that producing units outside the central city are given adequate consideration. It is also important to note that the delineation procedure throws heavy emphasis on *daily* contact relationships, an important indicator of economic interdependence. Contact is, moreover, measured not only in terms of physical commutation movement but also in terms of communication based on a frequency factor.

Another general advantage of the standard metropolitan area approach is the fact that in principle it is adaptable to any geographically independent urban community and to any variety of base within such a community. To this combination of advantages must, of course, be added the idea of the county-unit approach which increases the availability of pertinent data necessary to most base studies. In this same connection the point should also be made that when independent checks are made of relative volumes of business done by firms between the local and outside market these are in most cases far easier to estimate and compute in terms of county boundaries than in terms of the boundaries of minor civil divisions.

Finally, it may be said that the "respectability" of the standard area is very great. This is due first of all to the thorough fashion in which it adapts to the needs of a suitable base area definition. There is also present the idea that the standard area is the product of many years of thought and research on the part of a highly competent technical government bureau. These factors represent strong bids for the general acceptance of this area concept for base area description purposes for the time being.

However, there are points, though few, on the negative side of the argument. There is, for example, the objection that the standard metropolitan area has fixed population minimums and does not, therefore, pertain to cities below the minimum size level. This is, of course, not a damaging criticism since the population limits might easily be removed and the basic principles of delineation on a proportional basis would still remain for the most part. However, in the case of metropolitan-area suburbs under economic base analysis, even the proportional technique might not be entirely appropriate. Criticism might be raised as to the commutation proportions adopted. In a situation such as this, arbitrary limits must be set. Obviously, the proportions cannot decline to a base of 1 percent or zero for, below a point, economic integration may become too weak to be significant. Only those persons and authorities such as the Bureau of the Census who have long familiarity with such problems are in a position to render competent judgment as to appropriate limits and cut-off points. Finally, a question may arise concerning the county-unit, or its equivalent, as the most suitable building block for a base area. As was pointed out a few paragraphs back, and as the Census Bureau itself admits, the county is often unwieldly and imprecise for metropolitan area delineation purposes. Whereas these objections were met in part by the exigencies of data collection and the practical difficulty of introducing a high degree of precision into delineation work of this kind there does remain a bothersome question of the very small city in the very large county. Certainly, the small trading center cannot view the county in which it is located as its base area when a true economic evaluation of the situation indicates that practically all of the county represents the export market for that particular city.

CONCLUSIONS

Any thorough-going discussion of economic base areas and the manner of their description has at least two general goals in mind. One of these goals is a type of description or delineation that will best reveal the urban community as an economic and social entity whose mechanism of productive and distributive parts is interdependent to a very high degree. Subsidiary to this goal are such technical objectives as general applicability of a description system to community types and to base types. This second goal is concerned with the standarization of conception of an economic base area in order to increase the comparability of base studies and consequently to increase the reliability of generalizations relative to urban economies that may be drawn from such comparisons.

It is this writer's belief that at the present time those interested in actual field research on problems of the base should employ the Bureau of the Census Standard Metropolitan Area as the base area wherever this may be possible. This suggestion is made in the belief that the Census has made the closest practical approach to the goals mentioned above. While this may seem to many an obvious and over-simplified conclusion it is one that has to be stated for the sake of much needed emphasis. There has been a definite tendency for those cities which are large enough to qualify as standard areas to use this approach for base analysis. Others have employed independent techniques of delineation or combinations of independent and standard area approaches. Acceptance of the Census approach does not suggest that a standard has triumphed for all time. Quite the contrary, the standard approach must be subjected to constant testing and questioning. This becomes doubly necessary in a dynamic society where seemingly trivial technological devices and institutional developments can undermine what appear to be impregnable concepts. In this same connection it is appropriate to emphasize the idea that since the Census is on a one-analysis decennial basis it may describe the base area at a cycle phase which is highly atypical. This may mean that for base-area-analysis purposes a typical economic year or years within a decade should be selected for application of the standard area approach.

Adoption of the standard metropolitan area as base area leaves at least two disconcerting loose ends that must receive attention here. These problems are represented, first by the city which though geographically independent is too small to be considered as the core of a standard (county) area and second, suburban communities which are lacking both in size and geographical independence yet may require base analysis.

In the first case, that of the small independent city, one might say that as long as the city and area size closely approximate the standard area population minimum the Census technique might appropriately be used. But the reliability of the county unit measure of the standard area concept is very likely to diminish with great rapidity as city size declines. It is therefore suggested that where city size is substantially below standard minimum the old minor civil division approach be used for the independent city. This variation would involve an application of the standard area measurement proportions (no the *absolute* measures, with the exception of density) to the minor civil divisions rather than to counties.[16] Naturally there would be a loss sustained to such studies in the absence of county-data integration with base-area data. But a decided gain would be registered in the fact that the less-than-county area would far more accurately represent the community's base area. In this type of analysis it is not recommended that a return be made to the old 150 persons per square mile criterion which was used as a qualified standard approach for New England where towns rather than counties are the area units. Integration, economic and social, in combination (or alternating) with the density measure still appears the soundest test of base area extent. One conspicuous circumstance in which the ordinary integration tests would break down would be one in which the town or minor civil division was populated principally by persons on retirement incomes. It is felt, however, that this is such a specialized situation that it would be immediately recognized by the base area analyst and the civil division would consequently be included in the base area despite weak performances under regular communication tests.

---

[16] Unlike the standard metropolitan area concept this approach would not assume contiguity of minor civil divisions with one another and the central incorporated core. Gaps might well exist with degree of integration standing as the test of inclusion or exclusion of peripheral divisions.

One final difficulty of base area delineation which is not met by the standard area approach is that encountered where a metropolitan area suburb is subjected to base analysis. As was mentioned in an early section of this paper, one possible solution to this problem is an interpretation of the base area in terms of municipal boundaries. This approach would assume that all areas beyond the boundaries were those of another suburb or, if not incorporated, part of the central city's economic area. This does not seem to be a completely reliable conception, in large part because many suburbs have an independent pull or radius of dominance within the larger economic area. Consequently, it is here proposed that a better approach to the problem is one in which the base area of the suburb is determined by: (a) incorporation boundaries at those points where the suburb is contiguous with other incorporations; (b) standard metropolitan area integration proportions where the suburb touches unincorporated minor civil divisions.

Where analysis of the components of twin or multiple cities is desired the above approach is also feasible. However, the standard area approach may also apply in these cases in the event that incorporation boundaries are not contiguous. This point was emphasized in a recent article which said:

"A more difficult and more frequently met problem was that of competing cities. In the past, metropolitan cities in adjoining counties were in numerous cases included together in one hyphenated metropolitan district, as, for example, Scranton-Wilkes-Barre. In defining the new metropolitan areas these combinations as well as others were examined to determine whether integration existed, using the same principles followed for peripheral counties. Integration was demonstrated to be lacking for the following centers which previously had been combined: Scranton and Wilkes-Barre, Boston and Brockton,

Lowell and Lawrence and Haverhill, ... and Racine and Kenosha."[17]

These comments on urban economic geography have intruded into a field which is not the specialty of this writer. However, it is hoped that the problems and their suggested solutions have not been too simply stated and that they will contribute to the comprehension and manageability of a far broader concept, that of the urban economic base.[18]

---

[17] Robert C. Klove, "The Definition of Standard Metropolitan Areas," *Economic Geography*, April 1952, p. 102.

[18] While this paper was in galley proof Professor Harold Mayer of The University of Chicago, published an article on this same subject of base area delimitation. (Harold M. Mayer, "Urban Nodality and the Economic Base," *Journal of the American Institute of Planners*, Summer 1954, pp. 117-121.) The discussion is a contribution to the Chicago Region Project of the Department of Geography of The University of Chicago which is studying the reciprocal relationship between Chicago and its region, from the region inward. In line with this approach Mayer makes some very provocative observations concerning the base area-concept in terms of the relation of transport routes and traffic to a hierarchy of interrelated urban nodes. The "continuous hinterland," "gateway cities," "interchange areas," and "traffic watersheds" represent the detail focus of this approach.

Richard B. Andrews—Mechanics of the Urban Economic Base: The Concept of Base Ratios

Mechanics of the Urban Economic Base:
The Concept of Base Ratios*

Intensified urbanization throughout many parts of the modern world has brought city planners and social scientists to a greater realization of the need for a more complete understanding of the economic forces which represent the foundation of urban growth and change. The concept of the urban economic base is one of the cornerstones of the planner's economic understanding. According to present thought the urban economic base represents those activities of a community which export goods, services, or capital to consumers whose sources of payment for purchases from the community are outside the economic area in question. The base of each community has an economic complement commonly referred to as service activity. Service activities are those which market their goods, services, or capital to purchasers whose sources of payment are within the economic community. Their transactions are of an internal character as compared to the external transactions of the economic base. Few activities from an organizational point of view are pure base or pure service; in short, they are, typically, mixed.

The city planner's interest in the base and service activity data of his community is three-fold. On the one hand, data relative to these principal economic cogs give him improved understanding of the urban economic machine with which he is working. In another sense, base and service data have at least potential utility in predicting the economic course and health of the local economy under conditions of change whether those conditions find their explanation in external or internal causes. Finally, to shift the metaphor, it might be said that the base and service segments of the economic community represent control dials which can be consciously manipulated to obtain

* See Acknowledgements

desired quantitative and qualitative economic results.

It is the immediate purpose of this paper to present an out-line statement of the base ratio theory. This theory is concerned with the nature of the economic inter-relations of base and service elements and with the inter-relation of these elements separately and combined with total community population. In the process of making this statement the discussion will touch specifically on the causes of ratio differences among cities, the assumptions which appear to underlie the theory, and the difficulties of identifiying a normal or typical set of ratios for a particular community.

EXPLANATION OF THE BASE RATIO THEORY

The idea of arithmetic ratios, which found its first clear cut and explicit statement in the writings of Homer Hoyt, has not been greatly expanded or refined.[1] Early observations by Hoyt indicated that, when using employment as a measure, there occurred a ratio between the basic and service activities of cities that appeared to be about one to one. Upon further investigation he discovered that this ratio was actually a variable rather than the constant which he had at first observed.[2] This refinement of the original Hoyt theory suggested that under a variety of internal economic arrangements the base-service ratios of cities differed among themselves within a rather narrow range of whole numbers and fractions thereof; that is, 1 to $\frac{1}{2}$, 1 to 1, 1 to $1\frac{1}{2}$, 1 to 2, 1 to 3 etc. In this ratio arrangement it can be observed that the base activity component is always computed as a constant, or unity, while the service activity element is the one which fluctuates around the base component or, more precisely, is an economic function of it.

Whereas it was not explicit in Hoyt's early statements on the

---

[1] Arthur Weimer and Homer Hoyt, *Principles of Urban Real Estate* (New York: The Ronald Press Co., 1939).

[2] Letter from Homer Hoyt to the author dated Jan. 8, 1953.

ratios, later applications of the concept made the point that the ratio of base to service employment varied for different urban areas at different times. However, it has been assumed all along that in each community a "normal" ratio exists of between 1 to 1 and 1 to 2.[3]

Hoyt's thinking on the urban economic base and specifically on the base-service ratio further implied a relation of the ratio to the total population of the city in question. It is this specific relationship which is so important to the city planner in his thinking on problems of public works planning, zoning, and so forth. The idea is well expressed by the Detroit City Plan Commission when it points out that, "there is a somewhat constant relation between the size of the labor force and the size of the population which it supports. The supportable future population may, therefore, be computed provided the future employment can be estimated."[4] It is to be noted that this conception introduces the base and service activities in a combined role equivalent to total community employment rather than in the ratio relation previously under discussion.

There is, currently, more known of the ratio between total community employment and population than is known of the base-service ratios since the data for the former relationship are readily available in most cases and are frequently employed in other types of economic studies. The typical ratio of total community employment to total community population in this country is about 1 to 2. Speaking more precisely the percentage range of employment in the total of a community's population is characteristically between 40 and 50 with a strong tendency toward the 45 percent point.

What base ratio theory has done is to combine the thought

---

[3] National Capitol Park and Planning Commission, *People and Land*, Monograph No. 2, Washington, D. C.; June 1950, p. 10.

[4] Detroit City Plan Commission, *Economic Base of Detroit* (City of Detroit, 1944), p. 5.

behind the base-service ratio with the total employment-population ratio concept. When these two relationships are combined into a single set of ratios then the economic base assumes a key position in a set of economic reactions that provide the clue to quantitative and qualitative changes in population.

The complete set of ratios which have thus far evolved from investigation of, and thinking on the subject appear as follows:[5]

$$
\begin{array}{lll}
\text{B:S} & : : & 1:2 \\
\text{B:TE} & : : & 1:3 \\
\text{TE:TP} & : : & 1:2 \\
\text{B:TP} & : : & 1:6
\end{array}
$$

It must be re-emphasized before proceeding that these ratios in terms of the figures employed represent only typical conditions within an urban economy. Consequently, deviations from this average sample can and should be expected as the analyst shifts his center of attention from city to city. The causes of these deviations represent a considerable portion of the general explanation of the relation of an urban economy to its base. For that reason a short span of comment apropos of this idea is warranted by way of providing additional background to the ratio concept.

CAUSES OF RATIO DIFFERENCES AMONG CITIES

The causes of base ratio differences among cities are so numerous and have so many devious yet interconnected relationships that only a few representative situations will be described here.

The nature of the economic base itself is the central source of explanation of ratio differences. If, for example, the question relates to the fact that the B to S relation in Washington, D. C. is 1 to 2 as compared to 1 to 1 in Scranton, Pa., it may

---

[5]B = basic activities; S = service activities; TE = total employment or B + S; TP = total community population.

be answered by pointing to the fact that Washington's clerical, heavily female population is in sharp contrast to Scranton's heavy extractive, male population. Government service and commerce of the high order found in Washington represents its base and explain the sociological pattern of incomes, sex, age, marital status, religion, and education found there, which in turn explain the highly developed level of demand for service activities particularly in the forms of shopping goods, personal services, and recreation. This contrasts with the base-determined social pattern of Scranton which yields a less active demand for service activities. This line of reasoning might be supplemented by a closer examination of base-income effects on service activity and of the demand patterns of those persons within the service activity category itself.

Yet another important factor contributing to ratio differences is geographic location. This factor is a more appropriate explanation of differences within economic regions than between regions. Specifically, to take an extreme example, the S factor in a metropolitan area suburb might be as low as 1 to $\frac{1}{4}$ (B to S). This situation could be explained by the fact that the demand for service activities in the suburb is abnormally low due to the competitive geographic position of the suburb relative to the central city to which all members of the suburban commuter-community may have easy access. This same competitive relationship might also exist as between closely situated cities of more equal size. However, in the latter case, the disparity of competitive strength would be less marked; consequently the ratio difference would be less extreme than in the example of the suburb.

Regional economic cycles may contribute more light on the reason for ratio differences among cities. Here is suggested the situation in which the city of a region in depression or recession is compared to a city in a region where economic conditions are far sounder. If a judgment of ratios is made on the basis of data taken at only one time, the two cities may show striking ratio differences despite the fact that the economic bases and social patterns are very similar. Differences of this sort would be reduced or disappear in the event that an attempt were made to analyze the two cities at or near their economic norms or at comparable cycle points.

In this same connection it may be observed that the general status of the national economy (or of a regional economy) may, in the short run, influence TE, and therefore its ratio relation to TP, while the ratio relationship of B to S and B to TE or TP may remain the same. On the other hand, it should be emphasized that conditions of inter-regional trade and the competitive status of area locational factors, while tending to change the absolute volume of individual ratio components, need not always cause change in any of the originally observed ratio relationships in the long run.

An extension of these ideas as they might apply to the qualitative aspects of an area's population and its economy are found in the statement: "The labor force is not a constant fraction of the total population but varies with the proportion of the population in the prime of life or the number of women employed in gainful occupations."[6] This statement might be further qualified by pointing out that the TE to TP ratio will also be influenced by the degree of demand fluctuation for and availability of groups of marginal skill based on age, training, or physical condition.

Age may be another factor contributing significantly to base ratio differences among cities. The process of growth toward maturity, stability, and ultimate decline can apparently contribute to changes in certain of the ratio factors over time. In a sense this is only a special case of qualitative differences in bases among cities. However, as between two cities with

---

[6] Regional Plan Association, Inc., *Economic Status of the New York Metropolitan Region in* 1944, p. xv.

similar bases—let us say Brockton, Massachusetts and some younger western city in which the shoe industry has taken a major hold—there may well be differences in the B to S relationship. As a city matures there appears to be a tendency for the S factor to increase proportionately in its relation to B. This may result from a gradual increase in interest in more complete public services, as well as from a greater concern for local consumption of both goods and recreation services that are not so frequently found in the younger city—which tends to concentrate more on the productive export aspects of its economy. Although there is, thus far, inadequate data on the point, there is strong reason to believe that the TE to TP relationship may also change over time. The assumption here is that in the early stages of its development a city is likely to have a higher proportion of employed population than at a later period in its history. This assumption discounts, of course, secular trends toward a heavier proportion of employment due to the presence of more married women in the labor market. A limitation of this line of thought, however, is found in the employment measure which may not reflect growing capital export activity or other aspects of change in B and S.

ASSUMPTIONS CONCERNING THE MEANING OF THE RATIO THEORY

Thus far the discussion has centered around a very generalized description of the ratios. This is, of course, a necessary first step in building up an understanding on the part of the planner of the nature of the urban economy as viewed by the theory. However, before his understanding can be considered in any sense complete he must have a grasp of the implications or assumptions of the theory from a dynamic point of view. In other words, he must have an understanding of the assumed reactions of the ratio elements under pressure of change. Change is, of course, an unavoidable characteristic of the urban economy and of its social and physical structure.

One of the more important assumptions of the ratio theory is that when the B factor undergoes quantitative change, either positive or negative, sympathetic quantitative reactions take place in the other ratio factors. A further aspect or inference of this assumption is that the sympathetic reaction is an automatic though not necessarily an instantaneous one. For example, the statement has been made that, "every increase of 1,000 workers in basic manufacturing or other basic employment automatically increases employment by 1,500 in the service lines, making a total increase of 2,500 jobs."[7] There is assumed in this example a B to S ratio of 1 to $1\frac{1}{2}$; and, while the precise relationship to TP is not spelled out, it is more specifically stated in another report which says: ". . . each employee in basic manufacturing represents himself, another worker and three other persons in the total population. Thus, an increase in basic manufacturing jobs must be multiplied by 5 to find the resulting population change while a job increase in secondary employment must be increased by $2\frac{1}{2}$ times."[8]

The above passage also suggests a certain degree of independent influence of S over changes in TE and TP. Independent changes in S are a more recent addition to ratio theory and find partial expression in the Cincinnati report which points out that, "increasing opportunities in the urban growth (base) employment category is not the only impetus to the growth of an urban area. Growth is also induced through increasing real incomes."[9] The inference in this case is that increases in incomes will take effect in an increased demand for local goods, services, and capital. This demand reaction will, in turn, be

---

[7] M. Bodfish and H. Hoyt, *Savings and Homeownership*, Dec., 1947, Monthly Newsletter of First Federal Savings and Loan Association of Chicago.

[8] W. D. Bryant, *Housing Market Analysis of Greater Kansas City*, Report No. 6, Research and Information Department, City Hall, Kansas City, Mo., Dec. 1, 1945, p. 16.

[9] Cincinnati City Planning Commission, *Economy of the Area*, p. 23.

reflected in a rise in the employment volume of S. Also implicit is the idea that changes in S yield changes in TE and TP. However, cause and effect relationships are left in a rather nebulous state by the reasoning at this point. Questions immediately arise concerning the source of a real income shift within the community. Does it stem from B or S? Can a shift in general real income levels take place independently within S without an initiating push in the form of income shifts within B? Does not the question of income distribution, particularly the distribution of the real income change, again enter the argument at this point? Questions on income elasticity and the propensity to consume are also apropos.

A final assumption of importance in the base ratio theory which tends to follow from preceding assumptions but is not explicit in them relates to the readjustment of ratio factors following a change in one of them, particularly B. Simply stated, the assumption is that when a change takes place in B which disturbs the ratios there will occur within time a return to the original ratio relationships. For example, let us assume that the ratios of a community are as follows:

	Ratio to B as unity
B = 1,000 employees	1
S = 2,000 employees	2
TE = 3,000 employees	3
TP = 6,000 persons	6

If a positive shift is experienced in B via immigration to fill 1,000 new jobs, the ratios will be altered in the short-run thus:

	Ratio to B as unity
B = 2,000 employees	1
S = 2,000 employees	1
TE = 4,000 employees	2
TP = 8,000 persons	4

However, the long-run adjustment assumed by ratio theory claims a return to the ratios in existence before the rise in B thus:

		Ratio to B as unity
B =	2,000 employees	1
S =	4,000 employees	2
TE =	6,000 employees	3
TP =	12,000 persons	6

A negative shift in B is assumed to bring about repercussions within an urban economy in a direction opposite to that just described. The potential qualifications to the reasoning involved in this set of reactions is apparent from only a casual inspection.

Aspects of the base ratio theory sketched above indicate the rather profound assumptions that are made by the theory relative to its dynamic characteristics. In the opinion of the author the deepest meaning and utility of the ratio theory lies in its dynamics. For it is from an understanding of dynamics that the city planner can not only predict the action of his economy in differing circumstances but can also take steps toward more effective guidance and control. Before these broad ends can be accomplished, however, he must make a beginning at answering the maze of extremely difficult questions surrounding base ratio dynamics similar to those merely suggested at random in preceding paragraphs.

In the opinion of many the base ratios indicate only "rough magnitudes." These same authorities maintain further that, while the ratios are descriptive of the general economic-demographic relations of the community, they cannot be used with any precision.[10] This is undoubtedly the case at the present

---

[10] *Ibid.*

time. However, this situation reinforces the need for rendering a more exact statement of how the ratios work and of the nature of their planning applications. This is but another way of saying that we must gain through unrelenting research a more precise idea of the many ramifications of ratio dynamics while, through improved techniques of measure and identification, we move from a state of "rough magnitudes" to one of relatively precise and meaningful economic factors.

IDENTIFICATION OF THE RATIO NORM

A technical aspect of the ratio theory which has presented both theoretical and practical difficulties is that of setting a ratio norm for a particular urban area. If, for example, the B to S ratio of the community is discovered to be 1 to $1\frac{1}{2}$ a question arises as to whether or not the ratio reflects normal or average conditions of employment, production, income, competition, and population growth. It is certain that extremes of deflation or inflation will have a marked effect on the ratios, particularly if the data on which they are based are taken in the early stages of an economic shift before equilibrating influences have begun to take marked effect on the ratios. Apparently before the "normal" economic situation of a community can be determined certain value judgments must be made by the city planner concerning such matters as employment, production, and the like. When he feels from a preliminary survey of the situation that his local economy is very nearly in balance (or approximates his value judgments of a norm) he will be warranted in making a base analysis. Another approach to this difficulty may lie in the making of several base studies of the community over time. From the results of, let us say, six studies over twelve years either a definite ratio trend might be identified or, in retrospect, the planner might better understand to what particular conditions of local economic health the ratios which he had compiled applied. However, there is, aside from great expense, a hazard in this latter approach. If the time span taken is too long there is a chance that secular trends of the national economy or even of the region may influence the ratios. Secular trends of importance to the base ratios might take the form of an increasing proportion of married women in the labor force, the long-run influence of technological devices such as the automobile and automatic manufacturing production devices, the 40-hour week, the 8-hour day, and extension of the period of formal education.

Base ratios derived from proportional norms can, if properly determined, be of great practical value to the planner in that they provide invaluable bench marks on which his long-run policies of prediction and control may be based.[11] The ratio norm when used as a standard of measure, will, of course, indicate over-all degrees of short-run shift in an urban economy negatively toward depression and positively toward prosperity.[12] Proportional norms also provide a means of detecting secular change. It is assumed that, if the local economy shows differing ratios based on data both taken at norm points, it is highly likely that the difference in the ratios can be attributed to secular change.

SUMMARY AND CONCLUSIONS

The preceding discussion has outlined the principal features of the base ratio theory which indicates in essence that the economic base as element B stands in a ratio relation to the other elements of a local economy, S (service activity), TE (total employment), and TP (total population). Changes which occur in B, through free operation of the economy or conscious inter-

---

[11] Proportional norms refer to the planner's value judgment of his community economy, for example, 1 percent unemployment, operation at 90 percent of production capacity, 2 percent firm failures, firm maintenance of a ten-year employment and production average, etc.

[12] Comparisons of the normal ratios with depression or prosperity ratios may be meaningful only *before* the ratios return to equilibrium as base ratio theory assumes that they are destined to do in the long run.

ference, are assumed to carry in chain reaction fashion through the other elements of the ratios altering their quantitative make up and bringing them in the long run back to a position of equilibrium in terms of the original ratio. The ratio theory is assumed to be of utility to the city planner in that it gives him a better understanding of his economy, a better basis for prediction, and a promising means of judging the potential results of control policy.

The main limitations of the ratio theory rest first in the fact that no great care has been employed thus far in base studies in the identification of a base norm or base bench mark for a community. Consequently, the main basis of competent prediction and control has been diluted in its effectiveness. There is, moreover, the fact that to date too much has been assumed concerning the reaction of ratio elements to conditions of change. This part of the theory is actually extremely complex in terms of the diversity of situations that bear on each of the ratio elements. It is also apparent that B is probably not the sole source of ratio change. More theorizing and field investigation is necessary to explore the potential of independent change in the other ratio elements, particularly S and TP. One of the principal reasons that so little is known of ratio dynamics is traceable to the fact that there are extant no control studies of an urban community which are rendered in ratio terms at two or more points in time.

Richard B. Andrews—Mechanics of the Urban Economic Base: The Base Concept and the Planning Process

Mechanics of the Urban Economic Base:
The Base Concept and the Planning Process*

In all preceding articles of this series it has been assumed that the significance of the urban economic base concept lay in its efficacy, immediate or potential, in the city planning process rather than in its academic aptness as a means of classifying localized economic activity.[1] Earlier articles showed in a general way the planning significance of such technical factors as base identification and measurement. Discussion of the base ratios, particularly their dynamic characteristics, brought the relation of the base concept and planning into even stronger focus.

The present article will center its entire argument on the relation of the base to planning. Specifically, it will discuss by way of introduction the association of economic planning with the city planning process, an area of thought in which there exists considerable differences of opinion as to degree and kind of planner responsibility and action. An examination of current economic control techniques will be made with the objective of appraising the degree to which they are usable by formal and informal planning groups as well as the degree to which they are likely to attain meaningful and desirable results. Finally, the paper will turn to what might be called urban economic planning "frontiers." Here will be discussed those proposals for planning action which appear infrequently or not at all in formal planning reports but which may well hold great hopes for further rationalization of our urban economies.

---

* See Acknowledgements

[1] The economic base of a community is composed of those activities which export goods, services, and capital to individuals or firms whose source of payment is outside the urban economic area under analysis. Service activities which operate as an economic complement to the base in a community do not export their goods, services, or capital but sell them to local firms and the local population.

CITY PLANNING AND URBAN ECONOMIC
PLANNING

The general objective of city planning might be described as the process of making the city a better place in which to live, recreate, and work. Broad as this aim and consequent mandate is, its execution by the typical city planner is confined by the restrictions of budget, time, the realities of politics, and his own vision to the familiar, prescribed details of physical planning. The inadequacy of the physical planning approach as the only operating approach has been stressed by both planners and critics of planning for the past thirty years. It has been only within the last twenty years, following the lead of Hoyt and the FHA in housing market analysis, that practical applications of general urban economic data have been successfully made. Currently, community economic data, particularly as they refer to the base, are employed by the planner more and more as a check on the appropriateness of specific physical plans.

It appears, in fact, that over the years there have evolved two approaches to or interpretations of the role of general urban economic data in the city planning process. In one view, apparently the dominant one, general economic data are employed as mentioned in the preceding paragraph to verify the soundness of a specific physical plan or the community master plan. This procedure rests on the idea that the urban economic base has a direct long-run influence over the quantitative total and social qualitative makeup of the community population. The size and character of population in turn determine the detailed needs and demands for a special combination of land uses, specifically, housing, retail, manufacturing (service), recreational, school, transport, utilities, street use and so forth. The present status and anticipated trends of the urban economy, therefore, are the basis for forming and ultimately changing the detail of the community master plan. It is also here assumed that the desires of the population relative to the kind of community they wish planned have practical financial limitations set up by the nature of the local economy.

The second view of the use of urban economic data is different from the first largely in the fact that, whereas in the first instance the planner plays a relatively passive role—allowing his plans and those of the community to be guided by the present and estimated future of the local economic structure, he and the community in the alternative approach take an active role in fashioning the economy in order that it will more nearly accomplish the ends of living, recreating, and working which all desire. In many of those urban areas where conscious manipulation of the economy has been attempted, the economy rather than the combined planning objectives of the community have been considered the important end. This is, of course, a false emphasis which can lead to economic distortions and general frustrations of community growth.

As can readily be seen, these two views are not mutually exclusive and in all propriety should work together if a community is to gain the full benefit of its planning potential. However, there exists a substantial question concerning the role of the city planner as an active agent in manipulating his local economy.

In the opinion of this writer the task of the city planner, relative to the economy of his area, assumes different forms nearly all of which can be subsumed under the two general interpretations described in the foregoing paragraphs: (1) The planner has the duty of *understanding* his economy in order that he can make intelligent plans for the community which is in large part the social and physical outgrowth of this economy. Understanding includes not only the *status quo* of the urban economy but also its characteristics in movement, in short its dynamic character. (2) Understanding enables the performance of another obligation, that of *estimating* the secular trend, quantitative and qualitative, of the local economy. (3) In a broad sense the city planner also has the obligation of *protection*. The protective function can be thought of in terms of the protection of livelihood of the population; i.e., jobs, businesses, and local realty investments. Investments can be considered public as well as private; i.e., the tremendous investment in streets, parks, and public buildings. The protective function includes as well the concept of preservation from deterioration or decline of the economic competitive position of the community. It also embraces the idea of protection from the more severe economic shocks that result from cyclical variations in wages, profits, and rents. (4) An extension of the obligation of protection is undoubtedly that of *promotion* in the specialized rather than popular sense. Here is envisioned planning that results in fuller employment, a greater variety of employment opportunities, higher wage levels and investment returns.

The actual participation of the planner in promotion and some aspects of protection is open to question. One of the better statements of the case appears in the Cincinnati study. An excerpt of the point of view expressed follows:

"Public action is limited in scope. As far as physical developments are concerned, local governments can gear their programs for highways and other services such as water and sewerage in a manner calculated to aid best the future development of the area. Local governments also can, through their planning and zoning powers, where these exist, lay out the general patterns most suitable to sound future growth in a physical sense.

"The stimulus for most economic development and its guidance in a balanced, systematic manner, however, must come from the leadership of private individuals."[2]

In this statement there is evident the traditional emphasis on

---

[2] Cincinnati City Planning Commission, *Economy of the Area* (Cincinnati, Ohio: 1946), p. 73.

physical aspects of planning insofar as public action is concerned. Economic corrective action is assigned to the sphere of private enterprise and citizen groups. However, it is of greatest importance to note that the Cincinnati economic study is one segment of the metropolitan master plan. Therefore one might say that the document *is* the economic master plan. Consequently we see in this study something rather unique in planning, a completely sketched picture of the economy rather than a set of miscellaneous recommendations which characterize so many planning reports. Apparently, therefore, it is the viewpoint of this planning group that detailed economic planning is the business of the city planner but that its execution should be divorced from local government and should not be progressive, closely controlled planning as is true of other elements of the master plan.

This separation of powers is, of course, consistent with the political and economic philosophy of many nations. However, from a technical point of view such a situation is known to be inconsistent and wasteful. Specifically, it is inconsistent to expect from a city planner plans which in the long-range view are intelligent and effective when he has no control over the principal determinant of the conditions for which the plans were made. In short, lacking power of guidance over economic plans he is at the complete mercy of capriciously controlled or uncontrolled economic forces which in their dynamic aspects may negate many of his proposals and cause gigantic social and economic wastes.[3]

There is no doubt that the citizen group is becoming an indispensable part of the planning process as city planning in terms of scope and complexity becomes a more awesome thing. It is the author's opinion, however, that citizen groups have lim-

---

[3] It is worthy of mention to echo a belief of Dennis O'Harrow that physical and even economic planning may be to little avail without more adequate planning of our urban political machinery from city executive and council through the jurisdictional jungle that now governs most metropolitan areas.

ited competence in the fields they attack even in those cases where they retain a permanent staff of professional planners and administrators. The citizen group should concentrate as it does in Chicago and many other large cities on the special problems of a restricted area or on a restricted phase of the city's economic development. This means that the city planner has the job of stating the problems and their relationships and then coordinating the efforts of all local citizen groups and government departments to the ends that appear to maximize the community's welfare.

In those cases where the citizen group assumes the principal responsibility for economic planning several significant objections or difficulties arise. It may be that the local city planner has presented the community with the facts necessary for economic planning and may even have recommended the outlines of a plan. However, it is likely that a citizen group, depending on its composition, may only pick and choose among the facts and proposals. Such eclecticism may be the result of ignorance of the interrelation of the net of facts and the resultant proposals or it may be in turn the outcome of varying degrees of disagreement with the ideas of the city planner. Such disagreement is proper in a democratic society. However, if the unity and effectiveness of complex economic plans are to be maintained, disagreements must be aired before public commissions and councils who may better appreciate the implications of omissions and changes.

Other objections to dominance of urban economic planning by citizen groups lie in more familiar directions. Continuity of membership, leadership, and financing appear to be more precarious with these groups than with public commissions and committees. Significant breaks in the prosecution of an urban economic plan are likely to have more serious repercussions than those which occur in connection with other varieties of plans. One of the commonest flaws in the approach of the citizen group is the tendency to consider economic improvement of the community in terms of more manufacturing plants. As a matter of fact, industrialization of this variety may be inappropriate or actually injurious to the community. It is likely, in addition, that concentration on expansion of the manufacturing function which is here assumed to be part of the base will lead to the neglect of a careful development of the service aspects of the economy. It cannot be emphasized too often that service activities are of signal importance to the successful operation of the base. Although service activity from a quantitative point of view will tend to expand automatically as the base grows, some of its qualitative characteristics may need considerable guidance if they are to complement the base in a proper manner.

Over-concentration on the manufacturing aspects of community economic planning is in part an outgrowth of the fact that businessman-representation on such committees is heavy and usually dominant. Economic planning should not be so concentrated in terms of the source of its guidance. The biases in even the public planning field are bad enough without placing the key planning area, *economic,* in the hands of a group-type that usually has relatively restricted interests toward the community at large.[4] It cannot be gainsaid that non-governmental groups have in specific communities been very effective in economic planning from time to time. However, the proper work of these groups is one of criticism and promotion of and assistance to the city planning commission and the plans of its technical staff.

---

[4] A citizen group which appears to overcome the last two specific objections is the Committee of 100 of South Bend and Mishawaka, Indiana. The efforts of this committee are directed at industrial-economic planning and development. This organization is composed of the leading business and professional men of the area with representation from education, local government, and labor. Although its primary objective is the location and expansion of industry in the area it also aims at a better rounding of community life. For more detailed comment see: Robert N. Gold, *Manufacturing Structure and Pattern of the South Bend-Mishawaka Area* (Chicago: University of Chicago Press, 1954), pp. 215-218.

CURRENT TYPES OF URBAN ECONOMIC PLANNING AND ADJUSTMENT

The objective of the present section of the discussion will be to make a brief review of the most familiar urban economic planning problems and their solutions or approaches as currently suggested by professional planners and as practiced for the most part by citizen groups. In the course of this description an analysis will be made of the ways in which the problems are stated and proposed solutions propounded in terms of their long-run validity for community welfare. This suggests, of course, an examination of the flaws and misuses of the ideas involved as well as their necessary interrelations. In more precise terms the questions to be covered will include those relating to the scale of economic activity within an urban area, the stability of that activity with emphasis on diversity and seasonality, and to more detailed problems such as the proportion of marginal firms, the linkage potential of the area, and the like. Throughout the relation of economic proposals to the base and service elements, their proper functioning and characteristics—when in the process of induced or automatic change—will be made clear.

Scale. The commonest variety of urban economic planning appears to be that which is concerned with increasing the scale of activity, more precisely the total volume of employment and total payroll within a community. The desirability of this objective seems obvious to all, particularly the traditional man in the street. Simplicity of the idea makes it seductive and hence may obscure its inadequacies in meeting the economic planning problems of a particular local situation. Service elements of the economy are sure to be strongly vocal in pushing broad programs of this kind. More local economic activity, particularly the large-scale additions that are usually promoted in connection with the base, will result in a growth of the volume of local retail sales and hence service profits. On a firm basis the eventual arrival of competitive service firms may reduce the early bonanza but a satisfactory net advance for the older firms is likely to remain. There is, moreover, a community-wide advantage from a property tax point of view. When, particularly, a new industrial firm of any great size is added to a small urban community, taxes may be lightened since industry pays an excess of taxes over cost of public services rendered. This assumes, of course, that tax abatement was not used as a device to get the new firm or firms into the community. In support of this general type of economic planning it can be said that employment and aggregate payroll increases are good for any urban economy regardless of who promotes them. There is no contradicting the fact that, up to a point, city economic and population growth is to be sought because of the community and business production efficiencies that emerge from increase in scale alone. Increase in scale may actually contribute to stability if it results in a larger number of firms as it is rather likely to do. Greater scale can also mean the development of industrial linkage potentials which may trigger a rather automatic cumulative growth. There is, finally, an apparent tendency for per capita income to rise as scale increases.

There are, on the other hand, a number of criticisms to be made of this shotgun approach to economic planning. To repeat an earlier argument, this is the type of program which is customarily in the hands of the amateur citizen promotion group. This fact may, in part, explain the other defects of the action plan.

Perhaps the outstanding fault of planning solely for scale is that the thinking involved is almost entirely on a quantitative rather than a qualitative basis. In urban economic planning the qualitative emphasis is almost a *sine qua non*.

Concentration on manufacturing in the promotion program is most likely to appear when greater scale is the objective. Community economic and population growth seem to be inseparably linked in the popular mind with more manufacturing which appears to be the only common meaning for "industrial activity." Overemphasis on manufacturing or possibly some other single variety of activity may stimulate conditions which lead either to instability or to aggravation of instability that was already present in the local economy.

In addition, there is the very real chance that the quantitative planning approach will lead to ultimate inefficiencies of scale as a point of diminishing returns is approached. The inertia of cumulative quantitative increase is certain to carry beyond the point of optimum efficiency because the entire program behind such increase is more likely to be promoted than managed.

Finally, from a broader point of view, it is evident that in this frame of reference little attention is customarily given to the question of integrating the quantitative additions to industrial activity with either the long-term needs of the community from a land use point of view or with the more immediate popular views concerning the kind of community ultimately desired.

While non-integrated quantitative expansion of B is usually explicit in the "scale" approach, there do occur special situations in which a portion of B in a particular local economic framework may be under-expanded in terms of its immediate potential. Where by careful analysis or obvious conditions this situation is recognized, adjustment is usually appropriate. An example of this type of problem is to be found in Albuquerque, New Mexico. This city which is at the heart of a major national tourist area has only four hotels. None of these is a resort hotel and all are located in the business district. There are, in fact, no resort hotels to be found in the vicinity outside the city.[5] Here, obviously, is a poorly managed portion of what is essentially potential economic base activity. While this is a

---

[5] Federal Reserve Bank of Kansas City and Bureau of Business Research, University of New Mexico, *The Economy of Albuquerque, New Mexico* (Albuquerque, New Mexico: 1949), pp. 56-57.

rather patent case there may be others which should give the analyst and policy-maker pause. Should, for example, a deficient portion of the base be earmarked for expansion if it is part of a nationally declining industry, an industry undergoing a geographical shift away from the area, or one which even with good management has been, locally, a marginal operation?

This last series of questions raises a query concerning the character of urban economic analysis content as well as corrective policy. More intensive attention must apparently be given in urban economic survey work to the position of the various local base activities in relation to the regional and national trends of each activity from an economic, technological, and geographic point of view. While the objective of such analysis, where it has been conducted, has been mainly that of providing raw material for population, income, and land use forecasting, it should be used increasingly with the objective of local economic adjustment. If certain elements of the economic base structure are in regional or national decline, if there is a significant volume of marginal operators, if there are many plants with poor employment experience records from the standpoint of strikes, wages, and working conditions, if many firms in the base are young with untested products and policies then, if one or all of these conditions prevail, careful and intensive corrective planning is imperative.

The quantitative scale approach to planning of the base is closely associated with another line of local economic analysis and development, that of the optimum expansion of S in both the goods and personal service lines. Here is contemplated both a quantitative and qualitative analysis which would reveal those activities of S which but incompletely supply local demand thus requiring importation of the deficiency. The principal objectives of expanding S on an independent basis along these lines is to increase local consumer amenities and conveniences

and community self-sufficiency.[6] While there is little doubt
that consumer and some producer convenience would in many
instances be augmented by this measure, there is a question concerning the whole concept of self-sufficiency and the reduction of
import dollar expenditures. Whereas most personal service activities should in principle be able to care for typically local
needs there is also no doubt that price and quality may be to
the advantage of the consumer when the item is imported. In
short, the locational advantages of specialization should perhaps be recognized rather than resisted for certain portions of
what might otherwise be S activity. This counter-view is, of
course, particularly forceful where the community in question
is small and under the regional dominance of a large metropolitan center. The larger center may, in fact, be so close in terms
of contract or delivery time that even the aforementioned convenience factor of purely local purchase would be largely
negated. Finally, there arises a question as to whether the
deficiency in S represents a sufficient volume and qualitative concentration of business to warrant either a new firm (or firms)
or profitable additions to plant by existing operations.

Stability. With the concept of urban economic stability a
transition is made from quantitative programs of scale to an almost purely qualtitative approach. The meaning of economic
stability as it applies to urban public planning policy refers for
the most part to the elimination or reduction of cyclical variations in the economic activity of a community. These variations
of the cycle, in turn, involve seasonal and business cycles of the
short-span variety. In the opinion of many economists the
degree of control possible over the effect of business cycles on
an urban community is greatly restricted due to the fact that
such cycles tend to be largely national in origin. The argument
runs that as cities grow the similarity between local and national
cycles increases. This is, of course, due to a growth in similarity

---

[6] Cincinnati City Planning Commission, *op. cit.,* p. 23.

of the local with the national economic composition. The conclusion of this line of reasoning is that local authorities should therefore direct their efforts to support of policies at the federal level which through their influence over wage rates, prices, credit terms, and government expenditure will tend to stabilize the entire economy and hence each urban unit of that economy.[7] Seasonal cycles, on the other hand, in the opinion of these same authorities are more subject to local control.

Opinion relative to the position of local planning and its capacities in the control of business cycle impact on the urban economy is certainly brought into question by the views stated above. It would appear that any attempts at manipulation are very nearly futile. However, there is certainly room for debate on this point. Must the industrial pattern of every major urban community ultimately reflect the proportions of the national economy? On the one hand, this question seems to suggest a levelling of locational differentials which may well be taking place with improvement in the means of transport, communication, and power distribution. Yet it would seem that the urban cells of the national economic organism have from a social and political point of view a sufficient potential autonomy to counterbalance, if they wish, the laissez-faire development of their urban economies. This influence apparently centers over control of entry. Use of this term does not suggest that communities would or could ban the entry of certain economic activities except by such means as zoning, taxation, and licensing. However, it does mean encouragement and promotion of entry of those industries specifically desired for better economic balance. Here again a question will arise concerning the architects and agents of control of entry. With these limitations in mind the discussion will proceed to a brief review of the better known programs of stabilization of urban economies at the local level.

---

[7] Frank L. Kidner and Philip Neff, *An Economic Survey of the Los Angeles Area* (Los Angeles: The Haynes Foundation, 1945), pp. 147-148.

Industrial diversification is one of the better known policy approaches to urban economic stabilization. Its objective is to so diversify the kinds of basic industrial activity within a community that negative swings of the business cycle as they impinge on the smaller economic unit will have the depth and rate of their plunge reduced. It does not appear to be an inherent part of this same argument that heavy positive swings of the cycle should also be avoided on the assumption that there might be a boom-bust relationship present. Among the various means of mitigating the depth of local cycle decline is the familiar policy technique of encouraging a local industrial pattern which has a minimum of activities which on a national basis are subject to excessively fast and deep deflation in periods of regional or national economic recession. This usually means a local industrial structure which gives preference to low unit price consumer non-durables as against the other extreme of high unit price producer durables. In some communities the distinction might be between the necessity and luxury classifications of consumer goods or services. Kidner and Neff make the point in relation to regions that diversification is no guarantee of economic stability:

"The real question has to do not with the existence of highly specialized industrial development and the consequent dependence upon one or a few principal industries, but rather it has to do with the particular composition of industrial activity in the region governed. One may argue that the particular pattern of industrial specialization is the important factor rather than industrial diversification per se."[8]

A similar observation was made by Roterus when he found that although Hamilton County and the Cincinnati Industrial Area showed good diversity in types of manufacturing and had an average proportion of employment in durable and non-

---

[8] *Ibid.*, pp. 148-149.

durable goods they suffered far sharper than average declines in manufacturing employment between 1929 and 1933. Further analysis indicated that the explanation for the situation lay in the fact that the composition of the durable goods manufacturing side of the local economy was made up of a very high proportion of extremely sensitive industries such as machine-tools and foundry and machine-shop products.[9]

That diversity per se is not to be pursued as a stabilization policy except in special instances is made clear by the "selective expansion" concept which originated, insofar as this writer can tell, with the Cincinnati study. Selective expansion has two general objectives: "(1) balancing appropriate job opportunities with the present and anticipated labor force of the area, and (2) achieving the highest possible stability of those job opportunities in order that incomes will be at a maximum."[10] The second objective pertains to both the seasonal and cyclical aspects of employment stability. By now the Cincinnati rating system of depression-resistant, seasonally smoothed, labor-force fitted industries is well known though, apparently, but infrequently used. It is important to note that great emphasis is placed in the selection system on covering the entire industrial field so that personal services as well as manufacturing activities important and suitable to the economy are favored. This is formal recognition of the fact that many of the desirable characteristics of urban economic cyclical stability lie in activities other than manufacturing.

Two other aspects of the diversity argument deserve mention. It is apparent, for example, that in times of depression the urban area which has an adequately diversified economic base will not feel the impact of decline all at one time but will absorb it gradually. This situation comes about due to the fact that the

---

[9] Cincinnati City Planning Commission, *op. cit.*, pp. 27-29.

[10] *Ibid.*, p. 64.

differences in timing, duration, and amplitude of change are likely to be very great.[11] In addition, local dislocations such as strikes can tie up a non-diversified local economy rather quickly, particularly in those cases where one or two unions dominate the employee bargaining of the main industrial firms.

There is, apparently, a belief in some quarters that in particular urban or industrial areas the rate of secular economic and population growth is so rapid that it can offset cyclical fluctuations in the contraction phase. According to students of the subject, the rate of secular growth while often spectacular in its early phases soon begins to level off as the local economy enters maturity, rendering it no less vulnerable than other areas to cyclical dampening.

No lengthy mention is necessary of the fact that if an urban community has an exceptionally heavy proportion of its industrial employment in the relatively non-sensitive consumer nondurable lines it undoubtedly has a great potential in the direction of the expansion of durables without risk of cycle difficulties.[12]

In smaller urban communities problems of scale and diversity (in a somewhat different sense than the one in which the term has been used thus far) appear closely related. An extreme example of this idea is the one firm base or one industry town. Vulnerability is obvious here and the need for planning action is imperative if any degree of stability is sought by the community. However, an increase in local economic scale if applied to the one firm would be planning folly insofar as stability is concerned. Here is a case where diversification per se is probably a sound policy to follow. Difficulties in executing diversification and increase of scale in cases such as this would be

---

[11] Chester Rapkin, et al., *Housing Market Analysis, A Study of Theory and Methods* (Washington, D. C.: Housing and Home Finance Agency, December 1953), p. 52.

[12] Homer Hoyt, *The Economic Status of the New York Metropolitan Region in 1944* (New York: Regional Plan Association Incorporated, 1944), p. 24.

evident in highly specialized instances such as isolated communities in which raw materials extraction was the single base activity. It might almost be concluded in this connection that the community with several separate firms all in the same industrial classification is in a more stable position than its neighbor with one firm whose total employment exceeds that of the many smaller firms in the other community.

While, therefore, diversity usually refers to a qualitative range of firms within a community it can also refer to quantity of firms with no qualitative range or a very narrow one. The latter condition while lacking cyclical or industrial stability does produce localized stability of a sort. This develops from the fact that the extremes of stranding or quick out-migration on the part of labor and some aspects of capital when a single firm shuts down is lessened and a redistribution of at least the unemployed labor factor within the community may take place.

Seasonal balancing of local industrial activity can be thought of as a special variety of diversification with, of course, the objectives of employment stabilization on an annual basis and increased purchasing power for the community. Smoothing of the seasonal cycle is considered to be the variety of economic manipulation most likely to succeed as a result of local efforts. If a community is dependent upon a single season base activity it is clear that the annual ups and downs of its economy are traceable to that condition rather than to the longer swings of the business cycle on a regional or national basis. Whereas much seasonal variation in the service sphere of the local economy is either traditional or the result of what is occurring in the base the variation of the base itself is more controllable. The classic Cincinnati study suggests several lines of approach within particular businesses and among industries. A firm can reduce seasonal fluctuation in many instances by "better scheduling of production in advance of orders, addition of new products which can be produced during the slack season in established lines, concessions to encourage customers to buy and stock out of season . . . ."[13] There are, of course, activities which are unable to smooth their seasonal cycle. In these cases it is possible "to dovetail their employment with those establishments whose seasonal fluctuations are contemporary."[14] Another alternative involves the attraction of new industry to the urban area which will accomplish the balancing desired. From earlier analyses in this base series it is perhaps apparent that seasonal balancing of the base may well mean stimulation of sales volume and therefore employment in S without a net addition to the employment total of B. Whether planning of seasonal industry adjustment is done by the local planner, a citizen group, or a combination of the two, the greater chance for immediate and visible results is a factor which makes the seasonal approach a logical first if economic planning of a qualitative character is to be attempted in a community.

In closing this specific set of comments it is appropriate to mention a recently developed institutional factor which may expedite seasonal balancing in some urban areas. This factor is the guaranteed annual wage. Already the automobile industry is contemplating further production integration (geographical as well as organizational) so that it would do more of its presently sub-contracted manufacturing, thus leveling seasonal ups and downs which should, of course, be avoided under a G. A. W. contract.

Yet another phase of the stabilization approach to local economy planning is the fitting or matching of present and future labor force characteristics to industrial jobs. The implication of this approach appears to be that the industrial pattern should be molded by the labor force. This is done in order to reduce the volume and duration of unemployment as well as the inefficiencies of poor fitting that will redound to the disadvantage of

---

[13] Cincinnati City Planning Commission, *op. cit.,* p. 32.
[14] *Ibid.*

producer and employee.[15] The Cincinnati study observed several tendencies of the labor force in its study area which would require matching adjustments in the future. These tendencies included such items as a proportional increase of women and Negroes in the labor force, a greater percentage of the force over 40 years of age, and substantial shifts of workers from the unskilled to semi-skilled class.[16] Although the concept of fitting or matching is a sound one there appear to be flaws in some of its policy proposals. An essential argument of base theory is that the base molds the character and composition of the urban labor force. It is, of course, recognized in this argument that the existent labor force of an urban area also has a locational pull over basic enterprises contemplating moves. Nonetheless the labor force of a particular urban area is not the only locational pull for most enterprises. Consequently, businesses may leave an area and other enterprises of a quite different character enter it, all because of changes in locational factors other than labor. If the character of the labor force is changing, as described in the Cincinnati report, it is probably in response to social secular trends that exist in part because industrial hiring practices and working conditions already encourage them. Although this is perhaps an overly free market type of argument it appears to this writer that the proper approach is one in which recognition is given to the fact that all or portions of a particular force may reflect an industrial pattern which is unsuitable to a stabilized community existence. Therefore, corrective changes in pattern may mean changes in force. Early changes in force may even involve importation of some personnel in those cases where other locational advantages combined

---

[15] It has been pointed out in this connection that certain varieties of diversification of industrial activity can implement labor force matching and increase local stabilization. Some activities are able, for example, to use the skills of otherwise unemployed but able wives and teen-age children of industrial workers thus broadening total employment, stimulating S, and stabilizating family group employment.

[16] *Ibid.*, pp. 64-65.

over-ride the disadvantages of assembly and training. Although this variety of solution will result in unemployment it will be of a localized variety resulting in gradual outmigration or other adjustment of the "unmatched" or unadaptable labor force elements.

Any discussion of urban economic stabilization must include at least passing mention of the fact that the shelf of public works advocates are still vocal in support of their plan to lessen industrial area cyclical swings by postponement of major projects until depression. Their arguments from a pragmatic point of view seem less forceful than before. This is traceable to the fact that postponement is often not practical from a public service point of view as for example the need for replacement of a public sewerage system, street resurfacing and widening, and the like. Moreover, the budget difficulties of holding reserve accounts of great size for many years in the face of rising tax rates have been found politically embarassing.

Linkage, Diversity, and Stability. One of the implied advantages of economic diversity within an urban community is the potential of industrial linkage which is likely to develop. In other words, as the range of industrial types grows the attraction of other associated or linked activities is encouraged. Linkage growth is, of course, not only a resultant of variety in industrial activity but also of sound locational relations and of adequate original local industry size within such diversity.[17] The direct relation of critical firm or industry size to the possibilities of linkage can be put forward as an argument in support of a qualitative "scale" approach in planning of local economic activity. However, as the Cincinnati report points out, it must not be assumed that the entry of associated industry is an auto-

---

[17] R. B. Andrews, "Mechanics of the Urban Economic Base: Causes and Effect of Change in the Base Ratios and Base Ratio Elements (III)," *Land Economics*, November, 1955.

matic process. The possibilities for linking may be far from obvious, appearing only after long and careful analysis. Linkage or "integration," as the report describes the condition, need not be dependent on a single industrial relationship:

"For example, it is necessary to determine not only the nature of materials, components and containers used in common by existing firms in the area, but also the overall quantities represented, in order to determine the feasibility of establishing a local source of supply. This supply source might take the form of a fabricating plant or merely a central purchasing organization which is able to secure the economies attendant upon volume buying . . . , other kinds of integration possibilities include: (1) The possibility of using one or more by-products of existing operations to make, or assemble into, a new product. (2) Complementing the production of existing products—for example, printing dress fabrics or making apparel findings. (3) Rendering repair or specialty services to existing production."[18]

While the employment and production efficiency advantages of linkage or integration are clear it is also true that the over-promotion of integration can possibly give a community a built-in sensitivity which will defeat the original objective of stability.

Description of the complexities of economic base linkage and integration in large industrial centers has been spelled out most definitely by P. Sargent Florence. Classification of urban industrial integration by Florence reveals four major groupings:

(1) Vertical integration describes industries performing a series of successive processes such as textile carding, spinning and weaving.

(2) Laterally integrated industries are those producing parts and accessories for an assembly industry or industries.

(3) Divergent integration involves industries which are de-

---

[18] Cincinnati City Planning Commission, *op. cit.*, pp. 71-72.

pendent upon a common local process for their raw material, such as the dependence of lock and gunmaking, chain, cable and anchor manufacture on the proximity of iron casting.

(4) Diagonal integration is descriptive of those industries which serve a number of industries within a community. In a heavy goods center it might involve die-sinking, stamping and galvanizing. Unlike the other classes of integrated industry it is to be identified more exactly with the service portion of the urban economy than with the base. Nonetheless these industries are rather unique in the service category in that their business contacts are almost exclusively with producing firms rather than with the general public. Diagonal integration also involves servicing operations that are absorbed on a rather large scale by single firms, for example, firms which have their own maintenance divisions, medical services and the like. This variety of diagonal integration can, in some instances, materially influence the ratio relationship of B and S.[19]

Florence's classification is, of course, useful in many ways. However, for the planner it provides a particularly valuable means of appraising qualitatively the direction in which his economy is moving or the direction in which he would like it to move in terms of industrial integration. It lends, moreover, further perspective to the field of dynamics of the urban economic base and underlines largely unresolved questions concerning chain reactions within the economy as discussed in other articles of this series.

---

[19] P. S. Florence, *The Logic of British and American Industry* (London: Routledge and Kegan Paul, 1953), pp. 44 and 45; and *Investment, Location, and Size of Plant* (Cambridge: The University Press, 1948), pp. 54-60: also, West Midland Group, *Conurbation, A Planning Survey of Birmingham and the Black Country* (London: The Architectural Press, 1948), pp. 131 and 132.

URBAN ECONOMIC PLANNING FRONTIERS

There appear to be several areas within the field of urban economic analysis which are, thus far, conceived in rather restricted terms. Before an adequate job of economic planning can be performed these areas must be expanded and in some cases redefined. It will be the purpose of this section of the paper, therefore, to outline the new directions and emphasis that the writer thinks necessary.

Analysis of the productive factors relating to the urban economic base has been standard practice for many years. This analysis has usually been combined with the other key locational factors of raw materials and markets. The intent has been two-fold. One objective was simply that of improving understanding of the local economy. A second purpose centered around the tracing of trends in factor demand, supply, price, and transport cost so that forecasts could be made of the future trends of base activity, of the service function, of population, etc. However, but little attention has been devoted over the years to comprehensive positive programs directed toward preservation of competitive locational advantage and more efficient use of the local factor pattern.

It must, of course, be remembered that local economic planning could hope to influence directly only a portion of the factor picture while it concentrated on support of state and federal legislation to bring about factor influences beyond its immediate control. Those productive and other locational factors which might in many instances be partly under the direct control powers of a locality include traditional land, labor, capital, raw materials, and local transport. The market relation is not included where B is concerned but can certainly be a very real consideration for S.[20] An important exception to this state-

---

[20] The degree of mix of B and S elements within a local firm may make the local market factor of great importance to B in an indirect manner.

ment in which the markets of B are involved pertains to communities that are trade centers where the customer comes to the community. The planner here has a chance to influence markets directly by specific planning programs for out-of-town customer parking, recreation, and general scale of personal services.

Preservation and promotion of locational advantage is, in a sense, a means of assisting and holding existing local industrial activity but it is more than that in that it is also a means of attracting new industry. The selectivity of new industry attraction will in this instance depend upon which factors are promoted or improved most efficiently.

In relation to the land factor, greater appreciation must be given in the planning process to the fact that zoning of adequate space for industrial and commercial areas, while of great importance, is not enough. More recognition is gradually being given to problems of integration, integration of such areas with streets, trucking routes and terminals, rail and siding facilities, belt lines, parking areas, water transport and harbor facilities, public storage and, finally, with complementary land use not directly involved in the production and distribution process. The entire question of utilities both public and private enters into consideration of the land factor. Whereas most city planning agencies are concerned with problems of sewerage extension and availability of electric power they must, again, give greater weight to questions of expansion potential and competitive interurban installation and operating costs of these items.

The same line of argument applies as well to water. Only here the tremendous modern industrial use (and pollution) of water has become a problem not only of adequate supply for the economic side of the community but one also of serious competition with civilian use, domestic and recreational. Within the past few years commercial and industrial redevelopment and renewal have come to be more specifically considered as techniques for protecting the local economy through rectification of mass structural, site planning, and locational obsolescence. Finally, there is the straightforward question of competitive raw land costs among communities. While this problem can be approached by zoning it may be solved in some instances only by public industrial estate planning. All through this listing of internal factor problems it must be kept in mind that many of the approaches mentioned may be currently executed simply because they are "good planning" in the abstract, the professional thing to do. But they are nearly useless or possibly even harmful if they are not linked to a tangible objective. In this particular case the objective should be not a vague "community economic improvement" program but a plan aimed at (a) holding and possibly advancing the competitive factor advantages of the community and (b) making every effort to correct the outstanding, or developing, weaknesses of those same factors.

Raw material as a productive factor is subject to planning control usually only when it is located in the community. Where this is the case the relation of public planning to the factor is uncertain. If the "raw material" is natural scenery or landmarks which attract a large volume of tourists the case is rather clear cut. Planning action, though it is not always so directed, should be aimed at conserving, developing, and beautifying with, again, the economic objective of maintaining and expanding the tourist flow.[21] There is also the case of extractive processes where the planner may be contending with questions that relate to oil, timber, and mineral supplies handled in the raw state by his community. If these resources are privately-owned and mined, as they most frequently are, the planner's job involves measuring the length of profitable operation life and working out the problems of industrial transition and substitution which must inevitably follow resource exhaustion. On the

---

[21] It is, of course, recognized that the objectives of planning in this direction should include the environmental welfare of the inhabitants of the community itself.

other hand, he has a chance, too infrequently exercised, of discovering or devising conservation measures that will prolong resource life and thus ease the process of transition. While the community and the planner may exert only the power of persuasion over the mining corporation they may have greater indirect influence via the revision of federal and state resource and tax laws. In many instances the "raw material" involved might be the finished parts or semi-processed output of a locally linked manufacturing operation. The role of local planning toward this particular factor situation might, in addition to appropriate approaches already mentioned, stress the efficiency of movement of goods to the local producer-user.

Capital in terms of the supply and price of loanable funds is subject to but little direct planning control. The community which wishes to increase the supply and reduce the cost of capital investment can attain its end within limits first by so planning its municipal governmental plant and operations that its public credit rating is of top quality. A second, perhaps longer term technique, is that planning approach which through selective expansion and other devices previously discussed develops an industrial climate of such stability and dynamism that capital at low rates and in adequate quantity is naturally attracted to it.

Dominance of private employment in most urban economies results in a limited sphere of planning control over the labor factor. Nonetheless, as with capital, the indirect measures of control can be of great importance in maintaining and improving competitive locational advantage. The problem here must, of course, be viewed from the standpoint of the desire of both business firms and labor force either to stay in the community, leave it, or enter it.

Wage levels and distribution are of importance to all in the labor force and to most businesses. While high comparative levels may attract labor they may repel industry. A "proper" wage distribution or one skewed to the right may, again, be sought by labor and, if not closely related to differential skills, be avoided by industry. A favorable cost of living index is viewed with favor by both groups and may cause labor to accept a lower money wage and less equitable distribution than might otherwise be the case. It can be said that both groups favor amicable labor relations and working conditions but the relations and conditions approved by one group are not always those approved by the other. Finally, labor efficiency, which is undoubtedly sought by all firms, may cause business to be more agreeable to high level wages. But if "efficiency" means speed-ups and sweated work it will be strongly resisted by labor.

The position of planning relative to these broad considerations involves several approaches. For example, selective expansion as a technique of urban industrial adjustment and fitting, in particular, has as at least one result of its successful pursuit closer approximation of the earnings and skills to the needs and goals of the local labor force. Implicit in the entire factor approach of planning should be, moreover, the idea that the pressure of industrial costs of operation (land, capital, raw materials) will be reduced or stabilized thus leaving more for profits or for an inadequately rewarded factor, in this case labor.

A specific local planning approach to the comparative cost of living status of a community, while involving the factor approach and others discussed earlier, is more directly concerned with manipulation of the S portion of the local economy. Proper analysis of S as of B will reveal its shortcomings such as monopolies, underdevelopment, inadequate management, and excessive factor costs. Certain cost of living elements like food, clothing and fuel—where importation of the finished product is necessary—will be rather diffcult to control except in the local physical access and distribution phase. However, others in which local processing plays a more prominent part like housing (cost *and* quality), food items in the class of milk and baked goods, manufactured gas, and water are more subject to control.

Public services are very much a part of the cost-of-living question. One community with a relatively high cost-of-living index may provide public services in quantity and quality to its citizens which more than compensate for the higher index. The efficient planning of public services so that they are kept up to date and even anticipate public needs while accompanied by relatively stable property taxes is thus a means of reducing labor force turnover and increasing the strength of competitive attraction of the area for mobile labor. This line of reasoning applies most directly to school systems, welfare services, cultural amenities, shopping facilities and recreational systems of a city.[22] Much the same approach may be argued for the firms of the base which in some instances are highly sensitive to the adequacy and quality of fire and police protection, street extension and maintenance, public storage, and the like. Traditional planning thought is deficient as it relates to the argument stated above in that its approach to public service planning is either too diffuse or too expedient. In short, there is no very specific yet comprehensive focus for it aside from a physical master plan. The need here, therefore, is for a master plan of public services based more forthrightly on social and economic considerations of preservation and promotion of the economic base and service complement.

One final observation on the factor approach to urban economic analysis applies to the question of sensitivity to cost changes. Adequate local analysis should reveal not only the tendency for a certain factor to dominate a firm or industry cost structure but should also show how sensitive to factor cost change (including property taxes) these economic units are. This does not suggest merely a study of marginal firms and in-

---

[22] William Manchester, "Louisville Cashes in on Culture," *Harper's Magazine*, August 1955, pp. 77-83. Where commuters represent a significant proportion of the labor force and base of an urban satelite area it becomes even more incumbent on the planner to preserve the living climate of the community in order to hold a group which is locationally rather mobile within the metropolitan region.

dustries but of all local activity, particularly B. With such data at hand, either complete or in sample form, it would be possible to anticipate more precisely the impact of operating cost changes on local economic activities in terms of expansion, contraction, or out-movement whether such changes stemmed from pressures of the free market, or from union or government action.

CONCLUSIONS

The mechanics of urban economic planning seem as of the present to be only imperfectly devised. An occasional base study (one per community), an economic inventory, a housing market analysis, all with but few exceptions, give a one-shot, balance sheet view of the economic city. This is adequate only as a starting point. For suitable planning in this sphere what is required is a progressive, year-to-year community economic accounting system. This system should compile a series of all the significant and accessible economic indicators and data that might be used as the raw material for frequent assessment of the local economy.[23] Frequent assessment is imperative if the economy is to be guided, if corrections in economic structure are to be made before it is too late, if scientific promotion of the economy is to be carried on when the competitive time is right.

If an economic master plan of a city is made, this system is one formal means of checking it, changing it if necessary, as might be done with any master plan. But even more important, such a system is one means of following and controlling if pos-

---

[23] The content of such an account system would be local series, with regional comparisons where appropriate, of firm arrivals and departures of qualitative employment and wage trends, of production, inventories, and sales volume, of shifts in the B and S content of the economy. Regular non-statistical observations would be necessary on the influence of institutional and technological factors, and of the decisions actual and contemplated of local government and business over the economic structure. Progressive estimates would also be required in this connection on the influence of state and federal legislative and executive policies and judicial decisions.

sible the dynamic characteristics of the urban economy. It will give the data for point-to-point comparisons in time so vital to dynamics analysis but now lacking. It should, if properly organized as a body of data, show the firm-to-firm, industry-to-industry, and B-to-S interplay that is the significant chain reaction detail which characterizes the whole field of dynamics. Finally, it will therefore give a far sounder basis for decisions as to cause and effect patterns in the process of urban economic change.

In the next paper John W. Alexander restates the economic base concept as a geographic-spatial concept and emphasizes basic activity as a tie between the city and the surrounding territory or even the rest of the world. Clearly, Alexander, is an enthusiastic supporter of the economic base theory. Although written primarily for geographers, this paper is of interest to other professional groups.

John W. Alexander—The Basic-Nonbasic Concept of Urban Economic Functions

The Basic-Nonbasic Concept of Urban Economic Functions*

Among geographers there appears to be an increasing interest in urban geography as evidenced in faculty research and the number of Ph.D. dissertations. The purpose of this paper is to analyze a concept which has particular value in the geographic study of urban settlements. It applies specifically to the economic functions of a city.

The traditional system of studying urban economic functions begins by measuring the livelihood structure. It determines the number of people employed in the city and tabulates them in such categories as trade, manufacturing, and government. This classification is based, not on any characteristic of space-relationships, but rather on type of service performed.

The concept discussed in this paper *is* based on a space-relationship; and it recognizes that cities develop in response to demands from other places. Indeed, as Mark Jefferson observed over 20 years ago, "Cities do not grow up of themselves. Countrysides set them up to do tasks that must be performed in central places."[1] No city lives to itself. It serves other areas which can be said to constitute the city's "market region." In turn, the region serves the city. Such functioning is of immediate interest to geographers because the interconnections between city and region are one type of spatial relationship. Thus, one aspect of urban geography is the analysis of those ties which bind a city to its region. For example, how extensive is the region served by a city? How far and in what directions does that region extend? What does the city do for that region? To what degree is the region dependent on that city for goods and services? Answers to these questions constitute useful criteria by which relationships between city and region are measured.

---

* See Acknowledgements

[1] Mark Jefferson: "The Distribution of the World's City Folks: A Study in Comparative Civilization," *Geogr. Rev.*, Vol. 21, 1931, p. 453.

One of the strongest ties between city and region is the economic bond, for the economic life of a city is inextricably interwoven with the economic life of its region. A portion of the economic effort in a city is supported by non-local demands. But these city people in turn have need for local services, and thus a second urban function is discernible—that which caters to the needs of local inhabitants.

The difference between these two economic efforts is of fundamental importance, because the former constitutes the city's economic foundation. As Jefferson observed, the city's life depends upon it. It brings money *into* the city and is termed "basic." By contrast, the second category (serving local demands) is termed "nonbasic" and simply involves an exchange of money which basic efforts have already brought in.

The concept of this basic-nonbasic dualism is recognized in several social sciences, particularly economics and geography. "The primary or 'city building' activities should be identified, i.e. those activities which bring into the community purchasing power from outside."[2] "The support of a city depends on the services it performs not for itself but for a tributary area. Many activities serve merely the population of the city itself. Barbers, dry cleaners, shoe repairers, grocery men, bakers, and movie operators serve others who are engaged in the principal activity of the city which may be mining, manufacturing, trade, or some other activity."[3]

The purpose of this study is principally to analyze the basic-nonbasic concept in terms of its relevance to urban geography. The paper is so organized as to present (1) salient points in the historical development of the concept, (2) an inspection of those qualities which recommend the concept for application by urban geographers, (3) a review of selected case studies in

---

[2] Richard U. Ratcliff: *Urban Land Economics,* New York, 1949, p. 43.

[3] Chauncy D. Harris and Edward L. Ullman: "The Nature of Cities," *Annals of the Amer. Acad. of Pol. and Soc. Sci.,* Vol. 242, 1945, p. 7.

which the concept was applied, and (4) questions which need to be answered or refinements which need to be made in maturing the concept for more fruitful application in geographical studies.

HISTORICAL DEVELOPMENT OF THE
BASIC-NONBASIC CONCEPT

The concept of a city's economic dichotomy has been recognized in theory for more than three decades. Various writers have identified it, often using different terminology such as *primary, urban growth, external, supporting* for "basic," and *secondary, service, internal* for "nonbasic." The first expression of the idea appears to be that of Aurousseau who wrote in 1921: "It is well known that towns have an extraordinary power of growth. This appears to be due to the relationship between the primary occupations and the secondary occupations of the townsfolk. The primary occupations are those directly concerned with the functions of the town. The secondary occupations are those concerned with the maintenance of the well-being of the people engaged in those of primary nature."[4]

The first urban analysis explicitly to identify a city's economic dualism was the New York Regional Planning Committee's *Regional Survey of New York and Its Environs* published in 1927. On pages 42-43 of this survey the concept was described in terms of "primary" and "ancillary" as suggested by Frederick L. Olmsted who described the economic activities of a city as follows: "the multiplicity of their productive occupations may be roughly divided into those which can be considered primary, such as carrying on the marine shipping business of the port and manufacturing goods for general use (i.e., not confined to use within the community itself), and those occupations which may be called ancillary, such as are devoted directly or indirectly

---

[4] M. Aurousseau: "The Distribution of Population: A Constructive Problem," *Geogr. Rev.*, Vol. 11, 1921, p. 574.

to the service and convenience of the people engaged in the primary occupations." A footnote in the text indicates that Mr. Olmsted first expressed this terminology in 1921 in a letter to a member of the New York Planning Committee. However, after defining the primary and ancillary components, the study did not proceed to apply the concept in very much detail in analyzing New York's economy, probably because methods had not yet been developed for applying the fledgling idea.

In subsequent years the concept received attention in different disciplines where scholars refined the theory or added new concepts. The most thorough analysis of this historical development is presented in a recent series by Professor Richard B. Andrews.[5]

As far as the author has been able to determine, the first geographer to apply this idea to a specific city was Richard Hartshorne in a study of Minneapolis-St. Paul published in the July, 1932, issue of the *Geographical Review*. On page 437 the author writes, "The conversion of this particular pair of towns . . . into a metropolitan district of three-quarters of a million in 1930 was based largely on the establishment of that district in the period of rail construction as the one all-important focus of rail lines of the central northwest. This may be readily seen from a brief analysis of the external functions of the urban district. In any city these tend to be obscured somewhat by the large number of functions developed to serve simply the residents of the city itself. In Minneapolis-St. Paul the 'internal' functions employed, in 1919, more than half the total number of men workers. Of the remainder, the railroads, including the car shops, employed more than a fourth—by far the largest single group." The author does not explain how he determined these proportions.

That a city's economy consists of two components was ob-

---

[5] Richard B. Andrews: "Mechanics of the Urban Economic Base," *Land Economics,* Vol. 29, 1953.

vious, but nothing appears to have been done in formulating a methodology for applying the concept until Richard Hartshorne worked on the United States manufacturing belt.[6]   Hartshorne reasoned that a part of manufacturing in every industrial city produces only for local consumption and that the most meaningful map of a manufacturing region would locate concentrations of industry producing over and above local demands.   To arrive at some measurement of this (which actually could be termed "basic" manufacturing) the author mapped industrial wage earners for all cities with over 10,000 population, subtracting from each city's total of industrial wage earners a factor of 10 percent of the population.   The assumption was that 1000 wage earners in manufacturing would be required to meet the needs of a city of 10,000 people.   Hartshorne subsequently concluded[7] that this factor was too high and probably should have been 8 percent.   Nevertheless his study was a pioneer effort to measure what is herein termed "basic" effort, applying it to a single type of endeavor, manufacturing.

The next advance in methodology was an analysis of the economic functions of Oskaloosa, Iowa by the research staff of *Fortune* magazine.[8]   By measuring the balance of payments between Oskaloosa and "the rest of the world" they arrived at a distinction between the city's payments to local creditors and to nonlocal creditors.

A third advance in methodology was Homer Hoyt's outline of six steps for measuring basic activity which appeared in a book published in 1939.[9]   In advancing this method Hoyt also

---

[6] Richard Hartshorne: "A New Map of the Manufacturing Belt of North America," *Econ. Geogr.*, Vol. 12, 1936, pp. 45-53.

[7] Personal conversation with the author.

[8] "Oskaloosa vs. the United States," *Fortune*: April, 1938, 55-62 ff.

[9] Arthur M. Weimer and Homer Hoyt, *Principles of Urban Real Estate*, New York, 1939.   The criteria here quoted appear in the text in Chapter VI, "The Future Growth and Structure of Cities," (pages 20-38 of this volume). For the background of Hoyt's experience which led to the formulation of his ideas see Richard B. Andrews' study in *Land Economics*, 1953, *op. cit.*

suggested new terminology: "urban growth" for "basic" and "urban service" for "nonbasic." The six steps are as follows:

1. From census reports, or from local sources such as chambers of commerce, local establishments, local trade associations, and employment offices, determine the number of persons engaged in the principal types of employment. It may be necessary to use estimates in some cases, especially in communities for which there are few published statistics.

2. Determine the number engaged in manufacturing, excluding those firms whose production is intended predominantly for the local market.

3. Determine the number engaged in extractive industry obviously intended for the nonlocal market.

4. Determine the number engaged in nonlocal governmental, transportation, or communication services and the number employed in lines of work catering to amusement seekers, tourists, or travelers.

5. From published sources (for example, the periodical *Sales Management*) determine the percentage of the national income that is earned by the city being analyzed. Then apply this percentage to the total number of persons engaged in trading, financing, professional, and related activities in the country, as shown by the figures of the Bureau of the Census and the Department of Labor. Assume that the number by which local employment in these lines exceeds this percentage is "urban growth" employment. For example, suppose 15,000,000 persons are employed in these activities in the United States and that the city being analyzed has 1 percent of the total national income. On this basis, it may be assumed that 150,000 persons will be required to perform the trading and related activities of the city. If 200,000 are so employed, then 50,000 may be considered as representing "urban growth" employment.

6. Total the figures arrived at in paragraphs 2-5 above and compute the percentage which each type of "urban growth" em-

ployment represents of this total. These percentages will indicate the relative importance of manufacturing ,extractive industry, trading, and the other types of activity in the economic development of the city.

In 1942 Harold McCarty expanded the concept to apply to regional economies as well as community economies. He described basic-nonbasic activities in relation to what he called
the *occupational pyramid*: "The base of the pyramid consists of
that group of occupations whose presence in the area is not predicated on the existence of other types of production. . . . The
base of the pyramid dictates the pattern of the remainder of
the structure. . . . The workers in basic industries are not self-
sufficing individuals, and the local economic organization must
provide them with many types of goods and services including
merchandising establishments, as well as transport facilities,
business, and personal services, and each of these groups in turn
requires workers to care for its needs."[10]

J. H. Jones, in a volume on national planning for Britain's
postwar reconstruction of damaged cities, introduced the idea
that city planners should give priority to basic activities. "These
industries (including services) are the foundation upon which
the town has been built, and may therefore be called 'basic' industries. Their size will determine the size of the industrial
structure and population of the town; no town can grow merely
by adding to an already adequate supply of local industries and
services. . . . Every area, large and small, must contain some
industries that 'export' their products to the world outside that
area . . . the inhabitants of the towns could not be expected to
live by taking in each others' washing."[11]

---

[10] Harold H. McCarty: "A Functional Analysis of Population Distribution,"
Geogr. Rev., Vol. 32, 1942, pp. 287-288.

[11] J. H. Jones: "Industry and Planning," pp. 126-127 in *Creative Demobil-
ization,* Vol. II, *Case Studies in National Planning,* edited by E. A. Gutkind,
London, 1944.

Robert E. Dickinson directed considerable attention to the concept in a book published in 1947 and pointed out the need for more urban analyses in terms of this economic dichotomy. He went further to suggest that analyses of cities could be based on this approach. "What is needed is a much more careful analysis of the urban community, not only as a seat of specialized industry and service serving a wide market, but also as a seat of industry and service for the 'regional' market over and above 'local' needs of the urban community itself, ..."[12] "While granting that in one and the same industrial occupation it is impossible to come to a quantitative measure of the relative importance of the nation-wide and international market, the local urban market, and the wider regional market, this is no reason why the last should not be adopted as a main approach to the study of the occupational structure of towns."[13]

In the past few years, since the publication of Hoyt's "six steps," there has been increasing interest in theoretical aspects of the basic-nonbasic concept. Students in various disciplines find it useful. Several features commend it, particularly to geographers since it is a meaningful expression of a fundamental space-relation between city and supporting areas.

FIGURE 1
ECONOMIC STRUCTURES

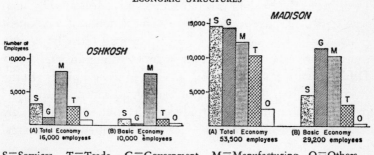

S=Services   T=Trade   G=Government   M=Manufacturing   O=Others

[12] Robert E. Dickinson: *City Region and Regionalism*, London, 1947, p. 24,
[13] *Ibid.*, p. 36.

GEOGRAPHIC QUALITIES OF THE
BASIC-NONBASIC CONCEPT

Traditional community studies based on employment data published in the Census or procured from employment agencies usually are seriously lacking in one respect: they provide no measure of basic activities because such employment data permit no reliable classification of activity in terms of the geographic areas to which the city's goods and services are sold. The local component is indistinguishable from the more fundamental (basic) component which supports the settlement. The conventional method of measuring "livelihood structures," informative as far as it goes, thus has a definite shortcoming. Much of this can be remedied by application of the basic-nonbasic concept which, by classifying economic endeavor in terms of market location, recommends itself to urban geographers for four reasons:

(1) The concept provides a view of economic ties which bind a city to other areas. The contrast between *total employment* and *basic employment* in this respect is shown in Table I (parts A and B) and Figure 1 which give data for two Wisconsin cities, Oshkosh and Madison.[14] The traditional livelihood structure (total employment) for Oshkosh reveals that manufacturing is the leading form of employment followed by services, trade, and government. But when the nonbasic component is removed, the structure of *basic* employment (part B) reveals more clearly the dominance of manufacturing in supporting Oshkosh, with trade displacing services in second place. In the case of Madison the structure of basic employment (part B) is markedly different from the traditional livelihood structure. By total employment, Madison's leading activities are services,

---

[14] John W. Alexander: *Oshkosh, Wisconsin, An Economic Base Study,* 1951, and *An Economic Base Study of Madison, Wisconsin,* 1953. Both were published by the Bureau of Business Research, School of Commerce, University of Wisconsin.

TABLE 1

EMPLOYMENT IN OSHKOSH AND MADISON, WISCONSIN

	Oshkosh	Madison
1950 Population	42,000	110,000
1940-50 Population growth	5%	28%
Total Employment	16,000	53,500
Basic Employment	10,000	29,000
Leading basic activity	Manufacturing	Government
Nonbasic Employment	5,900	24,300
B/N ratio	100:60	100:82
A. TOTAL Employment		
1. Services	3,100	4,500
2. Government	1,200	11,300
3. Manufacturing	8,200	10,100
4. Trade	2,700	3,000
5. Others	800	300
Number of Employees	16,000	29,200
B. BASIC Employment		
1. Services	900	14,500
2. Government	120	14,300
3. Manufacturing	7,880	12,100
4. Trade	950	10,200
5. Others	250	2,400
Number of Employees	10,100	53,500

government, manufacturing, and trade in that order; but the basic structure reveals services and trade to be far behind government and manufacturing in sustaining Madison's economy. This is a meaningful distinction producing an entirely different picture, one not revealed by conventional methods of studying livelihood structures. The rational of the basic-nonbasic concept is that the relationships revealed by data on *basic* employment constitute a more meaningful basis for analyzing a city's economy than do those comprised by *total* employment, that part B of Table I and Figure 1 are more significant than part A.

(2) Another value of the concept to geographers is that it permits the most satisfactory classification of cities in terms of

regional function. Cities are more accurately distinguished by their basic economy than by their total economy because the basics express a city's service to its region. For such a purpose, the nonbasics "cloud the picture" and therefore should be subtracted from the total economy as one endeavors to distinguish industrial cities from commercial cities from government cities, etc. Harris recognized this and suggested empirical estimates of percentages to achieve such distinctions.[15] However, it would seem that a measurement of basic activity would provide a more accurate method for defining urban regional functions.

Evidence from the Oshkosh and Madison studies reveals that the *nonbasic* employment structures were considerably different from both the *total* and the *basic* structures. (Compare Table II and Figure 2 with Table I and Figure 1.) Herein lies a corollary reason for subjecting a city's economy to the basic-nonbasic concept: segregation of basic and nonbasic components reveals an entirely different structure for each, a difference which the traditional system (by blending the two into one livelihood structure) fails to reveal.

Indeed, it even may be that the structure of *nonbasic* activities is substantially the same for every city. So far, not much is known about the nonbasic structure of city economies, but data

FIGURE 2
NONBASIC EMPLOYMENT

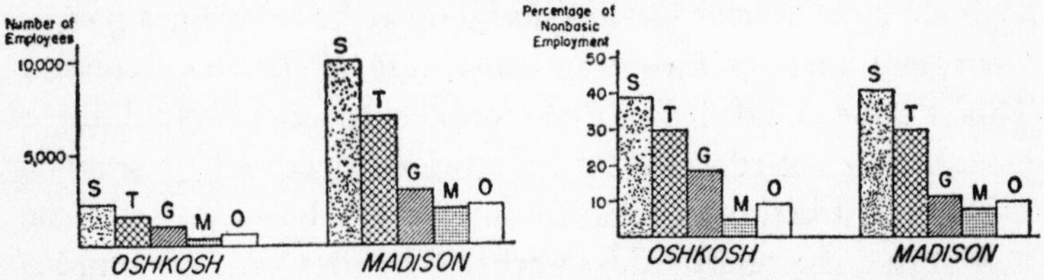

S=Services   T=Trade   G=Government   M=Manufacturing   O=Others

---

[15] For instance, ". . . only cities with more than 60 percent of their employment in manufacturing are classified as industrial, whereas cities with only 20 percent in wholesaling are classified as wholesale centers." See Chauncy D. Harris: "A Functional Classification of Cities in the United States," *Geogr. Rev.*, 1943, pp. 86-99; reference on p .87.

on Oshkosh and Madison reveal that their nonbasic structures are remarkably *similar* in spite of the fact that they are such different types of settlements. Table I shows that Madison is much larger than Oshkosh, is growing much faster, and is supported primarily by government while Oshkosh is mostly a manufacturing city. Clearly, these are different types of cities. Yet the nonbasic structure of each is revealed in Table II and Figure 2 to consist of the same activities *in order of importance*: In each city the leading nonbasic activity is service, followed by trade, government, and manufacturing. But the similarity is even more remarkable, for although Madison has 24,300 nonbasic employees and Oshkosh only 5,900, the *percentage* breakdowns are much alike. Table II and Figure 2 reveal that in spite of differences in overall size, each city has exactly the same percent of nonbasic employment in trade (30 percent), nearly the same in services (38 percent compared to 41 percent), and somewhat similar percentages in government and manufacturing. Thus, Table II and the graph of percentage employment in nonbasic activity are remarkably similar. To be sure, evidence

TABLE 2
Nonbasic Employment

	Oshkosh	Madison
Services	2,200	10,000
Trade	1,750	7,000
Government	1,080	3,000
Manufacturing	320	2,000
Others	550	2,100
Number of Employees	5,900	24,300

Percentage of Nonbasic Employment

	Oshkosh	Madison
Services	38%	41%
Trade	30%	30%
Government	18%	12%
Manufacturing	5%	8%
Others	9%	9%
TOTAL	100%	100%

from just two cities is insufficient to warrant the conclusion that nonbasic structures are constant from city to city. Nevertheless, the facts on Oshkosh and Madison are presented to suggest that if nonbasic structures *are* similar from city to city then they definitely should be isolated so that any functional classification of settlements can be based on the basic functions which *do* differ from city to city without being confused with functions which are *not* much different.

In any case, nonbasic activity should be culled out in order to provide an unobstructed view of the city supports, those activities which connect a community with its supporting territory and therefore serve as the best criteria for a geographical classification of cities in terms of function.

(3) The basic-nonbasic concept provides a new ratio which may have significance in differentiating types of cities. This is the "basic-nonbasic ratio" which, for short, can be termed the "B/N" ratio. Suppose, for example, that a city has a total of 50,000 people employed, with 25,000 engaged in basic and 25,000 in nonbasic activity. The B/N ratio then is 100:100, which means that for every 100 basic employees there are 100 nonbasic employees. But another city also with 50,000 employees might have 30,000 basic and 20,000 nonbasic giving a different ratio: 100:66.

As yet, this concept has not been applied in the analysis of enough cities to produce much evidence about the nature of B/N ratios. Moreover, the few case studies available have employed so many different methods for measuring the basic component that the resulting ratios are scarcely comparable. However, studies by the same analyst employing the same methodology in the case of the two cities already cited (Oshkosh and Madison) revealed that the B/N ratio varied from 100:60 to 100:82 (Table I). Madison's nonbasic component is a third greater than that in Oshkosh. Obviously, the ratio can vary considerably. More detail on its variation is presented in the following section on specific case studies. With the limited information as yet available it seems plausible that urban geographers will find the B/N ratio a useful criterion for the comparative study of cities.[16]

(4) Provision of the B/N ratio also enables a new classification for individual economic endeavors. To illustrate, a business which makes all of its sales to the local market is distinctly different from one which makes all its sales to the outside market. Both businesses might be factories. The traditional method of classifying economic activities would consider them to be in the same category: namely, manufacturing. And yet, in terms of spatial relationships with market areas they are opposites; one is *basic* activity, the other is *nonbasic*. One is tied to the local region for its sales; the other is tied to the surrounding region.

A second illustration: A mail order establishment employs 1500 people who fill orders originating in nearly every state of the nation. The local community generates a demand for less than 1 percent of the sales. Elsewhere in that community is a garment factory making work clothes. It also employs 1500 people who fabricate a product distributed through a market area covering several states. Again the local community purchases less than 1 percent of the company's production. By the traditional method of classification, these two companies would be different: One is *trade,* the other is *manufacturing.* Yet from the standpoint of areal relationships they distribute to surrounding regions, selling very little to the local market. They bring money into the city and are similar in that both are nearly 100 percent basic economic activities.

A third illustration: a city has 3000 employees in *education* —1500 of them in the local public school system, and 1500 in

---

[16] Homer Hoyt, leading student and advocate of the basic-nonbasic concept, says, "I believe that every city has its own distinctive ratio between primary and secondary employment or between basic and nonbasic." (From personal letter to the writer, December 27, 1952.)

a state-supported school of higher learning. The first group constitutes a nonbasic activity, bringing little money into the community; indeed, they are supported by local money. But

Category designation	Degree to which the organization is basic
B = Basic N = Nonbasic	
B	75%–100% sales to basic market
Bn	50%– 75% sales to basic market
Nb	25%– 50% sales to basic market
N	0 – 25% sales to basic market

the second and basic group brings money into the city. Such a distinction between basic and nonbasic can divide not only the education category but also manufacturing, trade, government, and every other category in the traditional classification system.

Data for such classification are not published but must be procured through personal contract with individual companies and institutions. Organizations providing information can then be classified in terms of basic effort. For example, four

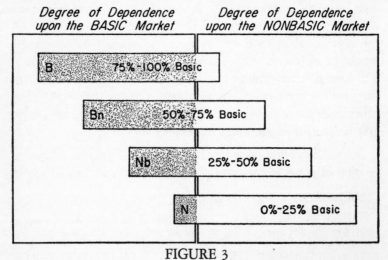

FIGURE 3

categories might be defined as above and illustrated in Figure 3.

Whether the economic activity is a factory, or a shoe store, or a state university, if over 75 percent of its service is in response to a demand from the non-local market region it is in category B (Basic). Category Bn (mostly basic, but at least 25 per cent nonbasic) includes stores, factories, theatres, and other enterprises which bring in more money from the outside than from the city but are more dependent on the nonbasic market than is category B. The two remaining categories depend for most of their support upon the local market, category N to a greater degree than category Nb.

An additional entry could indicate type of activity in terms of the traditional classification: "m"—manufacturing, "t"—trade, "g"—government, "s"—service, or any of several categories desired. Category "Bnt" would include trading establishments drawing 50-75 percent of their revenue from basic customers. Obviously, many other variations of this system are possible. Subnumerals could represent "tenths" of basic component: e.g., B1 for 10 percent basic and B8 for 80 percent.

The contention in this paper is that a discipline in which spatial relationships are fundamental should, in analyzing urban economies, augment traditional methods by a classification recognizing areal associations. Thus, a factory supported by non-local demands is, in the economic life of the city, more akin to a basic mail-order house, a basic store, a basic educational institution, or a basic government agency than it is to a nonbasic factory, albeit both are "manufacturing." Indeed, insofar as role in a city's economic life is concerned, it often is more important to know whether an enterprise is basic (B) or nonbasic (N) than to know whether it is manufacturing or trade.

By revealing components of the urban economy connecting the city with other areas, by providing a regional service criterion for classifying cities in terms of regional function, by providing the B/N ratio as another criterion for distinguishing between cities, and by a new method of measuring individual business firms—the basic-nonbasic concept contributes to the geographical understanding of cities.

APPLICATION OF THE BASIC-NONBASIC CONCEPT IN URBAN STUDIES

Although the concept has existed in theory for more than 30 years, efforts to separate basic and nonbasic parts of a city's economy have been relatively recent. Such studies have been marked by a wide diversity of methodology with a consequential variety of results. The purpose of the present section is not to analyze every case study in which the concept has been applied but rather to select a few which illustrate (a) various methods for measuring basic endeavor and (b) the wide variation in resulting B/N ratios. Readers interested in a comprehensive analysis of several case studies using the concept are reminded of Richard Andrews' series of articles "Mechanics of the Urban Economic Base" in *Land Economics*.

The pioneer case study apparently was by the research analysts of *Fortune* magazine who investigated the circulation of money into, through, and out of Oskaloosa, Iowa.[17] By numerous interviews and questionnaires data were gathered from both individuals and business firms as to the amount and source of income. Total business receipts were $13,942,000 of which $8,114,000 came from non-local buyers. This gives a B/N ratio of 100:72. Over $800,000 also came into the city via individual channels—e.g., Oskaloosa residents employed elsewhere. This increases the basic component so that the ratio becomes 100:65.

Another early effort to measure basic endeavor appears in Harris' study of Salt Lake City. In this, his Ph.D. dissertation at the University of Chicago in 1940, Harris observed, "The important basic occupations of the city are those which serve the

---

[17] *Fortune, op. cit.*

hinterland as well as the city. Two measures of the extra-city function in any given occupance are (1) the number engaged beyond the estimated local needs of the city and (2) the percent of the total state employment concentrated in Salt Lake City.

"The criterion of employment beyond local needs suggests that about 10,000 of the 54,000 people employed in Salt Lake City are engaged in activities of primary regional significance. . . . The other 44,000 are of local or secondary regional significance in that they serve partly the population of the immediate hinterland of Salt Lake County and partly the people of the city or county who are engaged directly in regional activities. [Thus there are at least 10,000 basic employees, and a portion of the remaining 44,000 apparently might be ascribed to basic effort. See Table III in this article.] . . .

"In each occupational group the relation of the total employed in Salt Lake City to the total employed in the state gives a clue to the regional importance of the city in that occupation. . . . [E.g., Salt Lake City contains 28 percent of Utah's population but 71 percent of the state's employment in wholesale trade.][18]

In 1944 Homer Hoyt applied to New York City the method he proposed in the 1939 edition of the textbook already cited.[19] Employed by the Regional Plan Association of New York to make an economic base study, he determined that for every 100 basic employees in Greater New York there were 215 nonbasic employees. He explains his method as follows: "For wholesale trade it was assumed that all the workers in the Region in excess of the number of wholesale workers employed on the average by the same population in the United States outside the Region, could be attributed to wholesale activities for the

[18] Chauncy Harris: *Salt Lake City, A Regional Capital,* University of Chicago, 1940, pp. 8-9.
[19] Weimer and Hoyt, *Principles of Urban Real Estate.*

benefit of persons outside the Region. For manufactures it was estimated that the New York Region would consume its share of the total national production based on its percentage of the total United States population (9.8 percent) or purchasing power (14.7 percent), and that the excess of its production above this percentage of the national production was attributed to production for persons outside the Region. For clothing it was assumed that the New York Region consumed slightly more than its percentage of the national income, or 15 percent, because expenditures for clothing tend to increase with income; but for food it was assumed that the New York Region consumed more than its percentage of the total population but less than its percentage of the national income. In this

TABLE 3
GENERAL OCCUPATION ANALYSIS OF SALT LAKE CITY*

	Number Employed in Salt Lake City	Estimated surplus over local in the city minus the estimated needs. Number actually employed local need for Salt Lake County. The latter is taken arbitrarily as employment on the assumption 38.2 percent of the total state that the occupational need is proportional to population.
Clerical	8,097	3,100
Wholesale trade	4,137	2,000
Retail trade	9,565	1,600
Other trade	3,176	1,000
Domestic, personal service	6,527	1,200
Public service	1,813	700
Professional service	5,691	500
Manufacturing and Mechanical Industries	13,522	....
Transport, Communications	5,656	....
Others	1,821	....
	54,069	10,100

*Adapted from Harris, *op. cit.,* p. 4.

manner, the number of persons working in New York for persons outside the Region was calculated, and it is estimated . . . that approximately 1,500,000 persons, or about 32 percent of the total number employed in 1940 in the Region, were working on goods or services to be sold outside the Region. This means that for every 100 persons so engaged, another 215 persons are employed in local manufacture or in service lines."[20] Hoyt later concluded that the nonbasic component of this ratio was too high because many people were on relief. Since relief payments are a form of basic support, they could be considered to represent the equivalent of a certain amount of basic employment. Thus the 215 nonbasic employees in the foregoing ratio should be linked with a figure exceeding 100 for the basic component. Or, the ratio could be 100: a figure less than 215.[21]

Also in 1944 the Detroit City Plan Commission issued its *Economic Base of Detroit* which states that for every 100 primary employees in Detroit the city has 117 secondary employees. No specific explanation is made of the method by which these ratios were determined, but it appears that *all manufacturing* is considered to be primary and that all other employment is considered to be secondary.[22] Indeed, "service" activities are specifically declared to be entirely secondary, "Detroit has no primary employment in services."[23]

An analysis of Cincinnati in 1946 sponsored by the City Planning Commission, with Victor Roterus as research director, estimated that the ratio was 100:170 between "urban-growth" (basic) and "urban-serving" (nonbasic) activity. The ratio was derived by much the same technique as that used by Hoyt

[20] Regional Plan Association of New York: *The Economic Status of the New York Metropolitan Region in* 1944, p. 6.

[21] Personal letter to the writer, December 27, 1952. Mr. Hoyt credits Professor Richard U. Ratcliff with observing this discrepancy in the ratio.

[22] Detroit City Plan Commission: *Economic Base of Detroit,* 1944, pp. 5, 47.

[23] *Ibid.,* p. 15.

in New York, "Urban-serving employment for each activity can be calculated by assuming that the population of the area will consume its proportionate share of the national production of goods and services. For example, if in the United States in 1940, 25.2 persons per 1,000 population were employed in supplying professional services, then professional employment in the same ratio (amounting to 19,830) in the Cincinnati area would be classed as urban-serving. Employment above the figure would be considered urban-growth (serving persons outside the area)." This study made clear that the formula would have to be varied with each activity because urban consumption differs in many instances from the national.[24]

In 1949 Homer Hoyt released *The Economic Base of the Brockton, Massachusetts Area* in which he identified the two components as "basic" and "service" ("nonbasic") and observed: "Every person employed in a basic industry normally supports approximately one other person in the service or nonbasic activities. Due to the instability of employment and to the number living on unemployment compensation, there were only 21,600 in the service lines in the Brockton area, compared with 26,500 in basic lines."[25] This is a ratio of 100 to 82 in favor of the basic endeavors. The report estimated employment in basic activity apparently on the basis of replies to questions submitted to various economic enterprises.

The analysis of Albuquerque, New Mexico, in 1949, undertaken jointly by the Federal Reserve Bank of Kansas City and the University of New Mexico's Bureau of Business Research, arrived at a ratio of 100:103 between "supporting" and "service" effort. This study actually is of the economic base of Bernalillo County: "where economic data is concerned, Albu-

---

[24] City Planning Commission, Cincinnati, Ohio: *Economy of the Area,* 1946, pp. 22-23.

[25] Homer Hoyt Associates: *The Economic Base of the Brockton, Massachusetts, Area,* 1949, p. 15.

querque can be considered as synonymous with Bernalillo County since no less than 95 percent of the population lives in and finds employment in the urban area." The number in supporting employment was estimated by two steps: (a) sampling representative business establishments to determine the proportion of business each did with people living outside Bernalillo County and (b) pro-rating total employment data for each type of activity (manufacturing, wholesale trade, etc.) according to the percentages determined by the sample.[26]

The "firm-by-firm" approach was used in the economic base study of Oshkosh, Wisconsin.[27]   Data tabulation began, not with total employment figures for the city as a whole but with individual business firms each of which reported its total employment and the percentage of sales to local and nonlocal buyers.   Accordingly, employment was pro-rated into basic and nonbasic components.   For example, a company with 100 employees depending on the basic market for 70 percent of its sales would have 70 employees ascribed to basic endeavor.   Another company making 90 percent of its sales to local buyers and employing ten people would have nine ascribed to nonbasic activity.   Three-fourths of the city's employment was thus tabulated firm by firm; the numbers of employees in basic and nonbasic categories were accumulated with a final addition, an estimate, for the quarter of the economy not contacted in the survey.   By this method, the basic-nonbasic ratio in Oshkosh was determined to be 100:60.   The same method applied to Madison, Wisconsin, in 1951 revealed a B/N ratio of 100:82.[28]

It is not the purpose of this paper to review every urban study employing the basic-nonbasic concept, since Andrews'

---

[26] Federal Reserve Bank, Kansas City, Missouri, and Bureau of Business Research, University of New Mexico: *The Economy of Albuquerque, New Mexico,* 1949, p. 23 ff.

[27] Alexander: *Oshkosh, Wisconsin—An Economic Base Study.*

[28] Alexander: *An Economic Base Study of Madison, Wisconsin.*

work is a comprehensive digest of these studies. Rather the purpose here is to observe some distinctive methods which have been used and the difference in B/N ratios resulting.

It would seem that none of the methods used in the foregoing studies is entirely satisfactory for application to all cities. Tabulation of employment by individual companies is accurate but tedious and generally impractical for large settlements. Use of national proportions as factors for multiplying a community's employment in specific activities is acceptable as a method of estimating but probably permits a large degree of error since it cannot discriminate well between types of communities. Its application to small cities might result in considerable errors.

The variation in the reported B/N ratios is considerable, from the one extreme of 100:215 (New York) to 100:60 (Oshkosh). Are these cities actually that different in their economic nature? Or were the methods used to determine the ratios that different?

The need is for more case studies which apply the basic-nonbasic concept. Surely the refining of the concept in terms of what should be included in "basic" and "nonbasic" activity, and improvement of the methodology for delimiting the two functions are worthy objectives for urban geographic research.

QUESTIONS FOR FURTHER RESEARCH

After various methods have been tested for measuring basic enterprise and reliable techniques have been proved, answers to the following questions should be available to further the understanding of urban settlements:

(1) Is the B/N ratio truly a meaningful characteristic for distinguishing cities? If so, a method for classifying cities could be in terms of B/N ratios. How many cities and what types would have ratios of 100:100? What proportion and what types of settlements would have ratios of 100: less than 100? of 100: more than 100? Or will it be demonstrated that

all cities have substantially the same ratio and that variations cited in the foregoing case studies are coincidental, resulting from flaws in imperfect methodologies?

If the B/N ratio is found to be a meaningful variable, additional questions await investigation.

(2) Does the B/N ratio vary with size of settlement? Is there a distinctive ratio for a hamlet, for a small town, for a city of 10,000 people, of 100,000, of 1,000,000? From the case studies cited it would appear that the larger the city the larger the proportion of nonbasic activity. Communities compared in this study are here listed according to population as reported in their analyses:

Community	Population	B/N Ratio
New York	12,500,000	100:215
Detroit	2,900,000	100:117
Cincinnati	907,000	100:170
Brockton	119,000	100:82
Albuquerque	116,000	100:103
Madison	110,000	100:82
Oshkosh	42,000	100:60

The correlation between size of city and size of nonbasic component in the above data is not entirely consistent; perhaps the relationship would have been clearer if there had been uniformity in methods of measuring the ratio. Nevertheless, in the case studies cited the larger city was found to have the larger proportion of nonbasic employees where: (a) the same method was applied, even by different analysts, viz., New York and Cincinnati; (b) the same analyst applied different methods, viz., Homer Hoyt in New York and in Brockton; and (c) the same analyst applied the same method, viz., Oshkosh and Madison. Not until the same method is applied to numerous cities can evidence be advanced for this hypothesis, but the question can be raised to challenge investigation: Does the B/N ratio vary with population?

(3) Does the B/N ratio vary with *type* of settlement? Would a manufacturing city of 50,000 inhabitants have a different ratio than a trading center or a government center of the same size?

(4) Does the B/N ratio vary not only with *size* and *type* but also with *location* of settlement? Other things being equal, would a city of 40,000 people located 30 miles from a metropolis have a ratio different from a counterpart located 300 miles from a similar metropolis?

(5) Does a city's B/N ratio vary from *time to time?* Would a city's ratio during a depression be different than in a period of prosperity?

(6) Does a vigorously growing city have a different ratio than a stagnant city of the same size?

(7) Are nonbasic activities similar from city to city? Or is the similarity between Oshkosh and Madison merely a coincidence?

(8) How does one delimit an urban community for application of the basic-nonbasic concept? The United States Census provides one useful definition in terms of settlement density, essentially that an "urbanized area" includes not only a municipality of 2500 inhabitants but also areas with a population density of 2000 per square mile (as long as the agglomeration has at least 100 dwelling units). However, the economic functions of an urban agglomeration usually are rendered by not only the locally employed inhabitants but also by commuters who reside elsewhere. These people are *not* part of the settlement in terms of residence; they *are* part of its economic function. Conversely, residents of a community working elsewhere are not tabulated with employees in the settlement's economic activities, yet their endeavors bring money into the city. Should an analysis of a settlement's economy be in terms of those who

work in it, who live in it, or both? Research endeavors in this field need to clarify the method of delimiting an urban settlement in terms of economic function.

(9) What is the best method for applying the basic-nonbasic concept to a settlement, once it has been delimited? What is the best definition of "basic"? Surely the concept needs refinement and the methodology needs improvement. In any case, the need is for an accurate method for measuring basic activity applicable to a metropolis as well as a small city. Surely, the search for such techniques is a profitable expenditure of a scholar's time.

SUMMARY AND CONCLUSIONS

For several years students of "urbanology" have recognized a dichotomy in urban economies, based on geographical location of markets for the urban efforts. A city's *basic* activity links the settlement with other portions of the earth's surface; *nonbasic* endeavors link the settlement with itself.

This concept has merit for urban geography because it classifies economic functions fundamentally on the basis of space-relationships, it reveals one group of economic ties which bind a city to other areas, it permits a classification of and comparative analysis of settlements, and it provides an additional method for classifying individual economic activities within a city.

Case studies in which the concept has been applied have reported a wide difference in B/N ratios which appear to vary with method of measurement and size of settlement. There is a need for more case studies as a means of improving the methodology.

Urban analysts in a discipline where spatial-associations are fundamental can augment their traditional methods of studying urban economies by application of a concept distinguishing between economic endeavors on the basis of location of the demand area. Application of the idea in more case studies should not only improve the methodology but also provide answers to numerous questions, contributing to the body of knowledge about urban settlement. This is a frontier challenging geographic analysts wishing to advance the borders of their discipline toward a mature fruition of economic geography.

II. OBJECTIONS TO THE ECONOMIC BASE THEORY AND AN ALTERNATIVE THEORY.

Well-reasoned objections to the economic base theory have been appearing in recent years. Most of these objections are aimed at the basic-service concept itself. The selection that follows differs from later selections in that it attacks the base service ratios as planning and forecasting techniques. The view is expressed by Gillies and Grigsby that the techniques have been developed beyond the ability of the economic base theory to support them. They also point out that using the base-service ratios in prediction implies a prior prediction concerning the change in basic industry, even if the economic base theory is accepted.

James Gillies and William Grigsby—Classification Errors in Base-Ratio Analysis

Classification Errors in Base-Ratio Analysis*

In a recent article in the AIP Journal Mr. Hans Blumefeld carefully analyzed the development and some current uses of the base-ratio method of forecasting changes in metropolitan areas.[1] He concluded that the limitations of the underlying theory restrict the usefulness of base-ratios for practical analysis and indeed suggests that undue consideration of base industries as prime sources of changes in the metropolis is unrealistic and incorrect.[2] It is not the purpose of this paper to take issue with Blumenfeld's conclusions, but rather to direct attention to another aspect of base-ratio analysis—errors which result as a consequence of improper classification of industries as either basic or service.[3]

THE BASE-RATIO METHOD DEFINED

Fundamental to the base-ratio approach is the assumption that economic activities within communities may be divided into two classes which are different both with respect to the forces which activate them and with respect to the contributions which they make to the urban economy. The first class is composed of "base" or "town building" activities which, according to theory, are industries which export goods beyond the boundaries of the metropolis. The second class is composed of the "service" or "town filling" activities, which are purely local in nature. They complement the base and react to changes in it. The forces of change, however, according to the theory, develop

---

* See Acknowledgements

[1] Hans Blummenfeld, "The Economic Base of the Metropolis," *Journal of the American Institute of Planners,* Volume XXI, Number 4, pp. 114-132.

[2] *Ibid.,* p. 132.

[3] For an example of detailed work in determining the exact nature of base ratios see Working Denver, An Economic Analysis by the Denver Planning Office, 1953.

in the base industries, and therefore for purposes of analysis, the base industries are the more significant.[4]

The first step in the application of the base-ratio technique is the identification of activities as either basic or service. Unquestionably, the manner in which this classification is done may have considerably effect on the results of the analysis, for it is the relationship between base and service activity which determines the base-ratio. For example, if there are 2000 persons employed in service activities for every 1000 in base industries, the ratio of base to service is 1:2. Given this ratio it has been argued that if the base employment increases by 500, service employment will increase by 1000 and total employment in the community will rise by 1500 as a result of the initial increase of 500 in base activities. The ratio may be measured in any one of several units, but it is usually computed from employment figures as they are easiest to obtain.[5]

SOME LIMITATIONS OF THE BASE-RATIO METHOD OF ANALYSIS

It is not surprising that the base-ratio method has received widespread acceptance as an important analytical device by those concerned with the dynamics of city growth and structure. Utilizing this method, it is believed, facilitates the preparation of estimates of future population, potential requirements for various services provided by a community, land use patterns and other information crucial to far-sighted planning. This knowledge of base-ratios permits estimates of the total potential effects brought about by changes in primary industry within the community. In addition to shedding light on some of the most difficult problems planners have to face, it has an aura of simplicity and finality which gives it a peculiar attractiveness.

---

[4] A. M. Weimer and H. Hoyt, *Principles of Real Estate* (New York: The Ronald Press Co., 1954) Chapter XVIII.

[5] See R. B. Andrews, "Mechanics of the Urban Economic Base: The Problems of Base Measurement," *Land Economics,* Volume XXX, Number 1, p. 53.

On close examination, however, some of these advantages appear to be more apparent than real because of limitations both in the concept and in the degree of precision which can be obtained through its use.[6]

NUMERICAL PROPERTIES OF BASE-RATIOS

Changes in the economic base of an area, when base is defined in terms of export industries, develop either through expansion and contraction of existing industry or through the development of new industries. The base ratio merely tells what will happen to the community *if* the base industries expand or contract or *if* new industries immigrate. Consequently, before the ratio may be applied, there must be a prediction of what will happen to the base. Thus the key factor in the analysis is accurate predictions of change in the base industries. Strangely, therefore, while a great deal of written material is available on means of separating base from service activities, very little is available concerning methods of making predictions. Similarly, in actual studies there appears, on the surface at least, to be more time spent in identifying base and service activities than in making predictions about them. Apparently the prevailing opinion is that the most serious errors in base-ratio analyses flow from inaccurate identification of base and service activities, or in other words, from inaccurate ratios. The numerical properties of ratios, however, suggest that this is not always so.

To illustrate these numerical properties, reference is made to Table 46, page 64, of *The Economic Status of the New York Metropolitan Region in 1944*, a well-known study made by Dr. York City. (See Table 1).

The most significant figures which can be derived from the table are the base ratios for New York City in 1940 and 1946. The ratio for 1940 is 1:2.16, and is found simply by dividing total base employment of 1,500,000 by the total service em-

---

[6] Hans Blummenfeld, *op. cit.*, p. 116-118.

TABLE 1

The Approximate Number of Persons Needing to be Employed in the Various
Lines of Activity After the War if We Are to Avoid Mass Unemployment

	1940 Actual Employment	Suggested Goals For First Post-War Year (Assumed to be 1946)	Increase
Population	12,500,000	13,000,000	500,000
Total Labor Force	5,700,000	6,000,000	300,000
Unemployed	955,000	200,000	755,000
In Armed Forces		200,000	200,000
Employed Total	4,745,000	5,600,000	855,000
In Basic Employment			
Manufacturing (non-local)*	900,000	1,067,000	167,000
Banking, Insurance, Management	220,000	250,000	30,000
Wholesale Trade (non-local)	190,000	218,000	28,000
Transportation, Rail, Water, Air (other than local)	150,000	190,000	40,000
Hotel & Entertainment (non-local)	40,000	55,000	15,000
Total Basic Employment	1,500,000	1,780,000	280,000
In Non-Basic Employment			
Retail Trade	723,000	780,000	57,000
Manufacturing (local)*	458,000	558,000	100,000
Professional Services	422,000	500,000	78,000
Personal Services	410,000	456,000	46,000
Local Transportation & Utilities*	255,000	255,000	
Construction	240,000	450,000	210,000
Local Government	200,000	200,000	
Business & Repair Services	135,000	150,000	15,000
Real Estate & Local Banking	120,000	140,000	20,000
Wholesale Trade (local)	110,000	126,000	16,000
Hotels & Lodgings Houses & Entertainment (local)	90,000	100,000	10,000
Agriculture, Mining, Forestry	55,000	60,000	5,000
Federal & State Offices	25,000	45,000	20,000
Total Non-Basic Employment	3,245,000	3,820,000	575,000

* Note — The total employment in manufacturing — for local and non-local consumption combined, was 1,358,000 in 1940. The program for full employment in the New York region calls for a total of 1,625,000 to be employed in Manufacturing in 1946 or 1947. This is composed of 1,067,000 in non-local manufacturing. The table is reproduced by permission of the Regional Plan Association, Inc., 205 East 42nd Street, New York 17.

ployment of 3,245,000. By a like computation the ratio for 1946 is found to be 1:2.15, or the same as the 1940 ratio for all practical purposes.[7] This is but another way of saying that the base and service sectors were expected to increase at the same rate. Since the idea of a fairly constant ratio in any given community is practically axiomatic by base-ratio theorists and since constant ratios can be found in other studies by Hoyt,[8] it can be safely assumed that the stability of the ratio from 1940 to 1946 was not a chance occurrence.

The second significant group of figures to be derived from the table are the predicted growth rates of the various industry categories. They vary from 0% (Local Government) to 87.5% (Construction), although the base and service sectors as a whole are assumed to increase at the same rate. This could happen only if the predictions for the various service categories were made *after* an estimate had been made for the total service sector. If the individual growth predictions for the service categories were not made within the context of a predetermined over-all increase, it would be a rare occurrence for the new ratio to be the same as the old one.

Hoyt's precedure in the New York study, therefore, may be summed up as follows:

A prediction was made about each base industry, and these were totalled to obtain the predicted increase for the entire base sector. The 1940 base ratio was applied to the predicted base increase to obtain the total increase for the service sector. The total estimated increase for the service sector was divided among the various service categories, using as criteria for this division

---

[7] If the ratio had stayed exactly the same the estimated total employment increase from 1940 to 1946 would have been 3.5 per cent greater.

[8] See for example Homer Hoyt Associates, *A Report on the Economic Base of the Brockton, Massachusetts Area,* (Brockton, Massachusetts, January, 1949), p. 79, Table XLV. Various theorists have mentioned causes of gradual secular change but have not assigned them too much importance and in practice have assumed constant ratios rather than attempt to estimate the change.

whatever information was available about the service activities. A slight departure from the predicted increase for the total service sector was made to accommodate unusually large estimated changes of specific service categories.

It may be assumed that the various industrial, commercial, and professional groupings shown in the table have been correctly classified as between base and service, but what would have happened to the estimates of total employment increase had this not been the case? Suppose, for example, that because of a serious conceptual or computational error, the entire 900,000 basic manufacturing employment had been misclassified as service. How would this change the employment forecast?

First of all, by reducing the 1940 basic employment by 60% (1,500,000 to 600,000) and correspondingly increasing the service employment 27.7% to 4,145,000, the classification error would change the 1940 base ratio from 1:2.16 to 1:6.91. Secondly, it would reduce the total predicted 1946 basic employment from 1,780,000 to 713,000. Assuming that the base ratio remains constant from 1940 to 1946, total 1946 service employment would be 6.91 times as great as the 713,000 base employment, or about 4,926,800.[9] Total employment—basic plus service—would now be 5,639,800 as opposed to the original estimate of an even 5,600,000. Total estimated employment increase would be 894,800 as opposed to the original estimate of 855,000. The huge error in classification has changed the final estimated employment increase by only 4.7%. Similarly, it can be shown that misclassification of all basic categories except manufacturing would alter the estimated employment increase by only 3%.

Errors also result when service activities are misclassified as basic. In illustrating these errors, an assumption must be made as to whether the original predicted increases for the misclassi-

---

[9] The new figure for total service employment would, of course necessitate new estimates for the various service activities.

fied service categories would be changed by reason of the misclassification or would be left alone. For example, if Wholesale Trade (local) were misclassified as basic, a different prediction about it might be made simply because of the very fact that it had been erroneously identified. This fact is of no concern when a basic industry is misclassified as service because the new prediction, if there is one, is made *after,* not before, total employment has already been estimated. The necessity for the above described assumption when explaining the effects of misclassifying service groups somewhat limits the generality of the illustration.

Keeping this limitation in mind, suppose that Manufacturing (local) were wrongly identified as basic. This would reduce the 1940 service sector by about 14%, increase the base by 30.5%, and result in a new base ratio of 1:1.42. If despite this misclassification, it were not felt necessary to revise the original 100,000 estimated increase for local manufacturing, total basic employment for 1946 would be 2,338,000. Total 1946 service employment would be 1.42 times this figure or 3,327,000, and the combined total, 5,665,000. The new estimated employment increase of 920,000 would represent a change of 7.6% from the original 855,000. Thus although the misclassified Manufacturing (local) category is smaller than the previously misclassified base categories, the final error of estimated employment increase is somewhat larger. If, however, the increase for the misclassified Manufacturing (local) were assumed to be not 100,000 but equal to the percentage increase for the correctly classified basic manufacturing with which the service manufacturing group became merged by reason of the misclassification, the error would only be 2.5%.

As a final example, suppose that the export criterion for base-service distinction is abandoned and that Construction is identified as basic employment, as it is sometimes described in analyses of the national economy. Suppose also that despite this shift of Construction from the service group to the base group, its

210,000 predicted increase remains unchanged. This reduces the 1940 service sector 7.5%, increases the base sector 16%, and reduces the base ratio to 1:1.73. It simultaneously changes the predicted increase of total employment from 855,000 to 1,336,000—an error of 56%. The smallest of the misclassified categories causes the largest error in the total forecast.

The apparent inconsistency between the magnitude of classification error and the magnitude of final error may be explained by the differing predicted growth rates of the various misclassified industries as compared to the predicted growth rate for the total base sector. The predicted percentage increase for the total base sector is 18.7%. That of Manufacturing (non-local) is 18.6%. Thus its misclassification had very little effect upon the predicted growth rate of the total base, and likewise of the total community, since the community as a whole is assumed by definition, to have the same rate of increase as the base. The predicted percentage increase for Manufacturing (local) is 21.8%, so its misclassification caused a slightly larger error. However, when its predicted increase was changed to equal the 18.6% rate of Manufacturing (non-local), the misclassification error was correspondingly reduced. Finally, Construction with a predicted increase of 87.5% caused the largest error.

The above illustrations suggest and it can in fact be shown that when the base ratio method is used to estimate the change in total employment stemming from contraction or expansion of base industry, misclassification of activities as between base and service does not by itself cause errors in the final employment estimates. For error to occur, the misclassified base or service industry must have a predicted growth rate which is different from the predicted growth rate for the total primary sector. Thus misclassification of a base or service industry (as defined by the export concept) whose predicted growth rate is the same as the predicted growth rate of the total base will have absolutely no effect upon employment estimates made from the base-service ratio.[10]

Similarly, errors which do occur will not be proportional to the amount of error in the base-ratio itself, since the amount of error varies with both the size of the misclassified industry (as a percent of the total primary sector) and the extent to which its predicted growth rate deviates from that of the total primary sector. The larger the misclassified industry and the more its growth rate deviates from the average rate of growth in the area, the more erroneous will be the final estimates.[11] The percentage error caused by misclassification will always equal the percentage change in the predicted growth rate of the base sector.[12]

It becomes apparent that with respect to the classification problem, the industry about which one can be least concerned may be the largest one in the area. This is not true, however, of the prediction problem. If the misclassification itself should occasion a different sort of prediction than that which otherwise

---

[10] As mentioned previously, in the base-ratio method of analysis, errors in the final employment estimates will occur either as a result of erroneous predictions of changes in the size of the various industries or as a result of the misclassification of these industries and consequent error in the ratio. In order to isolate the effect of misclassification, it is assumed in this discussion that the predictions are 100 per cent accurate. Thus any errors in the employment estimates are a result of errors in the base-service ratio.

[11] Regarding the direction of the error it can be shown:
  (a) If a base industry which is not growing as fast as the average of all the base industries in the area is erroneously classified as service, the employment growth estimate will be too large. Consequently, if a base industry which is growing faster than the average for all the base industries is misclassified as service, the increase of total employment will be underestimated.
  (b) If a service industry which is not growing as fast as the average for all of the base industries is erroneously classified as basic, the employment growth estimates will be too small. Conversely, the misclassification of a service industry which is growing faster than the average for all of the basic industries will cause the increase of a total employment to be overestimated.

[12] This is not immediately apparent from the table because of the slight change in the base-ratio from 1940 to 1946.

would have been made, this could be troublesome. In any event, concentration of classification efforts on the few industries whose growth rates are expected to deviate materially from the community average and relatively little attention paid to those industries closer to the community average will result in more accuracy where more accuracy is needed. It will, in addition, reduce the total time required to classify industries and thus enable more attention to be paid to the important problem of making predictions about industries. Of course, just how much attention need be paid to the classification of even the most "deviate" industries is itself a question. Even very rough classifications would never be as erroneous as those assumed in the above examples, and seldom would the predicted growth rate of an industry deviate from the average as much as did that of Construction in Hoyt's New York study.

OTHER CHARACTERISTICS OF THE BASE-RATIO

It would seem from the above analysis that the task of continuously refining the base-service ratio is an unrewarding one. It may also be unrewarding for yet another reason. Even if absolute precision in classification were possible, employment estimates might be distorted by an inherent limitation of the ratio—its instability.

In most writings, as mentioned in the previous discussion, the base ratio has been represented as or assumed to be fairly constant. Each city is said to have its own unique number which is developed by careful study, and which is usually thought to be a function of the age and geographical location of the city, the economic structure of the surrounding area, and, most important, the nature of the city's economic base.[13] It is accepted that the ratio may fluctuate secularly, with changes in business activity, and with varying states of military preparedness, but it is considered stable enough for predictive purposes.

---

[13] Homer Hoyt, "Homer Hoyt on the Economic Base," *Land Economics,* Volume XXX, Number 1, p. 182-186.

This assumption of normative value is, however, questionable. It appears more likely that the base-ratio actually changes with the very growth it is supposed to estimate.

There are several reasons why growth itself may alter the ratio. The chief reason is that urban expansion is not simply a multiplication of cells, as is assumed by a constant ratio. Growth of a community does not imply that the various components of the base increase in the same proportion. Some of the primary industries will expand, but others may remain static and still others decline. New industries may move into the area. Now if it is true that the nature of the base itself is the primary reason for variation of base-ratios among cities, it is equally true that base-ratios must vary among different industries. Therefore, if each base activity has its own ratio and if the various base activities do not expand at the same rate, then growth is certain to result in a new community ratio.

Looking at the other side of the same problem, applying the area ratio, which is an average of all the base-service relationships within the area, to growth predictions of particular industries will result in errors which by themselves might cancel the benefits of more precise calculation of the ratio. It makes a great deal of difference to a community whether expansion occurs in an airplane industry or in a mail order house.

This same idea can be viewed in yet another way. The fact that each base industry generates a different amount of service activity per unit of income or employment expansion (i.e., has its own base-service ratio) implies that service activities differ in their response to base expansion. Some services expand in response to any increase in the primary sector, whereas others are tied primarily to a specific industry or industries, either basic or service, and grow only as these industries grow. Still other service industries grow independently of any base expansion.[14] Thus, although the population of an area may double, it does not necessarily follow that the number and variety of service activities must also double. There will be a tendency for some service activities to expand faster than others, for some service trades to develop "base" characteristics (i.e., develop export markets), and for new kinds of service industries to immigrate. If the various service activities exhibit different growth patterns, only by sheer chance would their total increase be such as to produce a new base-ratio equal to the old one.

If growth does indeed alter the ratio, then the very purpose for which it is used casts some doubt upon attempts made to refine it. If the predicted growth of an area ranges from insignificant to moderate, the area can accommodate the small amount of change without recourse to this sort of estimation device. On the other hand, where there is a forecast of more considerable expansion, it may be inadvisable to rely upon the ratio method because the growth itself distorts the ratio, and the larger the growth the greater the distortion. The very expansion which occasions the use of the ratio renders it inaccurate, and this inaccuracy increases in direct proportion to the need for accuracy.

It is true, of course, that the objections raised here concerning the stability of the ratio are of only theoretical importance unless quantitative tests indicate that an assumption of constancy causes significant predictive errors in situations of large and rapid growth. Where growth is not appreciable, the error would not be great, but neither would be the need for using the ratio.

Preliminary estimates of the base ratio of the Los Angeles

---

[14] Because of the inter-dependent nature of these various base-service relationships, it would seem that even with the present lack of data sources, more accuracy would be achieved via input-output analysis than by the use of base-ratio techniques.

Metropolitan Area for 1940 and for 1950 indicate that if the 1940 ratio had been applied to a completely accurate ten-year forecast of the 1940 primary sector, the total employment estimate for 1950 would have been 20% in error because of a change in the base-ratio. Although this example certainly does not by itself settle the question, it does show that in one area where an accurate ratio would seem to be most needed by reason of growth, efforts toward precision would have been abortive. Likewise it raises the question of whether large volumes of resources allocated for the development of precise ratios are productively spent.

WHY A BASE-RATIO?

If the base-ratio has so many defects why use it at all? One reason is that the ratio with all its limitations does permit a rough prediction. It may not be a suitable tool for the detailed analyses for which it has been used, but it is at least a starting point. A second justification for its use is the fact that it is easy to obtain. Since proper understanding of the local economy is an important perequisite to accurate prediction of its future, it follows that every economic base study will include an estimate of the volume of various types of exports, imports, and local trade. Once this information has been obtained, computation of a base-ratio is only a matter of minutes.

It is important to note, however, that in identifying and quantifying base and service activities for the purpose of understanding and making predictions about them, the degree of accuracy required is not necessarily the same as that which has been sought for the base-ratio. It may be more or it may be less. In any event, it seems apparent that determination of the level of accuracy to be sought should be based on what is necessary for good prediction rather than on a desire for a more accurate ratio. For predictions must be made about the base industries before the ratio can be applied, and the major errors in population forecasts involving the ratio technique probably stem from these predictions rather than from use of an inaccurate ratio.

SUMMARY

The base-ratio method, though only one of several tools available to city planners for estimating future population growth, is presently one of the more popular. Originally envisaged as a crude device helpful in quick surveys,[15] it has been refined through the years and now is felt by many to have considerable potential as a precision instrument. When there is lack of accuracy in predictions based upon this method of forecasting, such errors are ascribed to inadequacies in developing the ratio or to inaccurate predictions about base activities rather than to limitations which may be inherent in the method itself.

It has been the intent of this paper to point out various characteristics and weaknesses of the base-ratio method. Specifically it has been suggested that:

a. With respect to the forecasting of change in the base structure, large errors in classifying base and service activities will not necessarily cause large final errors.

b. The base-service ratio for an area is the amalgamation of many individual base-service relationships within the area. These individual ratios are reflections of various linkages of economic activities. As these linkages change with the expansion or contraction of the community, so do the ratios. Therefore, the base ratio, which is used to estimate future growth, is not stable in a growth situation, and this instability may cancel out the benefits which accrue from precise measurement of the ratio.

Concentration on the improvement of the base-ratio method has diverted attention and resources from an examination of the limitations of base ratio theory and from other and better forecasting devices. Hoyt had the right idea originally when he ap-

---

15 Homer Hoyt, *op. cit.*, p. 183.

plied the ratio in a situation where time was of the essence and he needed a rule of thumb with which to work. Some of the refinements in the method since then have been useful. Additional energy, however, should now be expended on the problems of obtaining superior prediction techniques.

One of the early protests against the economic base theory, both as a theory of urban growth and as a basis for planning techniques, is reprinted next. Economists might view this paper with surprise because it was clearly written by a non-economist (the approach, terminology and method of thought reveal its non-economic origin) yet it makes many of its points that the economist would make. The author, Hans Blumenfeld, is a noted and respected urban planner. If Blumenfeld ever subscribed to the economic base theory, he had clearly become disenchanted with it at the time of writing this paper.

Hans Blumenfeld—The Economic Base of the Metropolis

The Economic Base of the Metropolis*

CRITICAL REMARKS ON THE "BASIC-NONBASIC" CONCEPT — SUMMARY

1. The concept divides all employment in a community into "basic" or "primary" employment, working for export, and "nonbasic" or "secondary" employment, working for local consumption.

2. This method purports to serve two goals:
   a. Concentration of attention on the most important industries.
   b. Prediction of future total employment and population, which are to be derived from future "basic" employment by means of a "basic-nonbasic ratio" and of a "multiplier."

3. The method seeks the answer to two different questions, which it fails to distinguish:
   a. What is the balance of payments of the community?
   b. What are the most "critical" industries, i.e., those most vulnerable to outside competition and most capable of expansion into outside markets?

4. The confusion is increased by a widespread dual bias:
   a. A "mercantilistic" bias in favor of money-earning versus consumption-satisfying activities.
   b. A "physiocratic" bias in favor of food and raw materials versus manufactured goods and services.

5. The attempt to identify "basic" activities by the widely accepted method of proportional apportionment is misleading. The attempt to do it by actual market survey is costly and ends up by revealing the inherent contradictions of the method.

6. The method neglects the import side of the ledger which is equally important with the export side, both from the

---

* See Acknowledgements

"balance of payments" and from the "criticality" point of view.

7. As a result of its confusion of these two points of view, the method is unable to solve the problem of "indirect primary" activities. If a consistent "balance of payments" approach were used, the problem would cease to exist; if a consistent "criticality" approach were used, these activities would fall in line with all other activities.

8. The method fails to integrate into its conceptual scheme any payments received or made other than those for work performed.

9. Employment is not a usable unit of measurement for a "balance of payments" approach, which must use "value of product" and other value terms.

10. The proportion of "basic" activities increases with increasing division of labor between communities and decreases with increasing size of community and with increasing division of labor within the community.

11. The "basic-nonbasic ratio" is meaningful only in small and simply structured communities; the larger and more complex, that is the more "metropolitan" the community, the less applicable is the ratio and the entire method.

12. The "multiplier" varies not only with the "ratio," but also with the "family coefficient" of both the "basic" and the "nonbasic" employed, and with the percentage of the population which is not employed.

13. Because of these complexities the "multiplier" is not a useful tool for population prediction in a metropolitan area.

14. The identification of the "export" activities of each locality could be an important tool for a national agency planning industrial location. However, if local planning agencies use it as a guide to promotion, it will either be ineffective, or, if effective, result in a harmful distortion of the national locational pattern.

15. A large metropolitan area exists, survives, and grows because its business and consumer services enable it to substitute new "export" industries for any that decline as a result of the incessant vicissitudes of economic life.

These services are the constant and permanent, hence the truly "basic" and "primary" elements of the metropolitan economy; while the ever changing export industries are the "ancillary" and "secondary" elements. The relation assumed by the method is, in fact, reversed.

1. *THE CONCEPT OF THE ECONOMIC BASE*

The terms "economic base" and "basic" industry or employment are being increasingly used and discussed in planning and related fields.

Sometimes the term "economic base" simply stands for "economy," considered as the base of the life and growth of an area[1]; or, the term "basic" is simply used as a synonym for "important."[2]

Geographers frequently denote the region which serves as market and as source of supply for a given city as its "economic base." So Harold M. Mayer: "the area which appropriately may be considered as constituting the economic base of a large metropolitan city."[3] Similarly John W. Alexander defines the "Bases for the Oshkosh Economy" as "I. The Market Base. II. The Supply Bases."[4]

However, both Mayer and Alexander[5] also make use of the

---

[1] See, f.i.: *Economic Base Study of the Philadelphia Area*, Philadelphia City Planning Commission, August 1949.

[2] f.i.: Grace K. Ohlson in *Municipal Yearbook*: . . . that furnishes the major volume of employment." Quoted by Richard B. Andrews, The Urban Economic Base, *Land Economics*, 1953, p. 265.

[3] Harold M. Mayer, "Urban Nodality and the Economic Base," in *Journal of the A.I.P.*, Summer 1954.

[4] John W. Alexander, *Oshkosh, Wisconsin, An Economic Base Study*, Madison, Wisconsin, 1951.

[5] John W. Alexander, "The Base-Nonbasic Concept of Urban Economic Functions," in *Economic Geography*, July 1954, Worcester, Massachusetts.

term "basic" in the sense in which it has become increasingly accepted, as opposed to "nonbasic." This concept claims that all economic activities of an area can and should be divided into two fundamentally different and mutually exclusive categories.

Apparently the first American planner to formulate the concept was Frederick Law Olmstead, who said in a letter of February 21, 1921: "productive occupations may be roughly divided into those which can be called primary, such as carrying on the marine shipping business of the port and manufacturing goods for general use (i.e., not confined to use within the community itself), and those occupations which may be called ancillary, such as are devoted directly or indirectly to the service and convenience of the people engaged in the primary occupations.[6]

Haig and McCrea, in conformance with this concept, state: "It has been urged that a distinction should be drawn between "primary" and "ancillary" activities: that primary activities be given precedence in the city plan."[7]

In the same year M. Aurousseau wrote: "The primary occupations are those concerned with the functions of the town. The secondary occupations are those concerned with the maintenance of the well-being of the people engaged in those of primary nature. The more primary citizens there are, the more secondary, in a relation something like compound interest."[8]

Here we find the two ideas which have determined the further application of the "basic-nonbasic" concept.

1. Planning and promotion, with preference to be given to "basic" activities.

---

[6] Quoted in: *Regional Survey of New York and its Environs, Vol. I*, R. M. Haig and R. C. McCrea, p. 43, footnote.

[7] Haig & McCrea, *op. cit.*, p. 42.

[8] M. Aurousseau, "The Distribution of Population," *Geographical Review*, Vol. XI, 1921, pp. 567 ff. Quoted by Robert E. Dickinson, *City, Region, and Regionalism*, London, 1947.

2. Prediction, with total future population being derived from "basic" employment by application of a "multiplier."

The bias in favor of the "basic" activities, implicit in such terms as "basic," "primary," "town-building," "town-growth," versus "nonbasic," "ancillary," "service," "secondary," etc.,[9] is made explicit in such statements as: "the first task of . . . Letchworth and Welwyn . . . was to secure that 'basic' industries would be attracted; the inhabitants . . . could not . . . live by taking in each other's washing."[10]

We will return to the question, if, when, and why people can or can not "live by taking in each other's washing." For the development of the concept the second application—for population prediction—has been even more important. It was broadly used by Homer Hoyt in his work for the F.H.A. The method, as developed by Hoyt, includes five steps.[11]

1. Calculate employment in each basic industry
2. Estimate ratio of basic to service employment
3. Estimate ratio of population to employment
4. Estimate future trend of basic employment
5. Derive future total employment and population from future basic employment.

This has become the accepted formula; frequently steps 2 and 3 are omitted in favor of a rule-of-thumb formula of "population to basic employment equals seven to one."

Hoyt started by assuming that employment in manufacturing was "basic," that all other employment was "service," and that their ratio was roughly one to one. For the purposes for which

---

[9] An exception is the use of the terms "surplus" and "domestic" in the sophisticated study by John M. Mattila and Wilbur R. Thompson: "Measurement of the Economic Base of the Metropolitan Area," *Land Economics*, August 1955, pp. 215-228.

[10] J. H. Jones, "Industry and Planning," in E. A. Gutkind, *Creative Demobilisation*, Vol. II, London, 1944.

[11] See: A. M. Weimer and Homer Hoyt, *Principles of Urban Real Estate*, New York, 1939.

Hoyt developed his formula—a quick, rough-and-ready housing market estimate—it was serviceable. However, he soon discovered, first, the difficulties of identifying "basic" activities, and second, the existence of wide local variations in the "basic-nonbasic" ratio.

2. IDENTIFICATION OF "BASIC" WITH "EXPORT" ACTIVITIES

Hoyt defines his criteria for a "basic" activity as follows: "those industries and services which produce goods for people living outside the urban region being studied, and which bring in *money* (my emphasis, H.B.) to pay for the food and raw materials which the city does not produce itself."[12] Similarly, Richard U. Ratcliff defines "primary or city-building activities" as those "which bring into the community purchasing power from outside."[13] A Swedish geographer differentiates between "exchange (bytes)" production, which is regarded as "primary" and "own (egen)" production which is considered "secondary,"[14] and a Swedish planner has used this distinction to develop his method of population prediction.[15] Perhaps the most straight-forward explanation of the concept of "basic" workers was given by Andrews who calls them "the wage earners of the community family."[16]

The concept sounds simple and convincing enough: in order to live a community, like a family, has to earn money. The number of families is determined by the number of bread-winners; the number of "housewives" who "service" the bread-

---

[12] *The Economic Base of the Brockton, Massachusetts Area,* Homer Hoyt Associates, published January 1949, p. 4.

[13] Richard U. Ratcliff, *Urban Land Economics,* McGraw Hill, N. Y., 1949, p. 42.

[14] W. William-Olsson, *Stockholms Framtida Utveckling (Stockholm's Future Development),* Stockholm, 1941.

[15] Fred Forbat, "Prognos for Näringsliv och Befolkniny" (Forecast of Industrial Activity and Population), in *Plan,* Stockholm, 1948, No. 9.

[16] Richard B. Andrews, op. cit., in *Land Economics,* 1953, p. 161.

winners, and of dependents, can be derived from the number of the former.

There are certainly cases where the concept is fully applicable. Take, for instance, a copper mining village with 1,000 miners. There will be, say, 600 people employed locally in retail trade and consumer services; if the family coefficient is 2.5, the population will be 4,000. If the company hires another 1,000 miners, it is safe to predict that they will be followed shortly by about 600 more "secondary" employed persons and that the population will increase to 8,000. Inversely, if the company lays off 500 miners, the population will in due course shrink to 2,000. It is also safe to say that no attempt to promote development of any or all branches of "secondary" activity will make a noticeable impact on the economic life or the population size of the community.

Now, let us define the specific conditions of this experimental case:

1. There is no possibility of substitution of another "basic" activity for copper mining.
2. There is no source of income from outside other than wage payments.
3. Earnings of all "basic" employed are roughly equal (or at least average earnings for any group which may be added or subtracted are equal).
4. The family coefficient of all groups in basic employment is the same.
5. None of the product of any "basic" industry can be sold locally; or, looking at the same phenomenon from the other side, all goods and services (other than those which because of their physical characteristics can be supplied only locally) are being supplied from the outside.

It is evident that every one of these five conditions is the exact opposite of conditions characteristic of a metropolitan area. A metropolis is not simply a sum of villages, and it can not be analyzed by adding up studies of its parts.

3. LIMITATIONS OF THE "BASIC-NONBASIC"
CONCEPT IN TIME AND SPACE

As has already been pointed out, the literature on the subject is pervaded by a conviction that the "basic" activities are more important than the "non-basic" ones. Emphatic statements abound. "Basic employment is the same as . . . destiny."[17] Harold McCarthy goes so far as to call "the base . . . that group of occupations whose presence . . . is not predicated on the existence of other types of production."[18]

This is evidently untrue. No "basic" industry in a modern city could function without such services as water, transportation, and communication. Some students of the subject are aware of this. "Urban-Growth and Urban-Serving Employment . . . are both equally essential," says Victor Roterus;[19] and the U. S. Chamber of Commerce speaks of "a chicken-and-egg relationship," adding: "industrial growth stimulates the remainder of the local economy and the existence of the community makes possible industrial growth."[20]

Here a new and important point is being made: the community with its services is the basis of industry, as well as vice versa; and it is startling to find that this point is being made by a promotional pamphlet of the Chamber of Commerce rather than by planners. It is the more startling as—alongside with the goal of "strengthening" or "broadening" the "economic base"—the American planning profession also proclaims the

---

[17] *Working Denver, An Economic Analysis by the Denver Planning Office,* 1953, Department of Planning, City & County Bldg., Denver 2, Colo., 1953, p. 27—We will frequently exemplify our critique of the "basic-nonbasic" concept by reference to this excellent study, because it has developed the concept more completely than most others.

[18] Quoted by John W. Alexander, "The Basic-Nonbasic Concept," *op. cit.*

[19] Cincinnati City Planning Commission, *The Economy of the Area,* Cincinnati, December 1946, p. 22.

[20] Chamber of Commerce of the U. S., Washington, 1954: *What New Industrial Jobs Mean to the Community.*

goal of the "self-contained community." The Greeks had a word for it: autarchy.

Evidently, the two goals are mutually exclusive. In a completely self-contained, or autarchic, community, nothing has to be bought from outside and consequently nobody works to earn money for outside payments. There is no "basic" employment; all people live by "taking in each other's washing."

On the other hand, the higher the percentage of the labor force in "basic" employment, the greater the dependence of the community on outside markets and on outside supplies, the less "self-contained."

It may help to clarify our concepts to look at extreme cases. The copper mining village comes as close to maximizing "basic" employment as any community is likely to come. An employed bachelor, who does not make his own breakfast nor sew on his own buttons, would be the perfect example of 100 percent "basic" and no "service" activity.

At the other extreme, a subsistence farm—or a truly "self-contained" community like the ancient Indian village—has no "basic" employment. All occupations are "concerned with the maintenance of the well-being of the people" which, according to the above-quoted definition by Aurousseau, is the criterion of "secondary" occupations.

Also, and perhaps more significantly, the global community of mankind is engaged exclusively in "secondary" or "service" activities. A large nation is not far from this extreme; the "basic-nonbasic" ratio for the U. S. is probably about 1:20. The generally accepted applications of the "basic-nonbasic" method—preferential promotion of "basic" (i.e. export) activities and prediction of future population by applying a "multiplier" to expected future employment in export activities—would be as patently absurd for the U. S. as they are sensible for a copper mining village.

We may tentatively derive from the juxtaposition of these

extreme cases a first statement: the applicability of the "basic-nonbasic" concept decreases with increasing size of the community.

Size, however, is not the only factor to be considered. Let us return to the case of the subsistence farm. By any acceptable usage farming is its "basic" or "primary" activity. If the farmer or his wife engage during the slack season, in some cottage industry, selling the product for cash, such activity is to them strictly "secondary" or "ancillary." Here the concepts appear reversed: production for own use—"taking in each other's washing"—is basic, and production for sale is ancillary. This is characteristic of a "natural" economy, while the reverse holds true for "money" or "exchange" economy, which is dependent on division of labor. Hence our second statement: applicability of the "basic-nonbasic" concept increases with increasing specialisation and division of labor between communities.

Still another aspect may be illustrated by the ancient Indian village community, or, for that matter, by a village in medieval feudal Europe. Here a good deal of the economic activity was for "export," for the Lord of the Manor, the Church, or the King. But far from being basic in the sense of being indispensable for the economy of the village, this activity is the only one which contributes nothing to it. The reverse of this picture is the town which receives these payments without having to compensate by any "export" activity or employment. Richard U. Ratcliff quotes H. Pirenne as saying that the early medieval fortress town "produced nothing of itself, lived by revenue from the surrounding country, and had no other economic role than that of a simple consumer." Another historian characterizes the "economic base" of such cities as follows: "The principal, constituent elements of the town were those who are able by *power and wealth* (my emphasis, H.B.) to command a means of subsistence from elsewhere, a king who can tax, a landlord to whom dues are paid, a merchant who makes profits outside the town, a student who is supported by his parents. These are "town builders . . . ."[21]

Here the "basis" for the economy of the town is not "persons employed in producing goods and services for export," as the "basic-nonbasic" method assumes, but "power and wealth." It may here be recalled that in the "tableau économique," which Quesnay, founder of the "physiocratic" school of economics, developed in the 18th century, the urban middle class was called "classe stérile," as serving the ruling class rather than working for the "producing" class, the farmers. Thomas Jefferson shared this physiocratic view.

In our context it is important to keep in mind that "nonbasic" activities are supported by money gained from the outside regardless of its source, which may be "power and wealth" rather than any "basic" employment. To the extent that this is the case, the "basic-nonbasic" ratio loses its meaning.

We may therefore formulate a third statement: the greater the amount of "unearned" income (i.e. income derived from sources other than payment for work performed) flowing into or out of a community, the less applicable is the "basic-nonbasic" concept.

We will later deal with attempts to assimilate "unearned" income to the concept of "basic" activities. Leaving aside this aspect, for the time being, and concentrating our attention on the relation of "basic" and "nonbasic" employment, we may accept as valid the existence of two opposite historical trends noted by Forbat in the above-mentioned article:

1. Replacement of local crafts by large-scale industry working for a national and international market; hence greater share of "basic" employment.

---

[21] F. L. Nussbaum, *A History of the Economic Institutions of Modern Europe,* New York, 1933, quoted by Richard B. Andrews, *op. cit.,* 1953, p. 161.

2. Increase in services; hence greater share of "nonbasic" employment.

Both trends result from increasing division and specialisation of labor, the first between communities and the second within the community. It should also be noted that the increase in services refers not only to services to consumers, which are generally the result of commercialisation of functions formerly performed by the household, but also to services to business, which were previously performed as auxiliary services within other businesses, but have now become so specialised and complicated as to require special establishments.

This specialisation of business activities reaches its highest development in large and mature communities. As mentioned before, the same communities also are nearest to "autarchy," because they contain the greatest number of branches of production.

We may therefore summarize:

The "basic-nonbasic" ratio is highest in small, new communities, lowest in large and mature ones.

4. MERCANTILISTIC AND PHYSIOCRATIC OVERTONES OF THE "BASIC-NONBASIC" CONCEPT

The difference between "basic" and "nonbasic" activities is the difference in their role in the balance of payments with the world outside the community. Strangely, and rather inconsistently, the "economic base" studies dominated by this concept pay practically no attention to the other side of the ledger: no attempt is being made in these studies to differentiate between those locally consumed goods and services which are produced locally and those for which payments have to be made to the outside world. Yet, rationally, the money earned by "basic" activities is merely the means to make these payments, not an end in itself.

The idea, underlying the "basic-nonbasic" method, that the acquisition of money from the outside world is the "basic" purpose of the urban or metropolitan economy has its historical precedent in the mercantilistic school of economics which regarded only gold and silver as true wealth. While in a study of the U. S. economy it is today taken for granted that increased production of goods and services for the home market is the goal, in the "economic base" studies of American cities these activities are regarded merely as supporting the "basic" ones working for export.

This is, of course, explainable by the role played by size which has been discussed above. If the slogan "export or die" is true for sizable countries like Great Britain or Germany, it is even truer for a single city or region which evidently can not produce everything which it consumes. In particular many base studies stress the need of earning money in order to pay for imports of food and raw materials. "Basic Employment . . . goods or services in exchange for food and raw materials . . . (is) the critical or crucial employment . . . ; without it the city ceases to exist."[22]

Here, as in many similar statements, there is the implication that the export activities are "basic" because without them the city could not buy food, which is a "basic" necessity, while New Yorkers would not "cease to exist" without such locally supplied goods and services as millinery or theatre performances. But they would cease to exist very rapidly without water supply, which is also a "service" or "nonbasic" activity.

The belief that there is something particularly "basic" in the production of food and raw materials also has its historical precedent; the antagonists and successors of the mercantilists, the physiocrats, believed in the superiority of farming and mining over other branches of production.

Incidentally, when we deal not with 19th century cities, but

---

[22] New York Regional Plan Association, *The Economic Status of the New York Metropolitan Region in* 1944, p. 3.

with the emerging, much larger and qualitatively different form of human settlement defined by the U. S. Census as a "Metropolitan Area," a sizable part of the food may be supplied by "nonbasic" activities; that is, supplied by residents to residents of the area. The Philadelphia Metropolitan Area, f.i., containing 2.45% of the U. S. population in 1950, produced 1.03% of all dairy products sold in the U. S., 1.17% of all poultry, 2.28% of all vegetables, and 4.68% of all nursery and greenhouse products. Thus, dairy and poultry production equaled almost half, and vegetable production equaled almost the entire normal consumption of the area. Altogether about 14% of the area's proportionate (to population) share of all agricultural products were produced locally.

If the classification of economic activities attempted by the "basic-nonbasic" concept is to acquire scientific validity and practical usefulness, it will have to discard all explicit or implicit notions that earning money or buying food is specifically "basic." It should be clearly understood that we are dealing exclusively with a difference in the market; and the appropriate terms would be "export" and "home market" activities.

There is reason to pay attention to this difference. A product or service which has to compete in the national and international market is more vulnerable than one which, like local transportation or a corner drug store, by its physical nature is protected against outside competition; it is, for the same reason, also more capable of expansion by invading outside markets. But, by and large, the share of the national product which is sold locally is just as vulnerable to competition as is the part which is sold outside.

From the point of view of vulnerability by outside competition as well as of ability to expand into outside markets, both of which we may identify as "criticality," the only meaningful distinction is between activities which, *by the nature of their product* have to and can compete with outside producers, *re-*

gardless of the location of their actual sales, and those which
do not complete; and it is just as important to measure the imported and the locally produced share of total local consumption as it is to measure the exported and the locally consumed
shares of total local production.

5. DEVELOPMENT OF TECHNIQUES OF MEASUREMENT

a. Manufacturing versus services

The first studies, those made in the twenties for the New
York Regional Plan and in the thirties by Homer Hoyt for the
F.H.A., assigned entire activities to the one or the other category
according to their predominant market; as Frederic Law Olmsted put it in the letter quoted earlier, "primary"[23] are goods
for general use (i.e., *not confined to* (my emphasis, H.B.) use
within the community itself)." Consciously, they were satisfied
with a rough approximation; subconsciously, they were guided
by the criterion of competitive character rather than by that of
actual markets of an industry.

Such a rough approximation by allotment of broad categories
to the two classes of activities was also used—but only as a first
step—by the 1944 study of the New York Regional Plan Association. As "basic"—producing *in whole or in part* (my
emphasis, H.B.) for persons living outside of the Region . . ."
are specifically enumerated: manufacturing, wholesale trade,
banking and insurance, transportation, administrative offices,
hotels and amusements, federal and state employment. As
"service—producing *entirely* (my emphasis, H.B.) for persons
living within the Region" are enumerated: retail trade, profes-
sions, personal services, local transportation and utilities, con-

---

[23] The concepts of "primary" and "secondary" used in this type of studies
should not be confused with the concept of "primary," "secondary," and "tertiary," meaning "extractive," "processing," and "service" activities, as defined by
Colin Clark and other economists.

struction, local government, business and repair services, real estate and local banking.

Parenthetically it may be noted that many of these last-named activities do not produce entirely for the local population, but also serve many persons living outside the Region.

There is reason to believe that the motive for concern with "basic" activities was their competitive and therefore critical character. Had the authors of the New York Regional Plan study accepted this criterion, they would have sought further refinements along lines which will be indicated later. However they, like all others using the "basic" concept, interpreted it as meaning "export" and consequently sought to refine it by measuring the portion of each particular product or service which was sold outside the Region.

The measurement of this "exported" portion is easy in dealing with a national economy where exports and imports are counted at custom lines. In dealing with areas within a nation, however, no comparable data are available and other methods have to be developed.

b. Proportional apportionment

The method used by the N. Y. Regional Plan study and most others is to assume that the community consumes a share of the total national production of each category of goods and services which is proportional to its share of the national population (in some cases purchasing power or other yardsticks are substituted for population). The surplus in excess of this proportional share is assumed to be exported or "basic." Frequently the relation between actual and proportional share of a given category of production is expressed as a "location—or localization—quotient." The "location quotient" is the percentage of employment in a given local industry of total local employment, expressed as a ratio to the percentage of national employment in the same industry of total national employment;

ei . Ei

or — — ; e = local employment; E = national employment;

et . Et

i = employment in industry; t = total employment. "By means of the localization quotient . . . the extent to which an activity is basic . . . can be determined."[24]

The same method was applied by Victor Roterus in the Cincinnati study. "Urban-serving employment (was) calculated by assuming that the population will consume its proportionate share of the national production."

We have used this method in defining the "service" share of various branches of agricultural production in the Philadelphia Area. However, it would be quite erroneous to conclude from the fact that the location quotient of vegetable production for the Philadelphia Area is roughly equal to one, that Philadelphians eat no vegetables grown outside their area. They do, of course, and other vegetables are exported from the area.

To choose another illustration: the Philadelphia Area's share in the production of weekly periodicals may about equal its share of national population and (or) purchasing power. But it does not follow that all copies of the Saturday Evening Post are consumed in the Philadelphia Area and that Philadelphians never buy copies of the Reader's Digest. They do (unfortunately).

The method of proportional apportionment is based on the completely fallacious assumption that categories of goods and services—however fine the breakdown—can ever be uniform. International trade statistics show that most countries are both importers and exporters of the same categories of goods. The same certainly holds true to an even greater extent for the exchange of goods and services between areas within the nation.

Of course, if the location quotient is very high, it stands to

---

[24] Harold M. Mayer, *op. cit.*

reason that most of the product is exported. However, in such extreme cases the importance of that particular industry will be a matter of general knowledge. No location quotient has to be calculated in order to find out that Detroit exports automobiles or that Brockton exports shoes. On the other hand, if an area produces its "normal share of, say, electrical machinery, it would be completely erroneous to assume that this is a "nonbasic" industry working exclusively for the local market. It is entirely possible, and indeed quite probable, that most locally produced electrical machinery is exported, while at the same time most locally consumed electrical machinery is imported. Mattila and Thompson unwittingly demonstrate the fallacy of the method by presenting a completely absurd result: the "proportion of surplus ("basic," H.B.) to service ("nonbasic," H.B.) workers," calculated by means of the "location quotient," is given as 1:1.99 for Chicago and as 1:4.47 for Philadelphia![25] Are we to believe that one "basic" worker supports 2 "nonbasic" workers in Chicago and 4½ in Philadelphia?

This is not to say that the location quotient does not deserve careful study. By analyzing it, much can be learned about market areas and about competitive advantages and disadvantages. But as a measurement of the share of "basic" activities or employment it is completely misleading.

c. Breakdown of markets by survey

The obvious inadequacy of this method has led several researchers to embark on the difficult and time-consuming attempt to follow up the actual sales of each establishment in the area under investigation. This was apparently first done in 1943 by Fred Forbat in his study of the small Swedish town of Skörde.

In Alexander's Study of Oshkosh, f.i., establishments employing 75% of the labor force were asked for the percentage of their sales that was local; the same percentage of their em-

---

[25] *Op. cit.,* p. 226, Table III.

ployment was then allocated to the category of "secondary" employment. The same approach was taken by Maxine Kurtz in the Denver study.

In addition to its high cost this method obviously encounters two obstacles: first, unwillingness to disclose one's market, and second, ignorance of the location of one's customers. The first obstacle appears to have been overcome fairly successfully both in Oshkosh and in Denver. Interviewing of cash customers of retail stores and other techniques have been used to narrow the gap of ignorance. The result of the studies may be regarded as a reasonably accurate measurement of local and outside sales.

However, this is still far from finding the answer to the question: how does the community earn the money to pay for the imports it needs? Leaving aside, for the time being, the question of modifying the needs for imports as well as the possibility of paying for them by money derived from sources other than export, the main shortcoming is this: we know the *gross value of the exported goods and services*. What we want to know is the *"value added" by the community*. A flour mill may export 10 millions worth of flour; but if it has to import 8 millions worth of grain, it earns no more than 2 millions for the community. Employment probably has been adopted as the only available, though extremely rough, approximation to "value added." However, those using the method are apparently unaware of this relation and of its implications.

If "value added" is sought, other difficulties arise. Assume that the grain has been grown locally. It is sold in the local market, to the local mill, by definition its production is a "nonbasic" activity. Yet the payment received for its sale (in the form of flour) is a net earning of the community, a "basic" support of its economy. Or, to take another example: a community exports a million tons of steel. If this steel is produced in an integrated metallurgical plant, the "value added" is the difference between the cost of ore, coal, etc., and the value of steel; and all employment in the plant is considered "basic." But if the same steel is produced in a steel plant which buys its pig iron from an independent local blast furnace, then only the value added by the steel plant is considered "basic," and the value added by the blast furnace is, by definition, "nonbasic," because it is sold to a local customer. Thus the distinction between "basic" and "nonbasic" is a function of the inner organization of the industry: the higher the degree of specialization and differentiation, the breakdown of a process into parts performed by several independent establishments, the higher is the "nonbasic" share. This, incidentally, is one of the reasons why "nonbasic" activities appear to loom so large in metropolitan areas, where the process of differentiation reaches its apex.

This difficulty has given birth to the concept of "indirect primary" activities and employment. "Indirect primary" are all goods or services sold to a local establishment which in turn exports its products. But the steel mill does not only buy locally produced pig iron; it equally buys locally produced power, water, trucking services, banking services, local police and fire protection. Moreover, it buys locally produced labor power which in turn buys locally produced bread and movie shows. Once "indirect primary" activities are admitted as "basic," where can the line be drawn? The economy of an area is an integrated whole of mutually interdependent activities; the distinction between "basic" and "nonbasic" seems to dissolve into thin air.

d. "Criticality" or "Balance of Payments"?

Confusion worse confounded. The more we attempt to refine the "basic-nonbasic" concept, the deeper we get involved in contradictions. Whenever that happens, there is reason to assume that there is something wrong with the formulation of the question.

Let us return to the origin of the quest. It may be fairly illustrated as follows. If General Motors closes shop at Flint, no efforts to promote the development of department stores will save the town. On the other hand, if a Flint department store closes down, but the General Motors plant continues to operate as before, it will soon be replaced by other stores. Therefore, the thing to worry about, the "base" of the Flint economy, is the automobile industry; once that works, the "services" will take care of themselves. Also, once we know how many people G. M. is going to employ, we know pretty well how many people there will be in Flint.

Unquestionably true. But why is the situation of the G. M. plant so much more critical than that of the department store? Leaving aside the difference in size which is extraneous to our problem, it is because the G. M. plant has to compete with all other automobile plants in the U. S. and in the world, while the department store has to compete, in the main, only with other stores in Flint (though its customers might purchase some goods in Detroit, or from a mail order house in Chicago).

The difference in "criticality" is determined by the extent of the area of potential competition. In actual practice this is, of course, a range of areas from the locality through ever-widening regions to the national and international markets. A development and refinement of the "criticality" approach would have to go in two directions. First, as much attention should be paid to the *actual and potential* source of locally consumed goods and services, as to the markets for local products; second, the potential area of competition should be broken down into areas of varying size.

Actually, both steps have been undertaken by many "economic base" studies. Most studies pay particular attention to industries with a location quotient smaller than one, assuming that here may be opportunities for new local industries to compete with outside suppliers. And most go into detailed analysis of their market areas; the Denver study, f.i., found that 54%

of the sales outside the Metropolitan Area were made within the "region," defined as Colorado, Wyoming, and New Mexico.

This is contrary to the "basic-nonbasic" theory, which demands concentration of attention on the "basic" industries, those with a location quotient larger than one, and which regards all export activities as equally "basic," regardless of the size or location of the export market. Thus, the practice of the economic base studies has been generally more sensible than the theory which they claim to follow. This is, fortunately, not an uncommon occurrence in human affairs (vide the practice of American foreign policy versus the theory of "massive retaliation").

In our case the theoretical weakness lies in the confusion of the question of "criticality," that is the question concerning *potential competition* with the question of *"balance of payments,"* which is concerned with *actual sales.* Both questions are valid and important; but either can be clearly answered only if they are clearly separated.

The concept of the "balance of payments" is well understood; but the assembly of the relevant data is exceedingly difficult. Apparently the only attempt ever made was the famous *"Oskaloosa versus the U. S."* study undertaken by Fortune magazine in April 1938. In this study "a city of 10,000 people has been treated as if were a little nation."

A "balance of payments" study evidently must use dollars as units of measurement, not persons. The widespread use of the categories of "basic" and "nonbasic" *employment*—a consequence of the attempt to use the concept for population prediction by means of the "multiplier"—has no place in a study of this type. What matters, is not how many persons work at supplying the outside world, but how much money they receive from it. For this reason some studies have used payrolls (and net earnings of self-employed persons) rather than number of persons employed. But payments for goods and services go only partly into payrolls, partly into profits, interest, taxes, etc. The appropriate measurement would be the one applied in international trade statistics: gross value of goods and services exported and imported. To these would have to be added taxes and disbursements of larger governmental units, as well as interest and dividend payments in both directions. However, the latter are "practically unobtainable," according to Charles L. Leven of the Federal Reserve Bank of Chicago.[26]

Nevertheless, the New York Regional Plan study of 1944 did make an estimate that "nearly one-third of the region's basic income was derived from dividends, rents, interests, and profits." It would seem that with the amount of labor and ingenuity that went into the Denver study, f.i., it might be possible to arrive at estimates realistic enough to construct a model of "Denver versus the U. S. A." As Victor Roterus wisely remarks, no economic base study can achieve more than a rough approximation.

The attempts to "refine" the "basic-nonbasic" concept have destroyed its usefulness for the identification of "critical" industries, while making no more than a very partial and dubious contribution to an identification of the balance of payments.

To repeat:

There is a need for two types of studies, related, and using much of the same material, but different in their conceptual framework:

1. A "criticality" or "variability" study, analyzing all actual and potential branches of production in the area from the point of view of the size and character of the area in which they compete and their consequent vulnerability to outside competition and potentiality to expand into outside markets.

---

[26] Charles L. Leven, "An Appropriate Unit For Measuring the Urban Economic base, *Land Economics,* November 1954. This is the most concise study of the subject known to this writer.

2. A "balance of payments" study, including *all* types of payments, and giving equal weight to both sides of the ledger.

6. SPECIFIC PROBLEMS

a. Replacement of imports by local production

One of the purposes of the distinction of "basic" and "nonbasic" activities "consists in concentrating investigation on those industries and services which . . . bring in money to pay for the food and raw materials which the city does not produce itself," to repeat Homer Hoyt's formulation. But if the city would itself produce the goods which it now imports, the effect would be the same. Why should not investigation be concentrated on those industries and services, which do *not* produce a surplus for export, but, on the contrary, show a deficit in supplying the home market? Evidently, if Brockton, rather than increasing its capacity to produce shoes worth a million dollars annually, would build a clothing plant to supply its inhabitants with a million dollars' worth of clothing which they now have to import, the improvement of the town's balance of payments would be the same. It may here be noted that this might not be possible in Brockton, because, the local market may not be large enough to support an efficient plant. But it would certainly be possible in a large metropolis. The larger the community, the greater the possibility of substitution for declining industries, hence the less significant the identification of "basic" activities.

Actually even the Brockton study does examine the possibility of substituting new industries for the "critical" shoe industry. Similarly the New York Regional Plan study concentrates its attention on "industries in which New York's share of employment is far below its proportion of population and income," stating: "these industries might be explored to ascertain why they have not expanded to a greater degree in the Region,"[27] and the Cincinnati study considers specifically "local industries

---

[27] *Op. cit.*, p. 19, 20.

not meeting local demands." Charles L. Leven, in the aforementioned article, agrees that "efforts might be more profitably
directed at establishment of local industries (supplying) local
exporters."

The important point, in our context, is that the "basic-
nonbasic" method is of no help whatsoever in identifying such
industries. It rather tends to deflect attention from them and
to confuse the picture. Half a loaf is certainly better than no
loaf; but half a balance of payments study may well be worse
than none.

The reverse substitution is no less important: the replacement
of local production by imports. As Fred Forbat has pointed
out, this is one of the long-term trends of industrial society, a
corollary of increasing specialization and division of labor between regions. However, it still remains possible to substitute
local production for imports; especially where the growth of
the community creates a previously nonexistent large market,
imports may be replaced by locally produced goods and services.
In this way growth induces further growth. "He who has, to
him shall be given" is a basic law of economics.

b. An extreme case of the effect of the establishment of a new "basic" industry on the balance of payments

It is generally assumed that the opening of an establishment
which exports part of its products will always improve the balance of payments of an area. However, if such an establishment is a branch plant of an outside firm and works mainly
with imported material, and if the part of its products which is
sold locally displaces the products of a local industry working
largely with local materials, then the net effort may be the
opposite.

In the hypothetical case presented here, "A" represents a
group of local establishments producing $1,000,000 worth of
goods for the local market. "B" represents the new branch
plant which produces $2,000,000; of these $1,000,000 are ex-

ported and $1,000,000 are sold in the local market, displacing the local establishments.

Case	Item	Spent, Total	Spent Locally	Spent Outside	Net Payment to Outside
"A"	wages	$ 220,000	$220,000		
	materials	500,000	250,000	250,000	
	amortization	50,000	50,000		
	overhead	60,000	60,000		
	taxes	70,000	10,000	60,000	
	profit	100,000	100,000		
"A"	total	1,000,000	690,000	310,000	$310,000
"B"	total	$2,000,000	$590,000	$1,410,000	$410,000
	materials	500,000	250,000	$ 250,000	
	amortization	200,000	50,000	150,000	
	overhead	100,000	20,000	80,000	
	taxes	200,000	20,000	180,000	
	profit	200,000		200,000	
"B"	total	2,000,000	590,000	1,410,000	410,000

(It has been assumed that plant "B" uses more ordinary [more amortization] and fewer workers [less wages].)

In case "A" the community has to pay $310,000 to the outside world in order to procure the $1,000,000 worth of goods which it consumes. In case "B" it has to pay $410,000 ($1,400,000 minus $1,000,000 earned from export sales). Thus the establishment of the new "basic" industry has resulted in a deterioration of its balance of payments by $100,000.

Let us assume an average wage of $3,000 and an average per capita income of $1,500. Let us further assume that one third, or $500, of this per capita income has to be spent to import goods and services from the outside. Then the loss of $100,000 in means of payment to the outside has the result that the community can support 200 persons less than before.

According to the standard formula one half of the 100 workers in the new establishment, or 50 workers, would represent "basic" employment. According to the rule-of-thumb "multiplier" of 7 persons for every one person in "basic" employment, there should be a population increase of 350 persons. But actually there would be a decrease of 200 persons.

This may be an extreme and unlikely case. It has been developed to point up the problematical character of the "basic employment" method.

Parenthetically, while this case is not likely to occur in the U. S. A. in 1955, it may be fairly typical of the impact of the establishment of branch plants of modern international concerns in under-developed countries; here the result is frequently aggravated by related effects on income distribution. The resistance of these countries to such apparently beneficial improvements by foreign investors may not be entirely due to short-sighted nationalistic prejudices.

c. Indirect primary activity

The problem of "indirect primary" activity has attracted the attention of many students of our subject. Fred Forbat[28] refers to a study of a new oil refinery in Aarhus, Denmark, undertaken by the economist B. Barfod.[29] Barfod found that "the company's purchases of goods and services from local suppliers gave livelihood" to 70 persons for every 100 persons employed in the refinery. He classes these as "indirect primary" and derives the expected number of "secondary" employment by assuming that there will be 80 additional "secondary" workers for every 100 new workers in *all* "primary" employment, "direct" and "indirect" combined.

Andrews, in his series of articles in *Land Economics,* repeatedly returns to this question. He recognizes that "linked activity . . . the chain of production . . . makes *all* activities basic" and calls this a "very serious blindspot . . . unless the anachronisms (? H.B.) of this situation can be reconciled."[30]

---

[28] Fred Forbat, "Synpunkter pa Lokaliseringsmultiplikatorn," in *Plan,* Stockholm, 1948, No. 9.

[29] B. Barford, *Local Economic Effects of a Large-scale Industrial Undertaking,* (in Danish); E. Munksgaard, Copenhagen, 1938. (This writer has not been able to locate this study.)

When dealing with a concrete example, however, he says: "rigidly, we would classify the automobile-starter factory as a service activity . . . realistic (ally it) should be considered basic in that there exists only an organizational line between the starter and automobile manufacturer."[31]

Andrews seems to be unaware that "crossing an organizational line" is only a synonym for "sale" and that any method which—like the "basic-nonbasic" method—counts sales, consists in counting line crossings. He adds, however, the very pertinent remark: "the number of links involved may very well be in direct ratio to community size." But he again fails to draw the conclusion: that the applicability of the "basic-nonbasic" concept is in inverse ratio to community size.

Ullman also wrestles with the problem. He says: "a city with large basic plants might appear to produce many basic workers whereas . . . many small plants each feeding the other . . . appear to have many service workers." He then tries to compromise by stating that "some intermediate producers are classed as basic if they contribute directly to an export industry," but concludes finally that "in this light all activities appear indivisible."

Alexander is also troubled by the problem: "since these castings (made in a local foundry, H.B.) are fabricated into axles which are exported, it could be said that this . . . production is for the primary market. However, this leads to complications, and the arbitrary decision has been made to classify each activity on the basis of its own direct sales."[32]

We have already shown that the complications are implicit in the ambiguity of the question. If the question is, instead, clearly directed to the balance of payments, the decision to count

[30] Andrews, *op. cit., Land Economics,* 1954, p. 260 ff.
[31] Andrews, *op. cit., Land Economics,* 1953, p. 347.
[32] John W. Alexander, *Oshkosh, op. cit.,* p. 12.

only direct sales is by no means arbitrary, but a matter of course. Nobody thinks of including the steel industry in the export statistics of American automobiles, because the "value added" by the steel and all other "indirect primary" industries is, by definition, included in the gross value of the automobiles. Dollars, not persons employed, are the correct yardstick.

If, on the other hand, the question is directed to the "criticality" of each establishment, i.e., to the range of its potential market and its potential competitors, the "indirect primary" activities fall into place alongside all others.

d. Inter-urban transportation

Practically all studies, while treating local transportation as "nonbasic," regard all other transportation as "basic." However, actually only those transportation activities which serve movements between two outside points earn money from the outside. A tanker, bringing oil from Venezuela to a refinery in the Philadelphia Area, exclusively serves and is paid by the Philadelphia plant. Its work might be called "indirect primary," but, as we have seen, that does not remove it from the "nonbasic" class under any consistent definition.

Normally, of the total exchange of goods between two points about half will be paid at each end; thus 50% of it should certainly be classified as "nonbasic." The point might well be made that the entire interurban transportation system performs a service for, and at the expense of, the local import and export trade and should be classified as such.

From the point of view of competitiveness, or "criticality," interurban transportation (except for the portion serving movements between two outside points) is strictly noncompetitive; nobody but some form of transportation can move goods and passengers into and out of the city. It is true, of course, that if transportation is very poor, other branches of production may move to other areas that are better served by transportation; it thus may profoundly affect the competitive position of the area as a whole. It was probably this thought that caused people to classify it as "basic." Yet in this respect it is not principally different from supply of water, power, housing, or any other local service.

e. Public employees, students, etc.

A field in which the confusion of the "criticality" and the "balance of payments" approach has led to particularly glaring contradictions concerns those persons whose income, while clearly contributing to the economy of the community, is derived neither from sales to the local community nor from sales to the outside world. Andrews, Maxine Kurtz, Forbat, and others allocate employment in goverment institutions according to the population served (local or outside population); and allocate the staff of universities proportional to the number of local and "foreign" students.

From the "balance-of-payments" point of view, which these researchers are trying to apply, this does not make sense. From this point of view the only thing that matters is the source of the income, not who is benefited by the work performed. The income of *all* federal employees is a net gain to the community, whether they deliver letters to local residents or work on projects to deliver milk—or atom bombs—to the Hottentots; just as all taxes paid to the Federal Government are a net loss to the community. Similarly, if the university professor is paid by state contributions, by the G.I. Bill of Rights, by an outside foundation, or by outside parents of his students, his income is a gain to the community. But it is not if he is paid out of city funds, out of contributions of local alumni, or out of money earned by his students in the community. The home residence of his students has nothing to do with it.

Evidently these researchers were led astray because in the back of their minds, but not formulated, was the "criticality" approach. In a city of a certain size, post offices, local courts, elementary and high schools can indeed be taken for granted; while the city has to compete with other cities for a state university or for a regional office of the National Government, and also has to compete with them for students at its university.

f. Discrepancy between "basic" employment and outside earnings

If a given community with a given level of living depends for 50% of the goods and services which it consumes on outside sources, its size is evidently limited by the amount of money which it can pay to the outside. It is the standard assumption of the "basic-nonbasic" method that in this case 50% of its employment would have to be "basic." The contribution to the "economic base" is assumed to be proportional to the number of persons employed in each branch of "basic employment." "Wholesale trade accounted for . . . 12% of its total basic employment . . . *therefore* (my emphasis, H.B.) . . . about one-eighth of the economic base.[33]

This comfortable "therefore" contains—and conceals—a number of unspoken assumptions, which should be spelled out:

1. Average wages are roughly the same in all branches of production (the Denver study does touch on this question).
2. The ratio of "value added" to payrolls is roughly the same in all branches.
3. The proportion of the "non-payroll" section of "value added" going to local owners is roughly the same in all branches.
4. Moneys paid or received by the community other than payments for goods and services balance out.

It is improbable that any of these assumptions correspond to the facts of life in a metropolitan area.

From the Denver study, f.i., can be seen that average annual wages in wholesale trade varied from $3,100 in "petroleum

---

[33] *Working Denver, op. cit.*, p. 4.

[34] *Working Denver, op. cit.*, p. 68.

bulk stations" to $4,300 in "manufacturer's branches without stock."[34]

"Sales per employee varied far more than average wages: in retail trade from $8,150 in "eating and drinking places" to $35,800 in "automotive"; and in wholesale trade from $28,000 in "auto & equipment" to $610,000 in "farm products (raw)."[35] These differences reflect largely, but hardly entirely, differences in mark-up. If we assume, f.i., that the mark-up was 20% in "auto & equipment" and 2% in "farm products," the mark-up, or "value added," per employee would still vary from $4,700 to $12,000.

Evidently the greater part of these $12,000 represents return on capital, and how much it will contribute to the purchasing power (the "economic base") of Denver versus the outside world will depend entirely on the share of the capital owned by Denverites.

Andrews, f.i., recognizes the importance of this factor of "absentee ownership" of capital, saying: "if a dollar-flow measurement device were employed, the loss would be clear . . . (and) the community receiving the profits would count them."

Andrews, not employing such a "device," does *not count* these losses. But he *does count* the gains in the receiving community where he classifies the income derived from investments in other communities as "capital export."

This is indeed a classical example of the confusion resulting from the attempt to achieve greater precision by refining a basically confused concept. The *export of capital* puts the community in the red; it is the *return on the capital*—and return of the capital—which produces income. Nor is this return contingent on previous "export" of capital by the community; the wealthy residents of Plan Beach derive their income from

[35] *Working Denver, op. cit.,* p. 74.

capital which was not exported by Palm Beach, but either was exported from New York and other places, or was not "exported" at all, but accumulated out of the returns of "outside" investments. Andrews' concept of unifying all sources of income of the community under the term "export of goods, services, and capital" is an unfortunate attempt to force strange bedfellows into the procrustean bed of the "basic-nonbasic" concept.

Other important factors affecting the balance of payments of a community are the ratio of payments to disbursements of state and federal taxes and the "terms of trade," i.e., the price relations between imported and exported goods. Assume, for example, that the work of 10,000 persons employed in export industries is required to pay for the food imported by a community of 150,000 persons. If food prices were cut in half, these 10,000 workers could pay for the food for 300,000 people.

Because of these many factors, "basic employment" is a very inadequate yardstick for the measurement of the economic base of the community.

g. The "basic-nonbasic" ratio

As has been noted before, the attempt to distinguish "basic" and "nonbasic" employment has been made primarily in order to find the ratio of the second to the first.

Jones had made the rather naive assumption that "the majority of the town . . . are employed in providing goods and services . . . for other communities. It could not be otherwise."[36] In fact, it is otherwise. In most cases the ratio is considerably greater than unity, but it differs widely.

Roterus and Calef, in the aforementioned article, succinctly state the reason for the difference: "the basic-nonbasic ratio is a measure of the degree of economic interdependence."

In new communities the ratio may be very low because they

---

[36] J. H. Jones, op. cit., p. 125.

depend for most services on established neighboring communities. However, one "service" industry, construction, is usually overrepresented in such areas. In Lower Bucks County, f.i., in March 1952, there were for every 100 persons employed in manufacturing only 35.7 employed in service industries other than construction, compared to a ratio of 90.4 in the Philadelphia Metropolitan Area in 1950. On the other hand, the ratio of employment in construction to manufacturing was 71.5 to 100 in Lower Bucks County as against 9.6 to 100 in the Metropolitan Area.[37]

It has been noted that the ratio is generally higher the larger the community. The reasons may be summarized as follows:

1. A greater completeness of all branches of production; the community is more nearly "self-contained" than a small one.

2. Greater "round-about-ness" of production; the productive process is divided into a greater number of organizationally independent, though economically interdependent, units.

In addition, in most metropolitan areas there is:

3. Higher average income, commanding more consumer services.

4. A concentration of "power and wealth," drawing unearned income from the outside and spending it for local services.

The New York Regional Plan study of 1944 found the abnormally high ratio of 2.2 "nonbasic" for every one "basic" employed. However, the study also states that nearly one third of the region's "basic" income is derived from sources other than the export of goods and services. If it is assumed that a proportional number of service workers was supported by this source of income and only the remainder is related to the "basic" workers, the ratio is about 1.5, practically the same as

---

[37] *Economic Development, Lower Bucks County,* Bucks County Planning Commission, February 1954, p. 12 and table E-8.

the one found in Denver, which was 1.53.

The ratio also changes over time; nor can these changes be easily explained. In Cincinnati, f.i., between 1929 and 1933, the decrease in the number of factory workers was 29% above the national average, but the decrease in retail sales was 6% below the average for the nation.

A slightly different and rather interesting approach to the question of "service" employment has been taken by Swedish planners and geographers who have attempted to find the number of service workers required to serve a given population in communities of various types. Here the distinction of "basic" and "nonbasic" is used as a tool for identifying those industries which have to be studied directly and individually, while a global average figure is used for the prognosis of all "nonbasic" employment. Forbat found that in the three towns of Kristinehamn, Skövde, and Landskrona secondary employment varied only from 20.92% to 22.39% of the total population. Even this slight variation was due entirely to variations in agriculture, construction, and domestic service; after elimination of these three categories the range was 16.37% to 16.49%.

These are three towns with a population between 15,000 and 24,000. For villages of about 2,000 population, Forbat found a percentage of service workers of 15%, and for Stockholm of 27%. This correlation of percentage of service workers with the size is in accord with American experience.

Sven Godlund contributed to the discussion the concept of an "index of centralization" which is defined by the percentage of the total population employed in retail trade and consumer services. He found this to vary with size from 6.5% in regional centers down to 3.5% in villages, with even lower percentages in "special urban settlements," mainly industrial satellite towns.[38]

---

[38] Sven Godlund, *Studies in Rural-Urban Interaction*, Lund Studies in Geography, Lund, 1951.

h. The "multiplier"

Investigation of the "basic-nonbasic" ratio is used to find the "multiplier," the ratio of total population to "basic" employment. The multiplier is determined not only by the "basic-nonbasic" ratio, but by three additional factors which are not always clearly recognized:

1. Family coefficient of basic employed.
2. Family coefficient of nonbasic employed.
3. Percentage of nonemployed (incl. dependents) population.

Frequently a global ratio of population to employment is used. However, this ratio may vary considerably if any of these three factors change, or if their relative weights change.

In Denver, f.i., the ratio of population to "basic" employment—the "multiplier"—was 7.8 in 1940. Between 1940 and 1950, however, there were only 4.6 persons added to the population for every one person added to "basic" employment. It is evident that a population prediction based on the number of additional "basic" employed and using the "multiplier" found in 1940 would have overstated the decennial population increase by 70%.

Variations in the family coefficient between various "basic" industries are very significant. In the anthracite mining regions of Pennsylvania, f.i., the addition of a mining job would usually mean the addition of a family. The addition of a hosiery job generally means employment of a female former dependent of a miner's family.

Generally the family coefficient is low in industries with high female employment and in communities with a high rate of employment and with low percentages of the population in the extreme age groups, i.e., children and old people.

Forbat[39] found that the family coefficient in the Swedish

---

[39] Fred Forbat, "Untersuchungen über den Lokalisierungsmultiplikator" (investigations on the "localisation-multiplier"). In *Raumforschung & Raumordnung*, 1953, No. 2, pp. 97-101.

countryside varied from 1.54 for textile workers to 2.49 for construction workers; for Stockholm both figures were considerably lower, 1.30 and 2.06, respectively. He also found that the family coefficient in trade and service employment averaged 1.7 to 1.8.

Forbat has developed a formula which takes into account the differences in the family coefficient for different types of employment. The formula is:

$$P = \frac{E_p \cdot C_p}{1 - R_s \cdot C_s}$$

$P =$ population
$E_p =$ employed, primary
$C_p =$ family coefficient of primary employed
$C_s =$ family coefficient of secondary employed
$R_s =$ secondary employment as % of population

If E_p equals 1, the "multiplier" becomes:

$$M = \frac{C_p}{1 - R_s \cdot C_s}$$

By applying this formula, Forbat found the following multipliers:

villages:	2.1 to 3.2
towns:	2.5 to 3.7
Stockholm:	2.3 to 3.3

These are large variations. They would be even larger except for the fact that high service employment and low family coefficient are generally associated, because both are correlated with high female employment, and that their influences tend to cancel each other. Thus, the multiplier is low in villages despite the high family coefficient, because the villages depend for services largely on neighboring towns; it is low in Stockholm, despite high service employment, because the family coefficient is low.

A further difficulty in deriving the "multiplier" stems from the fact that there is a sizeable and highly variable group in most communities which is neither in "basic" nor in "nonbasic" employment nor part of the families of either group. These are the "independent nonworkers," who may derive their income from a great many sources: investments, pensions, social insurance, relief payments, etc. Forbat classifies these as "primary" ("basic"), because their number is not dependent on the number of those in other "basic" groups. In the little town of Skövde their number was equal to one quarter of all other "basic" groups. In many American cities it may be even higher. On the other hand, in new or rapidly growing communities their number is low; in some cases practically zero. Also, their number may vary widely and abruptly with changes in the labor market.

Swedish statistical data make it possible to derive a separate family coefficient for this group which is, of course, lower than that for employed persons. In Stockholm, f.i., it was 1.30 versus 1.63 employed persons; in the Swedish countryside 1.43 versus 2.14.[40]

American statistics lump "independents" and "dependents" in the categories "unemployed" and "not in the Labor Force." They also present no data from which family coefficients for specific industries in specific localities could be derived. This writer, in attempting to apply the Forbat formula to American cities, has therefore substituted for both C_p and C_s (family coefficient for "basic" and "nonbasic" employed) what might be called a "community-wide family coefficient;" that is, the ratio of total population to total employed. The resultant multipliers are 5.5 for Philadelphia and 6.46 for Denver; the latter being practically identical with the 6.6 found by Maxine Kurtz.

The fact that these figures are about twice as large as those

---

[40] F. Forbat, *Untersuchungen* . . . , *op. cit.*, p. 100, Table 2.

found in Swedish towns is only partly due to the different classification of the "independent nonworkers." In a letter to this writer, of September 26, 1955, Forbat has recalculated the "multiplier" for five Swedish towns on the basis of the "community-wide family coefficient." The resulting figures are between 3.5 and 4.1. The difference between these multipliers and those found for Philadelphia and Denver are due first, to the fact that in Swedish cities employed persons average 49% of total population against about 40% in American cities; and second, to an unusually high percentage of "basic" employment which in the five Swedish towns was 53.3% to 60.0% of all employment. This, in turn, is partly due to actual differences in economic structure, and partly to differences in classification. Forbat classifies *all* "big" industry (as distinct from handicraft industry) as "basic." This appears quite permissible in small towns, but would lead to very serious distortions if applied, f.i., to the New York garment industry.

Barfod, in the above-mentioned study of the impact of a new oil refinery on the population of Aarhus, apparently ignored all these problems. He found a "multiplier" of 8.8. for every person in "direct basic" employment and of 5.5 for every person in all (including "indirect") "basic" employment.

The enormous range in multipliers—from 2.1 to 8.8—found by various methods shows that the multiplier is not the simple, unequivocal device for population prediction as which it appears at first sight.

7. APPLICATION OF THE "BASIC-NONBASIC" METHOD TO THE METROPOLIS

a. The "multiplier"

One of the main purposes of developing the "basic-nonbasic" method was its alleged usefulness for population prediction. Future population was to be found by multiplying future "basic" employment with a figure which could supposedly be derived from past experience.

We have seen that past experience does not and can not yield any figure applicable to future experience unless a great number of variables are known, in addition to the future number of persons in "basic" employment. The most important variables are:

1. Average level of living of the community.
2. Percentage, in terms of value, of the goods and services constituting this level which have to be purchased from outside.
3. Net gain or loss to the community from money flow due to causes other than payments for goods and services.
4. Family coefficient of persons in "basic" employment.
5. Family coefficient of persons in "nonbasic" employment.
6. Percentage of total population who are not employed, nor dependents of employed persons.

These variables make it difficult to determine the multiplier for any community. But in metropolitan areas it is even more difficult to predict the figure which is to be multiplied: the future number of persons in "basic" employment.

The illusion that "basic" employment is better predictable than many other variables stems from the fact that future employment of individual enterprises is, indeed, frequently known with reasonable certainty. If a new steel work requiring 5,000 workers is being built, it is highly probable that after its completion there will be 5,000 steel workers living in the community. If the community is and will remain a company town, it is indeed possible to find its population by adding to the steel workers and their dependents those persons (and their dependents) who service the steel workers.

But in a metropolitan area there are many plants, big and small, which open up or shut down, expand or contract their employment. We have seen that "basic" employment, by definition, is critical, competitive employment. It is the part of the economy which is most vulnerable, most likely to disappear or contract as a result of outside competition, and also most dynamic, most likely to spring up or grow as a result of invasion of outside markers. As the most vulnerable and most dynamic part of the metropolitan economy, "basic" activities are its most variable, least predictable element.

In addition, there is the practical impossibility of measuring "indirect primary" employment. Moreover, as Walter Isard and others have emphasized, a new "basic" industry attracts not only those which supply it, but also those which it supplies: not only "indirect primary," but what we might call "primary indirect" activities. Here another complication arises. Assume that a new steel plant, producing a million tons of steel, attracts, over the years, steel fabricating plants which buy half of its production. Then one half of its workers must, by definition, be transferred from the "basic" to the "nonbasic" category, because they now work for the local market. In other words, the more the steel plant contributes to the community's economic base—in the commonsense meaning of that term—the less "basic" does it become according to the standard formula.

Some, like Isard, believe that, while application of the multiplier formula for prediction of the entire metropolitan population may not be practicable, it can be used to estimate the population to be added as a result of the impact of a specific known development, such as the new steel plant at Morrisville, Pa., for instance.

Isard's study of the impact of the Morrisville plant clearly shows two difficulties inherent in this method:

1. Within what area will the added population live?
2. To which figure is the "new" population to be added?

The first difficulty is relatively minor: the region of impact comprises several metropolitan areas.

The second difficulty is fundamental. Obviously it makes no sense to add the "new" population simply to the present one, or to what the present one would be, as the result of natural increase, at the end of the impact period. The addition must be made to a figure predicted on the basis of past trends.

But these trends reflect the dynamic nature of the metropolitan economy, the never-ceasing shrinkage of old industries and expansion of new ones. In the Philadelphia Area, f.i., they reflect the coming and growth of the oil refining industry, an event closely comparable to the coming of the steel industry, and even due to the attraction of the same locational factors. Thus the figure derived from the trend already anticipated the coming of new industries, and if their impact is added separately, it will be counted twice. It is impossible thus to isolate the impact of single factors in and on the metropolitan complex.

It is worth nothing that even the Denver study, which had lavished so much care and ingenuity on the identification of "basic" employment, finally bases its prediction of the future growth of the economy and population of the area not on these figures, but on long-term trends and on estimates of the importance of locational factors.

We may conclude:

As a tool for predicting the population of metropolitan areas the "basic-nonbasic" method is useless.[41]

b. Promotion of "basic" industries

The other main purpose for developing the "basic-nonbasic" method is its alleged usefulness in concentrating attention on those industries whose promotion will do the most good for the well-being of the community, which is supposed to depend primarily on improvement of its balance of payments.

We have already pointed out that the method, strictly applied, tends to divert attention from many industries which might contribute most to an improvement of the balance of payments, namely those whose products the community now imports, but might produce itself. We also noted that most

---

[41] Forbat, who has probably developed the "multiplier" method of population prediction more successfully than any other planner, informs this writer that he recently advised against applying it to a big city, because "in the economy of the big cities there evidently exists a different hierarchy."

authors of "economic base" studies have had the good sense to forget their theory and to give a good deal of attention to just these industries.

But suppose communities did succeed in advertising their locational advantages for all those industries which are not by their physical nature restricted to a local market and who therefore have a choice. What would be the effect on the national distribution of industry? Would it be more efficient than it is now?

There are two possibilities. If *all* communities do an equally effective job of industrial promotion, their efforts will cancel each other out and the net effect will be zero. If some communities only do a good job, industries will learn of and be attracted by their locational advantages. By the same token they will ignore and neglect equal or greater locational advantages in communities which do less or nothing for promotion. The net result can only be a less efficient national distribution than would result from the functioning of the market without benefit of local planning.

Location of industries working for the national and international market is a legitimate and most important function of national planning. Local planning organizations could make valuable, indeed indispensable, contributions to such national planning by discovering the potentialities and limitations of their areas.

Without such a national plan the value of their promotional efforts is highly dubious. Most likely they will be ineffective; if effective, they are more likely to do harm than good to the nation.

We can conclude:

As a guide for the concentration of local promotional efforts the "basic-nonbasic" method is not a useful tool.

This is not to say that all results of the work done in the framework of this method are to be discarded as worthless.

They can be of great value, first, for the development of "balance of payments" studies, and second, for the exploration of the "criticality" of various industries.

c. The real economic base of the metropolis

What, finally, is the relative importance of "basic" and "nonbasic" activities in a metropolitan area?

We have seen that the percentage of persons employed in "basic" activities decreases as a community becomes more "metropolitan" quantitatively and qualitatively: that is the larger it is and the greater the variety and differentiation of its activities.

The more metropolitan the community, the more its inhabitants do "live by taking in each other's washing." Still, it remains dependent on the outside world for many goods and services and will have to pay for the major part of these by the products of its export industries. Is it not legitimate to worry about these more than about the "nonbasic" ones?

Certainly, from the point of view of sales there is nothing to worry about the "local service" industries, because they cannot be replaced from the outside. For the same reason there is everything to worry about them from the point of view of the welfare of the consumer. If the Philadelphia subway system goes out of business, it cannot be replaced by the New York subways. Inversely, from the point of view of sales there is everything to worry about the "competitive" industries; but from the point of view of the consumer's welfare there is nothing to worry about them. Their goods and services can be replaced by purchasing them from the outside; and the money they earn from the outside may be earned by other competitive industries which may be substituted for those which are lost.

The *ability to substitute* one activity for another is the crucial point. Most economic base studies touch on it in one form or another.

"Gold mining created service jobs, but when it 'petered out,' catastrophe was averted by local enterprise substituting for the erstwhile gold mine . . . ghost towns are evidence, however, that the substitution did not always occur," says the Denver study.[42] However, it does not inquire under which conditions substitution does or does not occur.

Part of the answer is given by Alexander who explains that Oshkosh owed its origin to sawmills which later disappeared, but only after having attracted the millwork industry. "The reservoir of labor persisted and became the dominant factor in the survival of the woodworking industry.[43]

Homer Hoyt adds other factors: "What does Brockton have to offer as attractions to existing and new industries? . . . Adequate power and transportation; decentralisation; skilled machine operators; a location within the world's greatest concentration of buying power; and proximity to a great pool of technical knowledge.[44]

These advantages can be summarized under three headings:
1. Labor force of various skills; its presence is dependent on *local consumer services*: housing, schools, stores, local transportation.
2. *Business services*, including transportation with its terminals.
3. *Markets*, local and regional.

The more developed these three factors are, the more favorable are the conditions for substitution; and it is easy to see that all three are strongest in metropolitan areas, and the stronger, the more metropolitan the area, that is, the larger and the more diversified it is.

The competitive advantage of a large home market is too

---

[42] *Working Denver, op. cit.,* p. 27.
[43] John W. Alexander, *Oshkosh, op. cit.,* p. 34.
[44] *The Economic Base of Brockton, op. cit.,* p. 6.

well known from the field of international trade to require further elaboration.

The importance of a large and diversified labor force also needs little comment. Only some special aspects may be mentioned here. Edgar M. Hoover, Jr., says: "the more abnormal the sex and age requirements or the more pronounced fluctuations, the more (such industries must be) located near others with complementary labor demands or in a large diversified labor market,"[45] that is, in metropolitan area. Hoover also shows that the big city is the natural habitat of the small plant which is most strongly dependent on the services of other plants. The average number of wage earners per manufacturing establishment in industrial areas in 1937 was 43 in central cities, 61 in major satellite towns, and 95 in the remainder of industrial areas.

The reason for this concentration of small plants in big cities is "external economies." Hoover says: "Many of these 'external economies' are based on the availability of more and more specialized auxiliary and service enterprises, with increased concentration of the main industry . . . the availability of service enterprises makes possible a very narrow specialization of function in relatively small plants."[46]

This development soon reaches a point where the "primary" industry is as dependent on the "auxiliary" ones as these are on it. "Often the number and variety of ancillary establishments clustered around some primary industry is such that the locational dependence of the primary industry on the ancillaries, though small in respect to each one, is great in respect to the total."[47]

---

[45] Edgar M. Hoover, Jr., "Size of Plant, Concern, and Production Center;" *National Resources Planning Board, Industrial Location and National Resources,* Washington, 1943, p. 251.

[46] Edgar M. Hoover, Jr., *op. cit.,* p. 245.

[47] Edgar M. Hoover, Jr., *op. cit.,* p. 276.

It is this high development of "business services" and other "secondary" industries which, together with the availability of labor of all kinds, enables the metropolis to sustain, expand, and replace its "primary" industries.

It is thus the "secondary," "nonbasic" industries, both business and personal services, as well as "ancillary" manufacturing, which constitute the real and lasting strength of the metropolitan economy. As long as they continue to function efficiently, the metropolis will always be able to substitute new "export" industries for any which may be destroyed by the vicissitudes of economic life.

We have seen that such substitutions may occur even in small towns such as Oshkosh. In metropolitan areas they are the rule rather than the exception. The history of the past 40 years in Europe has given eloquent proof of the ability of metropolitan communities to survive not only physical destruction, but also the disappearance of those functions on which their existence had been based in the past. They developed new functions and survived. Vienna and Leningrad are only two particularly striking examples.

It is worth nothing that this is a new phenomenon. The capitals of oriental empires soon turned into dust, once a new ruler transferred his court to a different location. Even Rome was little more than a village after the Western Empire had been destroyed. These cities were mainly centers of consumption, based on the concentration of "power and wealth." The modern metropolitan area is primarily a center of production, based on a concentration of productive forces. It is qualitatively different from the city as it has been known throughout history. It is a genuinely new form of human settlement, and, contrary to predictions of its approaching transformation into "necropolis," it is showing a greater vitality than any previous form of settlement. As far as this writer is aware, no community that during the last century has passed the half-million mark—a truer border line for the metropolis than the 50,000 adopted by the U. S. Census—has fallen below that population level.

The basis of this amazing stability are the business and consumer services and other industries supplying the local market. They are the permanent and constant element, while the "export" industries are variable, subject to incessant change and replacement. While the existence of a sufficient number of such industries is indispensable for the continued existence of the metropolis, each individual "export" industry is expendable and replaceable.

In any commonsense use of the term, it is the "service" industries of the metropolis that are "basic" and "primary," while the "export" industries are "secondary" and "ancillary." The economic base of the metropolis consists in the activities by which its inhabitants supply each other.

In the next selection a well known, young economist, Charles M. Tiebout, examines the economic
base theory. He suggests, in effect, that economic
theory is applicable to the urban economy and that
the economic base theory can be transformed or
modified to be consistent with economic theory. This
paper was one of the first, if not the first paper, to
point the way toward the application of existing
economic theory to the urban economy.

Charles M. Tiebout–The Urban Economic Base Reconsidered

The Urban Economic Base Reconsidered*

Like old shoes, traditional concepts in economics are more comfortable. New ideas and tools are apt to be upsetting. Eventually, if the concept has merit, the resistance wears and the idea becomes part of the economist's medicine chest, perhaps in modified form. This is one path in the development of doctrine.

In recent years the concept of "the urban economic base" has appeared. Certainly among those people concerned with urban economics, the concept of the base has made some impression. Writers on and users of the base technique do not claim perfection, for both the theoretical concepts and empirical methods are not much past the embryo stage.[1] But the core of the idea seems to be well developed. It is vital that we see how it fits within the general framework of economic analysis before complete acceptance.

This paper will attempt to place the concept of the base within the more conventional framework of modern economic analysis. We believe our analysis will place the base theory in a perspective, more valid as a description of urban economic reality and more operational in terms of urban economic research. The development of the paper is: (1) the objectives of base studies are set forth; (2) an analogous situation for national economy is presented; (3) the theory of the base, and (4) some misgivings about current usage of the base concept.

OBJECTIVES OF BASE STUDY

Properly speaking there is no single criterion for using the base concept. Any urban investigator is free to use the base for whatever purpose he has in mind, subject only to the restraint that the use makes sense. Yet the use of the base

---

* See Acknowledgements

[1] For a fair appraisal of the weakness of the base, conceptually and operationally, see: Richard Andrews, "Mechanics of the Urban Economic Base," *Land Economics*, May 1953 continuing.

idea, even in modified form, necessarily commits the researcher to certain, albeit implicit, statements about the urban economy. This is merely another way of saying that the urban base approach is a framework of analysis. It is, of course, impossible to study all aspects of the urban economic totality in detail. Some method of aggregation is essential. The simple listing of urban employment by industry types according to the Standard Industrial Classification is one type of aggregation. The conceptual framework of an input-output table is another. The classification according to exports vs. local use is still another. Which technique one uses depends on the nature of the study.

The basic vs. non-basic method is one more framework. Supposedly, it is useful because it points up cause and effect relations in critical areas of the urban economy. As usually discussed, these areas deal with employment and/or income, somehow measured, in the urban community. These are items which relate to the general health or general economic welfare of the area. Thus it may be argued that the base approach is useful in pointing up the forces determining the level of general economic welfare in the community.

In turn, this leads to the question of just what magnitudes best indicate the level of general welfare. This issue is old hat to economists. It is delightful since it has no solution. Probably, if a vote were taken among economists, some form of income measurement would win. Insofar as other variables, such as employment, industrial production and the like, move in the same direction, it does not make too much difference which measure is used. But income, especially per capita with some knowledge about its distribution, is probably the best single measure.[2]

Forgetting for the moment the statistical problems involved,

---

[2] For a discussion of other, but associated criteria see: Richard Andrews Measuring the Urban Economic Base," *Land Economics*, November, 1954, pp. *Land Economics*, February 1954, pp. 52-60.

we can say that the base approach is a useful framework because it helps to explain the level of income of the economy. Not only does it measure, when basic and non-basic activities are added together, the level of income, but supposedly it helps to explain sources of variation in income. Since so many of the activities of a community, both public and private, are tied to the level of income, this can be a powerful tool.

Yet a word of warning is in order. The base concept cannot explain everything, and in one case is weak in explaining income level. This is the case of secular growth and factor endowment. By analogy, we know two things happen in the national economy: (1) we grow in possible levels of output and (2) we do not always produce at capacity. In fact, we rarely do. If one is talking about income levels in India vs. the United States and seeks to explain the difference, the obvious answer is poor vs. rich factor endowments. On the other hand, if one is concerned with changes in income (cycles)—given the factor endowment—the level of investments, consumption and so forth, are the key variables. A third way of viewing this difference is to consider the level of income in Chicago vs. some southern city. This is again a question of factor endowment. In Chicago changes in income from year to year, however, may be considered another problem. This base concept is useful in the case of income change, but of much less use, as will be shown, in the case of secular income discussion.

In summation, the base concept is useful as a framework of analysis in aggregating urban economic activity. Its advantage over other frameworks is that it points up the interactions of the local economy in a meaningful manner. At least, that is what the base technique is supposed to do.[3] The only problem is, as

---

[3] To argue that in order to understand the local economy one must study the demand for its exports is merely carrying the base approach one step further. This is not our concern at this point.

usually formulated, it does not. In order to see why it fails to provide a meaningful aggregation, it will be necessary to look at the same problem the base approach is trying to solve at the national level.

NATIONAL INCOME FORECASTING

One of the favorite hobbies opened to economists is that of predicting national income. Obviously, in prediction one must explain something about the nature of the changes which raise or lower the national aggregates. In other words, one must have some idea of how the economic system works. This does not imply that all forecasters use the same method. In general, there are two methods of predicting income levels. One uses selected indexes which seem to show leads in the terms of national income. New orders, common stock prices, are examples of indicators used. A second approach is to set up an econometric model of the economy. These may be simple systems or may involve many equations and unknowns. Implicity, most discussions of the urban base are simplified econometric models. It is worth a moment to explore the innards of these creatures to see their basic ingredients. In this manner base studies can be seen in a new light.

Simply stated, the basic conditions of an econometric model, as used in forecasting, are threefold. (1) The level of some activities depend on the level of other activities in the system. For example, the level of consumption is said to depend, in large part, on the level of income. (2) Some activities are independent of other activities in the economic system. That is, they have their level set by forces outside the system. Insofar as the level of government expenditures is set by Congress, it is an independent variable. (3) The economist, with the help of theory and data, can say something about the stability of the variables. For example, he may feel the relation between income and consumption are fairly stable over time. On the other hand, we may view investment as unstable and subject to change almost at random. These are statements about the nature of the real world.

A woefully simple example will illustrate this point. Suppose we take a simple Keynesian system: (1) Income = Consumption + Investment, (2) Consumption = f (Income) and (3) Investment = autonomous (i.e. set by forces outside the system). Let us further suppose the forecaster feels that, on the basis of historical data, consumption will be .8 of income. This it is assumed, is a stable relation. Further, suppose that from surveys of intended investment, the level of investment will be at 20. This is the independent variable which is, by assumption, set by forces outside the system postulated. Given the validity of these data we know that the income will be 100.[4] The addition of more equations and unknowns merely serves to elaborate the process and enhance the accuracy of the prediction. We need not fret about this issue. The point involved is that if this setup works and makes sense, then we have stated something about the workings of the economy. Our method of aggregation is useful.

Let us now turn back to the urban scene and see what this same sort of approach yields as a method of explaining income levels of the urban economy.

THE THEORY OF THE ECONOMIC BASE

The urban economy consists of hundreds of economic units all engaged in the task of creating income. Our problem, as stated above, is to combine these units into meaningful aggregates. The method will be similar to that of the national income forecaster.

First off, let us look at those activities with levels set by forces outside the community. Exports, of course, are the biggest item. The forces which determine the demand for the exports are out-

---

[4] The basic 3 equations: (1) $Y = C + 1$ (2) $C = .8Y$ (3) $1 = 20$ reduce to: (4) $Y = .8Y + 20$ by substitution, which yields: (5) $Y = 100$.

side the control of the urban area. But this does not mean all exports are independent. The exports of the City of New York to suburban towns in the form of retail goods may not be true exports. The reason this is so is that the people who buy these retail goods work in New York. Their level of expenditures is dependent on the income they receive from the city. In effect, the city is selling to itself. This is not true in the case of a shopping center where, say, farmers come to buy. Farm income depends upon the demand for farm products, and not upon the income of the shopping center. In the latter case the retail exports are true exports similar to manufactured goods. In the former case they are not. But in general, it is safe to assume most exports are independent of the local community.

To stop here, as most base studies do, would be a mistake. Other income-creating activities in the urban economy are also more or less independent of the level of income. Residential housing, business investment and local government expenditures appear to be largely independent of the level of local income. If they are, then they function in the same capacity as true exports. For a small area these may not be of much importance as a percentage of total basic income, but this is not true for larger areas.

On the other side of base-type division are the non-basic or dependent activities. As usually pointed out, these activities consist largely of local services, retail trade, and professional as well as other services. The assumption is that these activities have their level set by the level of community income.

Now all that the theory of the economic base does is bring these two sets of activities together into an urban multiplier. An over simplified but useful example parallel to our national income example would run as follows: (1) Total urban income = income earned in independent activities + income earned in dependent activities. (2) Income originating in dependent activities = .5 total income. (3) Income originating in dependent activities = 20. In this case the income would be 40. In income terms this implies a basic to non-basic ratio of 1:1. If the function relating dependent activities to total income is constant, an increase of 10 in independent activities will give rise to a total increase of 20 in urban income. This is just a simple form of the well known economic multiplier. It is the arithmetic of the base approach.

In discussing national income forecasting it was pointed out that, in addition to knowing which variables are dependent and independent, something should be said about the stability of the variables. If, in the example of the preceding paragraph, at the same time the basic or independent activities level went up by 10, the function relating dependent or non-basic activities shifted, independently, from .5 to .4, any forecast of future income would be quite a way off. Thus it is important to state something about the stability of the variables.

The study of Alexander on Madison and Oshkosh gives some support in the "a priori" assertion that non-basic to basic ratios are stable.[5] To see this, consider the case of two communities of about the same size and income, located a given distance from the central city. In both communities people possess income and will spend it only on retail goods and services. Our knowledge of the consumers behavior would indicate that these two sets of consumers will spend their money in roughly the same proportions for various retail and service goods.[6] If this is true then it follows that the income flowing to dependent activities will be the same in both communities. Further we would expect the number of employees and firms to be about the same. The ease of entry into retail and service activities, compared with manufacturing, probably accounts for this feature.

---

[5] John Alexander, "The Basic-Nonbasic Concept of Urban Economic Functions," *Economic Geography,* July 1955, pp. 246-261.

[6] See the recent, Bureau of Labor Statistics, *Family Income, Expenditures and Savings in 1950,* Bulletin No. 1097, June 1953.

This is important. If consumption patterns in the urban economy are stable, as they tend to be for the national economy, then calling some activities dependent or non-basic is useful. Not only do they depend on the level of urban income, but they depend on the level of urban income in a predictable manner. If empirical studies such as Alexander's can support and quantify this thesis, it will be a major step forward in urban research.

Again on "a priori" ground one would look towards the independent activities for sources of instability. Local recessions do not start because of layoffs in the retail sector. Usually it is the manufacturer's business which folds, causing a downturn. Only further studies on the nature of demand for the various independent activities can point up the sources of instability in this area.

In summation, the base is simply a modified form of an old economic concept, the multiplier. Its usefulness is derived from the logic of the assumptions made concerning the behavior of the dependent and independent activities. These are yet to be tested fully by empirical research.

CURRENT PITFALLS IN BASE STUDIES

Using the above analysis as a frame of reference, some attention should be given to the current usage of the base concept. Although many items should be discussed, only four will be mentioned.

The definition of basic activities as the exports of goods, services and capital beyond the boundaries of the region can be misleading. If the object of a base study is to show the forces determining the level of income, this concept is too limited in its coverage. This follows from the fact that as the boundaries of a region are expanded, exports become less and less. Yet the boundaries are arbitrary, and the wider they are drawn, the less the amount of exports. For the world as a whole there are no exports, but a great deal of income instability exists. This is the danger of equating exports with the source of instability.

Another problem which comes up is the selection of units by which to measure the economic base.[7] For reasons argued above income may be the best method. But measuring income of a community is a tricky problem both conceptually and statistically. Conceptually the problem arises as to what is meant by income. The simplest measure is "income accruing to residents." This is the value of the income received by the residents from all sources. Except for some minor adjustments it resembles personal income in the national picture. If factor income is used then all sorts of problems come up. How to allocate corporate profits among residents vs. non-residents, rental incomes, and so forth, are problems. It is not safe to take "value added" in production for an urban economy and use it as the urban income analogous to national income. For the national economy, where all factors are owned by the residents, product and charges against product are good measures. The value of a unit of output must be somebody's income. But for a community the value of the output, of a local steel mill for example, need not be income to local people, even if the concept of value added is used.

Thus it seems highly desirable to use income accruing to residents as the measure of urban income. This income can be divided into incomes arising out of dependent and independent activities. In many cases the same individual will have income from both sources. Field surveys are needed to resolve this problem.

Another issue which comes up in base studies is that of secular growth. The concept of the base is essentially a short-run tool of analysis. If the desire is to explain future growth possibilities both in terms of the expansion of existing basic activities as well as the possibility of attracting new industry,

---

[7] See: Richard Andrews, "Mechanics of the Urban Economic Base," *Land Economics,* February 1954, pp. 51-60; Charles Leven, "An Appriate Unit for "Mechanics of Urban Economic Base: The Problem of Base Measurement," 369-71.

then an approach via location theory and the economics of regional development are called for. All the base type of analysis can do is point out what happens if you add more independent activities. It cannot say whether or not you will grow in independent activities. The failure of mining towns to attract new industries with the closing of the mines is evidence supporting this thesis. In like manner, the springing up of a retail sector around an atomic energy plant supports the thesis of dependent activities. The city planner interested in the possibilities of new manufacturers moving into a zone set aside for industry would do well to consider location theory and forget, in this instance, the economic base approach.

A final word may be in order about urban economic studies in general. The researcher may try to study everything about a community. This usually turns out to be an impossible task. Generally some logical framework is needed. The base approach is a framework. But unless this base approach is modified along the lines suggested above, it may not be too useful. Economics has a theory of the multiplier, both domestic and international, as well as a system of national income accounts. In modified form these can be of invaluable aid as tools of research in helping to understand the urban economy.

The next two papers represent the views of the Editor and, in the case of the second paper, a young collaborator, Erle T. Curtis. In each paper empirical evidence on the validity of the economic base theory is offered and in each paper the evidence does not support the economic base theory. An alternative theory is supported by each paper. In the first paper, use is made of elementary mathematics in presenting the theory, in the second paper the same theory is presented verbally and graphically.

Ralph W. Pfouts—An Empirical Testing of the Economic Base Theory

An Empirical Testing of the Economic Base Theory*

The major purpose of this paper is to report the results of a statistical testing of the economic base theory of urban development. Since the statistical tests do not support the economic base theory, a secondary purpose of this paper is to suggest some alternative directions of inquiry that may lead to an economic theory and an apparatus of analysis that would be of use to city planners and others interested in urban growth and development.

The economic base theory divides income-producing activities within the community into two groups basic or exporting activities and service or non-exporting activities. Emphasis is then placed on the basic activities since these are "city building" activities, and the inference is that an increase in the economic base will result in a growth of economic activity and of population. Without a continuing growth in basic activity the city cannot grow in population. "We cannot live by taking in each other's washing," etc. Although a rather extensive literature has grown up around the economic base theory, little in the way of systematic, empirical testing has been published.[1] The research reported in this paper is intented to overcome partly this lack.

Description of the tests

The tests included twenty-eight cities whose populations ranged from 100,000 to 300,000, as shown in Table 1. The cities were classified as diversified if a larger proportion of employees were engaged in retailing than in manufacturing. They were classed as manufacturing if a larger proportion were engaged in manufacturing than in retailing. All of the tests used were applied to each group and to the entire group of cities.

---

* See Acknowledgements

[1] For a comprehensive explanation, critique and extension of the economic base theory, see a series of articles by Richard B. Andrews that appeared in *Land Economics* beginning with the issue of February, 1953.

TABLE 1
Relationships of Change in Base-Service Ratios to Change in Rate of Population Growth for Twenty-Eight Cities, 1940-1950

City	Percent Change in Population, 1940-50	Change in Base-Service Ratio, 1940-50
Diversified Cities		
Duluth	−130	− 4
Des Moines	− 8	15
Salt Lake City	34	30
Tulsa	8	30
Spokane	108	35
Jacksonville	30	45
Wichita	− 2	55
Fort Worth	− 10	60
Sacramento	31	63
Miami	24	85

$r = .4767$; $t = 1.54$, 8 d.f.; $z_1 = − .2053$, $z_2 = 1.2423$

City	Percent Change in Population, 1940-50	Change in Base-Service Ratio, 1940-50
Manufacturing Cities		
Reading	20	6
Chattanooga	194	15
Utica	78	8
Trenton	58	17
Grand Rapids	−152	15
Peoria	1	18
Fort Wayne	− 27	19
Flint	− 18	19
Canton	9	21
Wilmington	53	21
Erie	− 13	21
Richmond	33	23
Nashville	− 28	25
South Bend	− 7	27
Charlotte	16	30
Tacoma	416	52
Norfolk	232	72
Knoxville	81	27

$r = .6294$; $t = 3.24$, 16 d.f.; $z_1 = .2399$, $z_2 = 1.2411$

For all Cities

$r = .3289$; $t = 1.78$, 26 d.f.; $z_1 = − .0479$, $z_2 = .7209$

Sources: Data from *Census of Population*, 1940 *and* 1950. The classification of the cities, the base service ratios and the percent of population change are taken from James R. Crozier, *Economic Base of Cities and Their Rate of Growth*, Unpublished master's thesis, University of North Carolina Library, 1956. The bulk of the remaining calculation was done by Nancy Dahl of the University of North Carolina.

The rationale of the tests rests on the hypothesis, implied by the economic base theory, that a growth in basic activity causes a growth of population in a given city. To test this hypothesis the base-service ratios (number of service employees per hundred basic employees) were calculated for each city for 1940 and 1950. The differences of the base service ratios were then calculated for each city and these differences were correlated with rate of population change for each city. All data was obtained from Bureau of Census publications.[2] Of course, the city planner does not use base-service ratios to predict population changes; he uses them as a description of the local economy. But the statement that a high basic employment component implies a high population growth potential is merely a statement of the fundamental preposition of the economic base theory.

The base-service ratios were calculated by the methods developed by Homer Hoyt.[3] For each type of business or industry the percentage of national employment in that type of activity was calculated for each city. If the percentage was larger than the city's proportion of national population, the excess was counted as basic employment. Basic and service employees were totalled separately for each city and the number of service employees per hundred basic employees was found. These calculations were carried out for each city for 1940 and for 1950. The differences between the 1950 ratios and the 1940 ratios were calculated and these appear in Table 1. Percent changes in population were calculated for the same decade for each city, and these values also appear in Table 1.

It is customary to use the number of service employees per one-hundred basic employees as the base-service ratio. Thus if a city had 160 service employees for every 100 basic employees in 1940 and had 200 service employees for every 100 basic employees in 1950, it had shown an increase of 40 service employees for every 100 basic employees during the decade.

---

[2] The data was taken from the *Census of Population for* 1940 *and* 1950.

[3] Arthur Weimer and Homer Hoyt, *Principles of Urban Real Estate* (New York: Ronald Press, 1939).

Then according to the economic base theory we would expect a diminution of economic activity and population because of the relative shrinkage of the economic base, or because of the shrinkage of the growth potential of the city. On the other hand, if the relative number of service employees declined during the decade we would expect an increase in economic activity and in population, according to economic base theory. Consequently our two series should show a negative correlation if the economic base theory were valid. An advocate of the economic base theory could argue that an increase in basic employment would bring about an increase in service employment in a subsequent time period. If we took the base-service ratio at the beginning of this second time period and at the end, we would find an increase in service employment, and (assuming no increase in basic employment in the second time period) we would find an increase in the base-service ratio. There would be an accompanying increase in population and a positive instead of a negative correlation. This is, however, a short period adjustment. The ability of service-type firms to come into and go out of existence is well known. If service employment increases relative to basic employment over a ten year period, as population increases surely we have a contradiction of the economic base theory. If we do not, the economic base theory is so general as to be incapable of contradiction and hence cannot be viewed as a scientific hypothesis.

Inspection of Table 1 shows that in nine of the 28 cases a decline in relative number of service employees (a decrease in the base-service ratio) accompanied an increase in population. These cases support the economic base theory. In 18 cases an increase in the relative number of service employees (an increase in the base-service ratio) accompanied an increase in population. These cases do not support the economic base theory. In the case of Duluth, a decrease in the proportion of service employees accompanied a decrease in population, which is exactly the opposite of the results anticipated by the economic base theory.

Interpretation of the correlation tests

If the economic base theory were valid, the correlation of the differences of base-service ratio with the population changes would be negative. That is, an increase in relative number of service employees would accompany a decrease in population and vice versa. As may be seen from Table 1, this does not occur; all the correlations are positive. Hence, none of them supports the economic base theory. The correlation coefficient for diversified cities is .4767; for manufacturing cities it is .6294; and for both groups lumped together it is .3289.

It is informative to notice that the correlation coefficient is strongest against the base theory in the case of manufacturing cities, the cities with the largest basic components. This would seem to support the "chicken and egg" hypothesis that a city with an excess of basic employment will gain population more rapidly by adding to service employment, while a city with an excess of service employment can gain more rapidly by adding to basic employment. The fact that the correlation is weaker for diversified cities also appears to support hypothesis, but, as we shall see, this correlation is not significant.

The significance of each correlation was tested by use of the t-ratio. The formula for this test is

$$t = r \sqrt{\frac{(N-2)}{1-r^2}}$$

where r is the correlation coefficient, N is the sample size and N-2 is the number of degrees of freedom.[4] For diversified cities it was found that t = 1.54 with 8 degrees of freedom. This is not significant and leads to an acceptance of the hypothesis that there is no correlation in the universe. Thus we conclude from

---

[4] R. A. Fisher, *Statistical Method for Research Workers,* 10th ed. (Edinborough and London: Oliver and Boyd, 1946, pp. 193-6.)

this test that there is no correlation (between base-service ratios and population growth) in the entire set of diversified cities of the size studied. In other words the base-service ratios are unrelated to population changes. That the economic base theory does not influence diversified cities is our conclusion from this test.

We can use the t value in a slightly different way. Again we specify the null hypothesis that there is no correlation in the universe, but our alternative hypothesis is that the correlation in the universe is negative. Using a five percent criterion of significance, this "one-tailed" test leads to an acceptance of the null hypothesis. The alternative hypothesis, which we reject, would support the economic base theory. If we specified the same null hypothesis but now specify as an alternative hypothesis that the correlation in the universe is positive, we again accept the null hypothesis. If service industries were the primary generators of economic activity, the hypothesis that the correlation in the universe is positive would support this "economic service" theory. But our conclusion in the case of diversified cities is that neither basic or service industry is related to population growth. In other words the base-service distinction is of no importance in the case of diversified cities.

In the case of manufacturing cities it was found that t = 3.24 with 16 degrees of freedom. This is highly significant correlation that causes us to reject the hypothesis that there is no correlation between basic service ratios and population changes in the universe of manufacturing cities. But the correlation is significantly positive, just the opposite of what we would expect from the economic base theory. In other words, the test suggests that the opposite of the economic base theory is true for manufacturing cities.

Again for manufacturing cities, we can gain additional insight by considering one-tailed tests. If we specify the usual null hypothesis that the universe correlation is zero, we may also consider the alternative hypothesis that the correlation in the universe is negative. The acceptance of the alternative hypothesis would support the economic base theory. But in this case we accept the null hypothesis. If we try a second one-tailed test using the same null hypothesis and the alternative hypothesis that the universe correlation is positive we reject the null hypothesis in favor of the alternative hypothesis at any reasonable level of significance. This acceptance of the hypothesis, of a positive correlation in the universe, implies that for manufacturing cities service industry rather than basic industry is associated with population growth.

For all cities lumped together the value of t is 1.78 with 26 degrees of freedom. This value is significant at the 10 percent level but not at the 5 percent level and leaves us in a rather indecisive state of mind as to whether we should reject or accept the hypothesis of no correlation in the universe. In any case the correlation is positive which is contrary to the expectation one would entertain under the economic base theory.

The indecision of the two-tailed test in the preceding paragraph can be removed by use of two one-tailed tests in which we employ the five percent criterion of significance. If we state as the null hypothesis that there is no correlation in the population and as the alternative hypothesis that the correlation in the universe is negative, the test causes us to accept the null hypothesis. Conversely if we employ the same null hypothesis but state as the alternative hypothesis that the correlative in universe is positive, the test rejects the null hypothesis in favor of the alternative hypothesis. Consequently the two one-tailed tests suggest that for the entire group of cities, service industries rather than basic industries are associated with population growth.

To summarize the results of the significance tests we note that for diversified cities neither basic or service industries appear to be associated with population growth. In the case of manufacturing cities service industries, but not basic industries, appear to cause population growth. For all cities considered simultaneously service industries rather than basic industries are associated with population changes. Hence in the significance tests we find no support of the economic base theory, but in the case of manufacturing cities and in the case of all cities we do find some evidence that supports the views that a growth in a service industries accompanies a growth in population.

Another statistical test of importance involves the confidence intervals for the correlation coefficient. This interval is an "interval estimate" of the numerical value of the correlation coefficient in the universe. That is, we have a prescribed level of confidence (in our test 95%) that the calculated interval encloses the universe correlation coefficient.

It is well known that the distribution of correlation coefficients is not normal unless there is no correlation in the universe, in which case it is asymtotically normal. To overcome this difficulty we make use of the transformation embodied in the following equation:[5]

$$z = 1.15129 \log \frac{1+r}{1-r}$$

The distribution of z is a good approximation to the normal distribution. It may easily be verified that z has the same sign as r. To find the confidence intervals we must calculate the standard error of z by use of[6]

$$\sigma_z = \frac{1}{\sqrt{N-2.667}}$$

The 95% confidence limits (z_1 and z_2) can be found by use of[7]

---

[5] *Ibid*, pp. 197-204.

[6] Harold Hotelling, "New Light on the Correlation Coefficient and its Transforms," *Journal of the Royal Statistical Society*, Series B, XV No. 2, 1953, p. 220.

[7] For examples and discussion of the use of the z transformation see Frederick E. Croxton and Dudley J. Cowden, *Applied General Statistics*, 2nd ed. (New York: Prentice-hall, 1955), pp. 723-5.

$$z_i = z \pm 1.96 \, °_z, \; (i = 1, 2) \, .$$

For diversified cities the lower confidence limit is —.2053 and the upper confidence limit is 1.2423. This shows that a positive value of z in the universe is much more likely than a negative value, and consequently a positive correlation is more likely in the universe than a negative correlation. This militates against the economic base theory.

The results are stronger against the economic base theory in the case of manufacturing cities than in the case of diversified cities. Here the lower confidence limit is .2399 and the upper confidence limit is 1.2411. It is highly unlikely that the z, and hence the correlation coefficient, for the universe is negative. This is very strong evidence that for manufacturing cities the economic base theory is exactly and diametrically incorrect.

For both diversified and manufacturing cities lumped together the lower confidence limit is —.0479. In this case also the correlation in the universe is much more likely to be positive than negative, and the economic base theory is not supported by this test.

Thus in a considerable series of statistical tests we fail to get a single affirmation of the economic base theory. It is submitted that this is strong enough evidence to warrant a careful rethinking of the economics of urban development.

Critique of the tests

The purpose of this section is to attempt to set a perspective around the results of the statistical tests. To accomplish that it is important to realize that no statistical test is conclusive; they are all based on probabilities. Thus we cannot say that the foregoing tests prove conclusively that the economic base theory is unsound; the probabilities could be playing us false. But the evidence presented in the preceding sections raises very strong doubts as to the validity of the economic base theory. We should be taking an unbelievable whipping from chance if the interpretation of the preceding section is incorrect.

Questions may also be raised about the representativeness of the sample. Practical limitations of the availability of data always serve to call a sample into question in problems of the type discussed in this paper. For example, for purely practical reasons no New England cities are included. Nevertheless, the opinion of the researchers involved, before the tests were undertaken, was that the sample was adequate.

The most important of the possible difficulties with the tests is that they test the economic base theory by means of the base-service ratios. Thus if we accept the results of the tests we can, strictly speaking, only claim that the economic base theory as represented by the base-service ratios is not valid. In other words it is possible that the base-service ratios are invalid, but that the economic base theory is sound. But even if this is the case, the proponents of the economic base theory are forced to abandon the technical apparatus developed around the base theory. To the author, the technical apparatus appears to suit the theory quite well.

Finally it should be noted that the tests apply only to cities of the class tested. By themselves the tests say nothing about the economic base theory and the large metropolis or the small town. One would judge that in the latter case the economic base theory might have some application.[8]

Some suggestions for alternative lines of inquiry

Why should such great emphasis be placed on exports? This appears to be the primary question that should be asked about the economic base theory. Are exports of such overwhelming importance that such variables as imports, savings, value-added, etc. can be safely neglected? This is essentially a question of fact. The facts marshalled in this paper suggest that exports are not of such overwhelming importance as the economic base theory would suggest.

[8] Cf. Hans Blumenfeld, "The Economic Base of the Metropolis," *Journal of the American Institute of Planners*, XXI, Fall, 1955, pp. 130-2.

Surely it can be argued that imports, since they represent money leaving the community, should be given a place in considering the income stream within the community. Similarly the amounts that individuals within the community save represents money withdrawn from the income stream within the community. These observations suggest that simple income models similar to national income models can be drawn up for the individual community.[9]

If we let E designate exports and I designate imports then the balance of trade is indicated by

$$(1) \qquad B = E - I$$

We assume that the quantity of imports into the community depends on income within the community that is

$$I = F (Y),$$

where Y stands for income. To consider a specific case we assume

$$(2) \qquad I = e + fY,$$

here lower case letters indicate constants. Hence in this case the "marginal propensity to import" or the change in imports following a change in income is a constant, i.e.,

$$(3) \qquad \frac{dI}{dY} = f.$$

We also assume that consumption expenditure depends on income. Thus we assume a consumption function for the community,

$$(4) \qquad C = a + bY.$$

Then the marginal propensity to consume within the community is

$$(5) \qquad \frac{dC}{dY} = b.$$

---

[9] A somewhat similar suggestion has been made by Charles M. Tiebout, "The Urban Economic Base Reconsidered," *Land Economics*, February, 1956. pp. 95-99.

It is clear that both f and b are positive fractions, i.e.,

$$o < f, b < 1.$$

We shall now turn our attention to a consideration of what happens to the income stream of the community when "new money" enters the community because exports are larger than imports. As such money represented by B in (1), comes into the community it represents income to the members of the community who receive it. But these members of the community will spend part of the money within the community, part they will spend for imports and part they will save. The proportion of this income that remains within the community is given by $1 - f$. Hence we must multiply B by $1 - f$ in this round of spending to take into account the effects of importing.[10] Similarly, to take the effects of savings into account we must multiply by b. Thus after this round of spending the money left in the community income stream is B $(1 - f)$b. This last quantity of money must again be multiplied by $(1 - f)$b to take account of importing and saving in the next round of spending giving us B $(1 - f)$b $(1 - f)$b or B[$(1 - f)$b]^2. For each subsequent round of spending we must multiply by $(1 - f)$b. Thus the change in income within the community is shown by

$$(6) \qquad dY = B + B (1 - f)b + B[(1 - f)b]^2$$
$$+ B[(1 - f)b]^3 + \ldots + B[(1 - f)b]^n.$$

This last equation exhibits a geometric progression and the sum is given by

$$(7) \qquad dY = B \frac{1}{1 - (1-f)b} = \frac{B}{1 - b + bf} = kB.$$

---

[10] If f is the marginal propensity to import, 1-f is the marginal propensity to spend money within the community.

In equation (7) the expression $\dfrac{1}{1 - b + bf}$ is a community income multiplier similar to the multiplier $\dfrac{1}{1 - b}$ for a closed system. The multiplier will be larger than one if both b and f are positive fractions. The multiplier is larger for a larger value of b, the marginal propensity to consume, than for a smaller value b. The numerical value f, the marginal propensity to import, works in the opposite direction. That is, a large marginal propensity to import causes a lower net addition to the community income stream.

For purposes of illustration suppose b = .8 and f = .3. Then k = 2.3. Hence the circulation of money within the community increases the original injection of money by a factor of 2.3 by 130%. As a consequence it seems incorrect to emphasize exporting industries to the exclusion of industry that causes the circulation of money within the community. If b increases to .9 while f remains fixed at .3, k becomes 2.7, and the injection of income is expanded by a larger amount than formerly due to a decrease in savings. If b is .8 and f increases to .4 then k falls to 1.92 and due to the increase in imports an injection of income is not expanded by as large an amount as in the first example. Thus it may be seen that income generation within the community, imports and consumption (or savings) are important "city builders" as well as exports.

In the model outlined above, exports, the important manifestation of basic industry, are one of three variables taken into account. Imports and savings, the chief ways for income to leak from the community, are also given a place in the community income picture. Hence it can be contended that even this simple model gives a better picture of urban income generation than does the economic base theory.

If B is negative, that is if imports exceed exports, the multiplier works in reverse. In this case, dY will be a contraction in income, and will be larger in absolute amount than B. This observation cannot be taken as evidence that the economic base theory is sound, because a negative value of B depends on the relative size of imports and exports, and the multiplier effect depends on savings and imports.

The economic base theory emphasizes an important determinant of income in the community. But it is not the only determinant of income within the community. The flow of income inside the community also generates income and hence community development. It is true that we cannot live by taking in each other's washing, but if nobody is taking in washing, income opportunities are lost and the community is less pleasant place than it would otherwise be.

The purpose of the model developed in this section is to suggest in a concrete way some of the complications not taken into account in the economic base theory. Further empirical investigations are needed to gain some idea of what variables should be included and what the relative importance of those variables is. Actually it seems that income studies of communities could be an extremely rewarding type of investigation from the standpoint of city planners and municipal administrators, because it could offer data of primary importance for many types of economic problems facing a community.

It would be foolish at this time to argue that city planners should start estimating community income multipliers. This is true because sufficient experimentation to validate the practicality of such work is still lacking. Thus we find ourselves in the position of rejecting the economic base theory and the base-service ratios, at least for certain types of cities, without having a well-developed practical apparatus to offer as a substitute. But the rejection of the economic base theory implies that we should start looking for a substitute.

There are other types of investigations that might serve the needs of city planners and administrators better than the income model suggested above. For example, a study of value added by the community might prove important and useful. Such an approach would not give a view of the community income stream and would show nothing about the effects of consumption and savings on the community income stream. An income model making use of the income velocity within the community could also be used. Such a model would have the disadvantage of not specifying the leakages of income from the community. Income studies appear to offer a more specific description of the economics of community development, but this must be taken as a preliminary judgement.

Ralph W. Pfouts and Erle T. Curtis—Limitations of the Economic Base Analysis

Limitations of the Economic Base Analysis*

THE PROBLEM

The fact that some cities flourish while others remain stagnant or actually decline in size and importance has led to theories explaining the causes of such behavior. One of the most prominent among such theories is the economic base theory. This theory divides all employment within a given commuinty into two categories; the first is referred to as "basic" or "export" workers and consists of those workers who are supplying the goods and services to people outside the community. The second category is referred to as "service" or "city-serving employment" and is made up of those who supply goods and services to people within the community.

In most types of industry within a given area, the products of the industry are consumed by both people within the area and those outside the area as well. In any application of the economic base theory, a difficult problem is to determine the number of persons employed solely for the market outside the community. For example, a barbershop located in a resort city will cut the hair of vacationers as well as the hair of the local residents. In reality the barbershop may be almost entirely exporting its services because most of its business is obtained from transients. The general method of solving this problem of determining the number of workers engaged solely in exporting its goods and services is by comparing the actual number of persons employed in each industry, within a city, with the number of employed persons required to provide the goods and services of the city's residents. If the employment in a particular industry is great enough to supply more than the requirements of the city, then the excess is counted as export employment.

Essentially the economic base theory implies that those cities that have a greater portion of their labor force employed in ex-

* See Acknowledgements

porting activities will show greater economic growth than those which do little exchanging of goods and services with the outside world.

Obviously, the economic base theory is something of a blanket theory in that it attempts to cover and explain all economic activity by means of an employment or industry breakdown; it avoids looking into the effects of income and money-flows within the community and ignors the institutions and other characteristics of the community. Various proponents of the theory have suggested that the types and stability of industry and incomes should be considered in the analysis of the particular city, but specific methods of fitting these factors into the determination of growth potential is lacking.[1]

In order to ascertain the validity of this theory, 40 standard metropolitan areas have been tested. Each area contains one central city with a population between fifty thousand and one hundred thousand. The reason for narrowing the selection to a standard metropolitan area is apparent; people and industry outside the immediate city but within a reasonable distance are generally closely tied in with the economy of the city.

For the purpose of determining the basic or export population of the areas one of the better known practices is to make the assumption that the areas would require the products of a given industry in accordance with its proportion of the total U. S. population, employed workers, or disposable income. In the case of necessities like food, where consumption is closely related to human population, the use of population figures would be justified, while the consumption of luxury goods would be more dependent on disposable income. If the city's employment in a particular industry group is greater than its consumption from that industry, then the surplus is counted as

---

[1] Arthur Weimer and Homer Hoyt, *Principles of Real Estate*, 3rd ed.; New York: Ronald Press, 1954, pp. 343-360.

export employment.[2] As an example, if an area contains one one-hundredth of the nation's total population, then the assumption is that it would also require one one-hundredth of the nation's workers in the various occupations to support the area as an economic unit. This is an oversimplified example, but it preserves the spirit of the economic base calculations. There is a possibility of bias in such a calculation, because this method assumes that the city-serving portion of the employees of any occupation are always close to the national average of the occupation. It is, of course, an empirical question as to whether this is true.

THE EMPIRICAL TESTS

For the purpose of the test, the basic or export employment was calculated for the 40 metropolitan areas for the years 1940 and 1950. The basic employees were expressed as the number of service employees per 100 basic employees and the percentage changes were calculated for the period 1940-1950.[3]

According to the economic base theory, the areas which showed the greatest decrease in the proportion of service employees over the decade should also show the greatest increase in economic activity, including population. By separating our universe into two groups, (a) the most basic cities, i.e. those showing the greater percentage increases in export employees over the decade; and (b) the predominantly service cities, i.e. those showing the greater percentage increase in the number of service employees over the 10-year period; it is possible to compare the two groups by means of correlation methods. When these two groups, the basic cities and the service cities, were correlated with the changes in population for the years 1940

---

[2] This is essentially the method developed and used by Homer Hoyt and his associates and is explained in greater detail in the above reference.

[3] The ratio between basic and service employees has been given special significance by many authors. For a lengthy elaboration consult the series of articles by Richard B. Andrews, "Mechanics of the Urban Economic Base," *Land Economics* (1953).

and 1950, it was found that the basic cities had a coefficient of correlation of—.2359. The appearance of a negative correlation supports the economic base theory; however the results are not significant for size of sample tested.[4] The service cities had a coefficient of correlation of .5670 which is significant and militates against the economic base theory, and for the entire group the coefficient was .4923, which is significant at 5 percent. All in all, this implies that cities with a large component of city-serving industries are more closely associated with population growth than are cities with a large export population.

Recognizing that the entire results of the analysis depend on the method of computing the basic population, another method was applied. The amount of employment in a particular industry within a city should approximate the average of the particular industry employed in the 40 cities; if the actual amount employed is in excess of this average, than the surplus is counted as basic. There is also a possibility of bias in this method of calculating basic employment, for a reason similar to that in the previous method. There is no reason to assume that the average of the 40 cities is the actual city-serving part of any particular community. Although this method will be biased, it will be helpful in a comparison of the actual differences between the cities with large export population and cities with large city-serving populations. Using this technique for determining the export employment, the same correlation analysis was applied to the cities. The results are recorded in Tables 1 and 2. The export cities have a correlation of — .7219, which is significant; the cities with large city-serving populations have a correlation of .2020, which is not significant, and all 40 cities taken together have a correlation of — .3618, which is not significant.

These results are at variance with our previous findings. This

---

[4] R. A. Fisher, *Statistical Methods for Research Workers* (8th ed.; Edinburgh and London, 1941), pp. 185-190, 202.

TABLE 1

CITIES WITH HIGH EXPORT EMPLOYMENT

Percentage Change in City-Serving Employees 1940-1950	Percentage Change in Population 1940-1950	Standard Metropolitan Area	Predominating Industries*
—79.5	27.7	Lexington, Ky.	Medical, Retail, Education, Construction, Household
—51.9	78.2	Phoenix, Ariz.	Wholesale, Retail, Construction
—33.9	66.1	San Jose, Cal.	Food, Construction
—33.6	62.8	Mobile, Ala.	Administration, Household, Transportation (other than motor vehicles), Nondurables
—29.9	45.0	Austin, Tex.	Education, Administration, Construction, Household
—20.4	16.5	Racine, Wisc.	Machinery, Electrical mach., Fab. metal, Primary metal
—19.7	54.9	Fresno, Cal.	Retail, Wholesale, Construction
—19.2	15.9	Jackson, Mich.	Motor vehicles
—10.3	32.4	Lansing, Mich.	Motor vehicles, Education, Administration
—10.0	49.6	Stockton, Cal.	Retail, Administration
—6.8	25.6	Saginaw, Mich.	Motor vehicles, Primary metals
—6.8	17.7	Waterloo, Iowa	Machinery, Food
—2.9	26.0	Little Rock, Ark.	Railroads
—2.4	25.8	Rockford, Ill.	Machinery, Fab. metals
2.1	29.6	Madison, Wisc.	Education, Food
4.1	15.5	Topeka, Kansas	Railroad, Medical, Food, Administration
10.7	22.7	Evansville, Ind.	Machinery, Food
11.6	—0.6	Altoona, Pa.	Railroads
11.7	16.7	Springfield, Ohio	Motor vehicles, Printing, Machinery
12.5	26.6	Kalamazoo, Mich.	Nondurables, Chemicals

Coefficient of correlation for export cities .... $r = -.7219$

---

* Gunnar Alexandersson, *The Industrial Structure of American Cities* (University of Nebraska, 1956), Appendix 1.

TABLE 2

CITIES WITH HIGH CITY-SERVING EMPLOYMENT

Percentage Change in City-Serving Employees 1940-1950	Percentage Change in Population 1940-1950	Standard Metropolitan Area	Predominating Industries*
222.8	26.7	Durham, N. C.	Nondurable, Textile, Medical, Education, Construction
103.3	21.5	Montgomery, Ala.	Household, Administration
87.6	17.5	Shreveport, La.	Retail, Mining, Household, Construction
82.7	32.5	Jackson, Miss	Households, Construction
60.0	15.5	Winston-Salem, N. C.	Nondurable, Textiles, Households
55.9	14.4	Asheville, N. C.	Medical, Retail, Households
51.3	6.7	Atlantic City, N. J.	Hotels, Construction, Eating and drinking places
49.6	36.1	Charleston, S. C.	Transportation equipment, Household
44.7	28.4	Savannah, Ga.	Nondurable, Railroad, Household
44.5	24.6	Lincoln, Neb.	Retail, Education, Railroad, Administrative
39.2	19.0	Raleigh, N. C.	Administration, Education, Household
35.5	15.8	Springfield, Mo.	Railroads, Retail, Wholesale
34.5	36.0	Columbia, S. C.	Households, Textile, Construction, Administration
30.6	10.5	Lancaster, Pa.	Textile, Durables, Elec. mach.
26.8	11.4	Binghamton, N. Y.	Nondurable, Machinery
23.5	11.5	Springfield, Ill.	Administrative, Machinery
23.3	23.1	Greenville, S. C.	Textile
20.1	0.3	Sioux City, Iowa	Food, Wholesale, Retail
15.9	39.3	Galveston, Tex.	Transportation, (other than motor vehicles)
14.4	13.9	York, Pa.	Machinery, Fab. Metal

Coefficient of correlation .... $r = .2020$

Coefficient of correlation for all forty cities .... $r = -.3618$

---

* Gunnar Alexandersson, *The Industrial Structure of American Cities* (University of Nebraska, 1956), Appendix 1.

may be partly explained by the reliance on national averages in our previous computation.[5] These results indicate that perhaps export employment is more closely associated with population changes than is service employment, at least in cities having a large export employment. To investigate this point, it is helpful to employ an industrial breakdown of the two groups of cities. In this closer analysis it is found that the industries in the two groups were similar with one notable exception. The export cities had a predominance of high wage industries, such as metals, vehicles, and food. The service cities were seen to have an abundance of low wage industries such as, textiles, nondurables, and household servants. It is well known that low wage industries are generally located where there are ample supplies of labor, and economic growth would not necessarily involve the importation of new population, but rather the utilization of already available manpower. The employment, even at low wages, of a previously underemployed segment of the population is an aspect of economic growth: "the cure for low wage industry is more low wage industry." Southerners interested in economic growth in their region will surely understand this point.

With the cities that were used, the export-service distinction had the effect of dividing the cities into two types. The export cities were found to be primarily the highly industrialized cities of the North, together with several cities along the west coast, which saw rapid expansion during and since the second world war. The service cities were more scattered, but 11 out of the 20 cities were located in the South. Our second set of correlations implies that the more industrialized cities which specialize in manufactures would tend to show greater population growth than the more diversified cities. In the period 1940-1950 the opposite results have actually occurred. The

[5] Gunnar Alexandersson, *The Industrial Structure of American Cities*, University of Nebraska, 1956, pp. 16-17.

manufacturing cities, which tend to be the basic cities of the country have failed to keep up with the more diversified cities in population growth. This is particularly true in the northern states which have such a heavy concentration of manufactures.[6] This is a complete contradiction of what would be expected by exponents of the economic base theory. During the 1940-1950 decade, standard metropolitan areas as a whole increased in population by 21.8 percent, while those of the Northeast increased by only 10.3 percent. In the same period, the South increased its standard metropolitan area population by a rapid rate of 35.6 percent, or more than 50 percent faster than the average rate of metropolitan growth in the nation.[7]

The proposition that highly industrialized areas would have greater potential for prolonged and above average growth has been tested by other investigators. One manner in which this hypothesis was tested was by correlating rate of growth with the percentage of the labor force employed in manufacturing in 1940. It was found that the generalization was valid for standard metropolitan areas in the Northeast during the 1940 to 1950 decade, but the reverse of this proposition was found true for the South and West. In the South and West, the areas of most rapid growth were found to be those which, in 1940, were the comparatively less industrialized areas. The same investigators conceived that it might be even more likely that *industrial expansion* might be highly correlated with population growth. To test this hypothesis, the percentage increase in the number of wage earners engaged in manufacturing 1937 to 1947 was correlated with rate of metropolitan growth 1940 to 1950. Only in the South and West, where rapid metropolitan development has taken place, were the rates of industrial expansion

[6] *Ibid.*, pp. 27, 91, maps 1 and 17.

[7] Donald J. Bogue, *Population Growth in Standard Metropolitan Areas* 1900-1950, Washington, D. C.: Housing and Home Finance Agency, 1953, p. 26.

TABLE 3

A COMPARISON OF EXPORT AND CITY-SERVING CITIES BY TYPES OF INDUSTRY

Industry	Wage Level*	Number of Cities In Which the Industry Is Prominent†	
		Export	City-Serving
Food + Kindred Products	Med.	5	1
Motor Vehicles	High	4	0
Metals	High	4	1
Textile	Low	0	5
Household		3	8
Nondurable	Low	2	4
Administration		6	5
Machinery	High	6	4
Construction		5	5
Retail		4	5
Education		4	3
Railroad		3	3
Wholesale		2	3
Medical		2	2

* Wage Level Source: *Regional Trends in the U. S. Economy* (Dept. of Commerce, 1951), p. 88.

† Gunnar Alexandersson, *The Industrial Structure of American Cities* (University of Nebraska, 1956), Appendix 1.

closely related to the rate of metropolitan growth.[8]

The reason that significant correlation exists between the export cities and changes in population lies in the observation that the percentage change in city-serving employees has not varied over a very wide range in the industrialized cities of the north. On the other hand, the lack of correlation between changes in city-serving employees and changes in population in the cities with a large city-serving employment is due in part to the greater changes in city-serving employment over the decade in the southern cities, together with more uniform changes in population. This is due to the fact that industrialization was begun much later in the South and far West, with special emphasis on service-type industries. On the other hand,

---

[8] *Ibid.*, pp. 36-37.

New England and the Middle East regions have followed more normal growth trends.[9]

The import of our tests and of other tests suggests very strongly that urban growth is not uniquely a function of basic employment.[10] Indeed the tests suggest that in certain cities at certain times basic employment is either unrelated to urban growth or retards urban growth. We do not, of course, contend that basic employment is never related to urban growth or that it does not stimulate urban growth at most times. We do contend that it cannot be described as the single wellspring of urban growth.

The failure of the economic base analysis to seize upon the real basis of a community's problems has prompted the use of a Keynesian approach. The use of national income statistics as a means of economic analysis is well known at the national level, but the difficulty of obtaining data for the regional or community level has limited its use in these fields. There have been increased efforts to collect and tabulate such data, the 1950 census has included income breakdowns for the larger cities, and the Bureau of Labor Statistics and other governmental agencies have made specific studies to obtain information concerning the expenditure and saving habits of certain cities. Cities, too, have become increasingly aware of the fruitfulness of economic research in regard to their problems; in particular they have become aware of the need for stable and fuller employment for their inhabitants. This is evident from the attempts by cities to initiate employment-stabilization programs for private industry as well as the planning of local expenditures for public works to coincide with periods of low economic activity in the community. City officials have learned

---

[9] Charles A. R. Wardwell, *Regional Trends in the United States Economy*, U. S. Department of Commerce, 1951, pp. 1-13, 36.

[10] R. W. Pfouts, "An Empirical Testing of the Economic Base Theory" *Journal of the American Institute of Planners*, Vol. XXIII, no. 2, (1957), pp. 64-69.

that new industries within their cities may not necessarily increase income of the inhabitants, but the new industries may have adverse effects upon the continued growth and the future of the city.[11]

THE COMMUNITY MODEL, A SIMPLIFIED CASE

In a community as illustrated by Figure 1, the major flow of income into the community is in the form of payment received for goods and services exported to the outside world. The part of this income that is ordinarily of major significance to the community is the portion that goes to workers as income. The workers spend most of this income within the community. This demand for goods and services within the community determines to some extent the number of local city-serving businesses and the number of persons which these city-serving occupations employ. In turn, part of the income earned by the city-serving businesses is paid out to employees as income payments, and they, too, consume local goods. This respending multiplies the impact of income within the city, and this process is referred to as the multiplier effect or the multiplier. This circular stream of income flows is the actual purpose and function of a city; it is the economic aspect of community living, without which there is no city, but an isolated industrial complex dependent on another community for its services and goods.

Income leaves the community income stream in two ways: through savings and through importation of goods and services by both basic and city-serving industries.

If for some reason the community has insufficient community serving businesses, then the inhabitants will tend to spend their incomes for products outside the community. This, too, will

---

[11] This interest in community employment has been reported in a series of books by the W. E. Upjohn Institute for Community Research. For more detailed information, see *Full Employment in Your Community* (Chicago, 1947), or some of the later publications of the Institute.

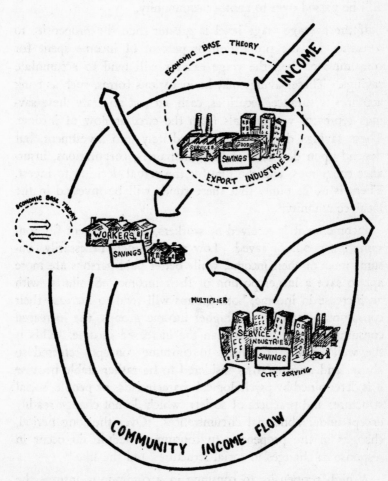

FIGURE 1. THE PATH OF INCOME FLOW THROUGH THE COMMUNITY

tend to retard the growth of local commercial establishments, and accompanying employment opportunities and income flows will be passed over to another community.

If the average wage level is greater than the propensity to consume, i.e. the proportion or percent of income spent for consumption, then the wage earners will tend to accumulate savings. These savings may be in various forms, such as bank accounts, insurance, securities, cash, etc.; at any rate these savings represent withdrawals from the circular flow of income. These savings do not enter immediately into investment, but depend upon decisions of bank managers, corporations, insurance companies, and the like for the actual decision to invest. There is no certainty that these funds will be invested in the local community.

Income, as it is received by workers, is either spent for consumption goods or saved. Low wage earners necessarily consume most of their income, while better paid persons are more apt to save a larger portion of their income. Similarly, with an increase in income, both groups will tend to increase their consumption and, in the higher income groups, the increased consumption will be less than the increased income. This is the well known propensity to consume concept, referred to above, and is generally considered to be rather stable because it is determined by psychological characteristics of people, social structures and practices of society, which do not change readily except under abnormal circumstances. Over the long period, changes in the propensity to consume schedule do occur in response to changes in social structures and the like.[12]

A high propensity to consume in a community insures the demand for service-type industries. On the other hand, a high propensity to save will tend to decrease effective demand within

---

[12] John Maynard Keynes, *The General Theory of Employment Interest and Money* (London, 1936), chaps. 8-10; Dudley Dilliard, *The Economics of John Maynard Keynes* (London, 1950), pp. 79-80, 84.

the community. The poor community characterized by low incomes will tend to have a high propensity to consume and a higher multiplier than a wealthy community. Any increase in incomes in the poor community will be spent for consumption and will be returned to the income stream via local city-serving businesses.

The wealthy community will have a lower propensity to consume and there will be large amounts of saving at the higher levels of income. This low propensity to consume makes the wealthy community dependent upon a large volume of investment in order to grow and maintain the income stream. In such a community, the inducement to invest locally would probably be weak because local demands for goods and services would be sufficiently supplied.

Saving in the community may be done by any of the three sectors as shown in Figure 1. However, the decision to invest (the actual expansion of plants and inventories, etc.) can be made by only two of the sectors, the export industries and the community-serving industries. The inducement to invest in a Keynesian economy depends upon the marginal efficiency of capital taken in conjunction with the rate of interest. The decision to invest locally in the export industries is based on the type of industry and the benefits to be derived from expanding in the same locale.

On the other hand, the decision to invest by the community-serving industries is based on local demand and market conditions, which are functions of the local incomes and the propensities to spend at the various income levels. The growth of the community is largely dependent upon continued investment by both of these two sectors. If for some reason the community has failed to develop its own community-serving establishments, then the community stands to lose the benefits of increased investments. Thus if the export industries decide to invest in local expansion and hire local workers, the income which these new workers receive is spent outside the community, because the community lacks the services which the workers demand because city-serving investment has been small. The income received by the other community is partly paid out to its own workers and they in turn respend their incomes and the circular flow continues; the community where the income was initially received has not benefited from the multiplier effect. In a similar manner an increase in consumption due to higher wages would not benefit the community, because it would be spent outside the community and the multiplier effect would take place outside the original source of increased consumption.

It can be argued that an increase in basic investment will ultimately call forth an increase in city-serving investment. To a limited extent this argument is true. But if city-serving investment has lagged, those who control basic investment will see little inducement to invest in the community. A city with inadequate city-serving activity is not an attractive place in which to live and work. It will be hard to persuade key personnel at all levels to live in a community insufficiently supplied with city-serving activity. Those of us in the south who are interested in economic growth must recognize the practical implications of this point.

Thus, it becomes clear that community-serving industries are vital to community life and allow the income to follow the circular path. The importance of this circular flow of income within the community has been largely neglected by the proponents of the economic base theory.

It has been shown that the economic base analysis neglects some vital aspects of a community's growth potential. Although the exportation of goods and services by a community is important, the existence of a well balanced city-serving component is also vital for continued growth.

The distribution of income within a community is indicative of the standard of living of the inhabitants and reflects the consumption and saving habits of the community. It is possible to determine and compare consumption patterns in various cities. In Table 4 such a comparison is shown.

It should be noted that the propensities to consume run considerably higher than would be normally expected. This is partly explained by the personal interview method used, which is affected by a tendency for the respondents to understate their incomes and to overstate their expenditures. Investigations of a considerable number of surveys indicate that here is a significant amount of under-reporting of income.[18] Quite obviously, more complete surveys of consumption patterns will be necessary before valid city comparisons may be made.

Even though it is possible to determine what portion of the worker's income will be spent for consumption goods, it is more

TABLE 4

A COMPARISON OF THE PROPENSITIES TO CONSUME IN
THREE DIFFERENT CITIES IN 1948

Income Group	Detroit		Houston		Denver	
	Number of persons	PC* %	Number of persons	PC %	Number of persons	PC %
Under $1,000	121,315	274	47,110	286	30,490	393
1-2	145,985	153	58,510	142	40,040	123
2-3	275,605	114	68,540	107	52,355	113
3.4	320,725	103	56,750	105	40,170	100
4-5	141,020	98	31,280	103	17,710	97
5-6	67,370	104	14,540	111	8,765	89
6-10	54,700	100	13,860	90	8,920	85
Over $10,000	24,080	59	7,460	81	4,920	72

PC = Propensity to Consume.

* This table was computed from statistics published in *Family Income, Expenditures and Savings in Ten Cities*, Bulletin 1065 (U. S. Bureau of Labor Statistics). The studies were based on a sampling technique, so that the results are not entirely satisfactory. There is some indication that the people interviewed tended to understate their incomes and overstate their expenditures. Also *Family Income*, Labor Statistics, 1953), pp. 6-8.

---

[18] *Family Income, Expenditures, and Savings in 1950.* Bureau of Labor Statistics, 1953, pp.6-8.

difficult to determine just what the city-serving establishments will do with their income. If the city-serving industries are labor intensive, a higher multiplier could be expected because more income would be passed out to a greater number of workers. If the industries are part of a large chain of department stores, then more income could be expected to leave the community and thus leave a smaller community multiplier.

It is recognized that export industries play a key role in the community, the expansion in this sector does undoubtedly have repercussions upon the city-serving industries. However, it is apparent that there is no simple solution for predicting growth potential for the community but, rather, various economic variables and indictors have to be compared and weighed for the community under observation. However, like any Keynesian system, the propensity to consume and investment are determinants of income and employment. In the absence of a healthy consumption function, investment will be all the more necessary for growth and stability.

The next paper was written by a respected young economist, Charles E. Ferguson, who does not ordinarily work in the field of urban economics. In this paper, Ferguson considers the logical validity of the economic base theory in dynamics and comparative static, i.e., as a theory having predictive value. He finds that the economic base theory is not a logical foundation for prediction.

Charles E. Ferguson—Statics Dynamics and the Economic Base.

Statics, Dynamics, and the Economic Base*

I.

INTRODUCTION

Discussions of the so-called economic base theory have appeared in the literature for the past twenty years, and the use of base analysis considerably antedates the first printed statement.[1] Both theoretical and empirical studies of the economic base concept have been reported and numerous claims regarding its applicability advanced. Some of these claims are quite modest and justifiable. For example, Andrews states that ". . . a general understanding by the planner of the planning significance of the two principal base classifications is important . . . from the point of view that an overall improvement in planning efficiency is to be gained."[2] Specifically, base analysis might contribute materially toward planning transportation and communication facilities, housing and zoning regulations, and peak-load parking requirements. Additionally, it has been suggested that studies of this type are helpful in determining land usage and community money flows.[3]

On the other hand, some writers urge that economic base analysis is applicable to significantly broader categories of problems. In particular, it is frequently claimed that residentiary employment, urban income, and urban population can be ex-

* See Acknowledgements

[1] Richard B. Andrews, "Mechanics of the Urban Economic Base: Historical Devolepment of the Base Concept," *Land Economics,* XXIX (1953), pp. 161-7. Professor Andrews has published a series of seven papers that provide a comprehensive discussion of the base concept and many of the technical problems involved in its utilization. In addition to the article cited, see *Land Economics,* XXIX (1953), pp. 263-8 and pp. 343-50; and XXX (1954), pp. 52-60, 164-72, 260-9, and 309-19.

[2] Richard B. Andrews, "Mechanics of the Urban Economic Base: A Classification of Base Types," *Land Economics,* XXIX (1953), p. 349.

[3] Homer Hoyt, "Homer Hoyt on Development of Economic Base Concept," *Land Economics,* XXX (1954), pp. 182-6. Unfortunately, all claims appearing in this reference are not so modest as these.

plained and predicted from a knowledge of employment in basic or export activities. Indeed, it is this form of the economic base theory that is most familiar.

Since there has been an adequate time period for both advocates and critics to formulate their statements carefully, it seems that a methodological analysis of the economic base theory is now appropriate. To provide this constitutes the objective of the present paper.

II.

FORMS OF THE BASE HYPOTHESIS

The economic base theory appears in two fundamentally different forms. The first of these is *static*. In this case, the economic base hypothesis states that residentiary employment, income, and population can be explained and predicted by reference to employment in basic activities. An important modification of the *static* hypothesis is that *changes* in employment, income, and population are attributable to *changes* in basic employment. Since time rates of change are introduced, it may seem that the hypothesis is, in this instance, dynamic. However, it is not, or at least it is not dynamic with respect to basic employment. Stated in this form, a trend term linear in time appears in the model; nevertheless, time change in the economic base does not enter the analysis in an essential way.[4]

Alternatively, it is possible to formulate the economic base

---

[4] The substance of the last two sentences is easily demonstrated. Let y represent residentiary employment (income, population), x represent basic employment, and t time. The hypothesis takes the form
$$dy/dt = f\left(\frac{dx}{dt}\right).$$
In the simplest (linear) case,
$$dy/dt = a\frac{dx}{dt} + b, \text{ a and b constants.}$$
Thus $y = ax + bt$, where bt is a linear trend line. More generally, since, by hypothesis, $f\left(\frac{dx}{dt}\right)$ involves, only the *first* time derivative, integration removes all time elements associated with basic employment.

theory in a truly *dynamic* form. To do so, one merely postulates that the rate of *change* in residentiary employment, income, or population is functionally dependent on the *level* of employment in basic activities. The *dynamic* base hypothesis is intuitively appealing, since it is one manifestation of the interesting stock-flow relationships that pervade economic dynamics. However, as we see later, the dynamic form of the economic base theory contains a serious methodological fallacy.

In the remainder of the paper, we first investigate the static form of the economic base theory and then, subsequently, the dynamic hypothesis. Generally, the results are negative as regards both the theoretical and empirical content of economic base analysis.

III.

COMPARATIVE STATICS AND THE ECONOMIC BASE

In what is undoubtedly the most carefully guarded and scientifically admirable statement of the static form of the economic base theory, Hildebrand and Mace write that ". . . the hypothesis asserts that an increase in community 'exports,' *ceteris paribus*, leads to an increase in non-localized employment; that such an increase in employment directly leads to an increase in community income, which as spent induces a derived and calculable increase in localized employment. Further, the increase in 'exports' increases the earnings of locally owned factors applied to non-localized industries in a fairly constant way, leading in this direction also to an increase in disposable community income and hence to increased localized employment. Accordingly, the hypothesis asserts a close and direct correspondence between the non-localized and localized employment variables."[5]

---

[5] George H. Hildebrand and Arthur Mace, Jr., "The Employment Multiplier in an Expanding Industrial Market: Los Angeles County, 1940-47," *Review of Economics and Statistics*, XXXII (1950), pp. 241-9. It will be noted that the authors use "localized" and "non-localized" just as we use the words "residentiary" and "basic."

Furthermore, the authors specifically state that the economic base theory is applicable only in the short run,[6] and more particularly, only for the selected period measured. And, of course, extrapolation occasions all difficulties inherent in projecting time series. "What we actually have, then, is a device for improved analysis of community employment problems, one that is reliable for the period analyszed and for limited future projections on *ceteris paribus* reasoning . . . ."[7] One would certainly not object to the first part of the expression; however, the latter portion is questionable on the grounds that those variables which must be impounded in *ceteris paribus* impose certain analytical limitations not generally recognized.[8]

Since the static base-analysis hypothesis proceeds from basic employment to income to residentiary employment, we discuss together both the prediction of employment and income. The prediction of population is then considered in light of the results obtained in the more elemental cases.

When the economic base hypothesis is stated in the precise form attributable to Hildebrand and Mace, it is seen that there are two possible justifications of the theory. In the first place, it may be argued that the economic base hypothesis provides a theoretical explanation of the generation of community income and employment. Secondly, even if theoretically unsound, base analysis might provide a satisfactory short-run prediction of income and employment. Such a result may, for example, be imputed to correlation of the common effects of some unspe-

---

[6] The economic base theory, as subsequently shown, is indeed more likely to be valid in the short run than in the long run. For a controversy in this regard, see Douglass C. North, "Location Theory and Regional Economic Growth," *Journal of Political Economy*, LXIII (1955), pp. 243-58, and Charles M. Tiebout, "Exports and Regional Economic Growth," with reply by North, *Journal of Political Economy*, LXIV (1956), pp. 160-8.

[7] Hildebrand and Mace, *op. cit.*, p. 242.

[8] For a good discussion of the dangers incident to *ceteris paribus* reasoning, see James M. Buchanan, "*Ceteris Paribus*: Some Notes on Methodology," *Southern Economic Journal*, XXIV (1958), pp. 259-70.

cified common cause. If this were the case, base analysis would be an invaluable empirical tool.

A. *Theoretical Content of the Economic Base Theory.*

The economic base hypothesis is theoretically valid if it can be shown that the dollar value of the community balance of trade fully accounts for the generation of income (and hence employment). Unfortunately for the theory, however, there are variables other than exports that are important determinants of income. Although this is a familiar proposition for national income accounting, there is no *a priori* argument for its applicability at the community level. Hence it must be proved; but our task is considerably facilitated since such proof has already been presented by R. W. Pfouts.[9]

Without considering the proof in detail, Pfouts shows that both the marginal propensity to consume and the marginal propensity to import are significant factors in the generation of community income. Or stated alternatively, both export dollars and dollars locally spent are "powerful dollars" in the determination of income.

Since the theoretical aspect of the economic base theory has been treated by Pfouts and Tiebout, the reader is referred to their papers for more intensive discussion of this point. We conclude this section with a quotation that is as true as it is trenchant: "The economic base theory emphasizes an important determinant of income in the community. But it is not the only determinant of income within the community. The flow of income inside the community also generates income and hence community development. It is true that we cannot live by taking in each other's washing, but if nobody is taking in washing, income opportunities are lost and the community is a less pleasant place than it would otherwise be."[10]

---

[9] R. W. Pfouts, "An Empirical Testing of the Economic Base Theory," *Journal of the American Institute of Planners*, XXIII (1957), pp. 68-9. For a similar verbal argument, see Charles M. Tiebout, *op. cit.*, pp. 161-2.

[10] Pfouts, *op. cit.*, p. 69.

B. *Predictability and the Economic Base Theory*

Let us turn now to an examination of the empirical aspects of the economic base theory. While several auxiliary issues might be raised, we shall focus attention upon the *ceteris paribus* reasoning incident to short-run prediction on the basis of linear regression analysis.[11] To do so, let us reiterate the hypothesis as stated by Hildebrand and Mace and then follow through the reasoning process.

The economic base theory asserts that an increase in community exports leads to an increase in basic employment. This, in turn, generates an increase in community income which, finally, serves to augment residentiary employment.

Now suppose that in the period of time analyzed, one obtains a reasonably high correlation between residentiary and basic employment. That is, the computed employment multiplier, when applied to the data from which it was estimated, yields results conforming to the residentiary employment data for the same period. Equipped with the employment multiplier, in order to make projections for the future, one must estimate the change in export activities. Then, if the production function for export activities is not altered,[12] one may predict the change in employment and income in the basic activities.

Next, consider this change as a *ceteris paribus* increase in community income. Hence, assuming a constant marginal propensity to consume and marginal propensity to import, the corresponding income-multiplier value of expenditures on residentiary activities is determinable. Finally, if an unchanging production function for residentiary activities is postulated, the

---

[11] G. Hildebrand and Mace, *op. cit.* The linear regression of total residentiary employment on total basic employment is found. The regression coefficient is the employment multiplier.

[12] The reader will notice that we speak of a "production function for basic activities" and a "production function for residentiary activities." Although these concepts are necessarily amorphous, we direct attention to the seemingly more important issues rather than to technical objections to the base theory.

resulting increase in employment in this sector may be estimated. Naturally, the process is reversible for diminished export activities.

Ignoring the fiscal and monetary influences of the government and the central bank, it has been necessary to make the following assumptions in order to proceed from the initial change to the ultimate result:

B.1.   An autonomous increase in exports occurs.

B.2.   The production function for basic activities is unchanged during the adaptation to increased exports.

B.3.   The marginal propensity to consume and the marginal propensity to import are constant, and there is no shift in "tastes" leading to a greater local consumption of goods produced for export.

B.4.   The production function for residentiary activities is unchanged during the adaptation to increased community effective demand.

B.5.   There exists some feasible means by which export activities can be expanded.   In light of B.2., this implies either the existence of excess productive capacity in the export activities, or unemployed laborers, or, more probably, both.[13]

At the outset, let us notice that assumptions B.3. and B.4. are tenuous, especially B.3.   However, despite the historical evidence of change,[14] there is no reason why these factors should necessarily be altered.   That is, these are parameters which can validly be impounced in *ceteris paribus*.   To observe the interrelations of the other assumptions, it is helpful to consider the expansion process.

Suppose that there is an increase in export activities.   By assumption B.2., this cannot result from improved technology or

---

[13] In case of fixed technical coefficients of production, a situation usually assumed in base analysis, both are required.

[14] See the issues of the *Review of Economics and Statistics* in the immediate post-war years.

a recently-acquired comparative cost advantage.[15] Therefore, the increase in export activity must be attributable either to: (1) an increase in the price of the good or goods in question associated with an increase in the general level of prices or the wage level for the specialized resources utilized in the production of the exported item, or (2) an upward shift in the national demand schedule(s) for one or more of the export commodities.

There is no reason to believe that Case 1 will result in an increase in community employment, although it would certainly augment dollar income. When there is an increase in the general price level, the dollar value of imports increases *pari passu* with the dollar value of exports. Therefore, an increase in the dollar value exports by means of an increase in the general price level will not lead to a favorable increase in the community balance of trade.

The second factor of Case 1 is not so readily interpreted. By assumption B.5, an increase in the wage level of specialized resources in the community is impossible. A national increase, unaccompanied by a local increase, tends to cause out-migration of the local factors. The diminished local supply, in turn, tends to cause an increase in the local price of the specialized factor. In any event, a national wage level increase for specialized factors must be explained by some other factor. Obviously, the likely candidate is a national increase in demand for the commodity produced by the specialized factor. This brings us to Case 2.

A national increase in demand for some one or more of the community export commodities is postulated, although by assumption B.3, a local change in demand is not permissible. Then assuming that the shift in demand is not attributable to

---

[15] A comparative cost advantage is gained if costs in other regions *increase* while local costs remain unchanged. However, this is a purely fortuitous circumstance: there is no way in which the urban area can initiate the change.

some force exogenous at the national level, the effective demand for some other commodity or group of commodities must decrease. These affected related goods might also be export goods of the community, in which case there is no reason to suppose that the export trade balance is changed. However, there is no presumption that the counterbalancing decline occurs. For this reason, we consider an exogenous increase in demand without corresponding decreases that impinge upon the local economy.

If compensating changes are not present, the economic base analysis describes the results attributable to the shift in national demand. But the predictive success of the technique in this special case is a dramatic illustration of the general predictive deficiency of the economic base analysis. From the standpoint of the local community, the national shift in demand is purely fortuitous. And what is important, when all *ceteris paribus* assumption necessary for the base analysis are made, the only available avenue for change lies in this fortuitous circumstance. I do not think that city managers, city planners, or civic minded residents of a community would be either pleased or correctly informed if they were told that commonity development depends entirely upon changes in national demand (and, hence, is beyond their control). On the other hand, they would be correctly informed if told that improved industrial high schools and service facilities promote community development more than itinerant shoe factories.

C. *The Prediction of Population by Base Analysis*

The static base analysis prediction of urban population is even more tenuous than the prediction of income and employment. The population estimate must stand, as it were, as a superstructure upon the foundation provided by the employment estimate and at least one further socio-economic assumption. The precise nature of this assumption is difficult to state, but, generally, it is as follows.

By assumption B.5 there must exist unemployed factors at

least sufficient in quantity to support an expansion of output in the basic activities. This satisfies the necessary assumption, but there could exist a larger volume of unemployment without violating the conditions of the problem. If the first case is applicable, *i.e.* only enough unemployed workers to support the increased production of export goods, then the additional assumption is:

C.1. The fraction of the population engaged in the labor force is constant, or at least it is not so elastic upward that the increase is residentiary employment resulting from the increase in export activities is met by an increase in the labor force drawn from the existing population.

Alternatively stated, in order for urban population to expand as a consequence of an increase in basic activity, it is necessary that the expanded labor requirements are not furnished by a shift in the existing population from the non-labor force to the labor force category. In the second case, however, the assumption is somewhat different. Here we suppose that the volume of unemployment is sufficiently great to supply both the initial increase in basic employment and the concomitant increase in residentiary employment. If urban population is to expand commensurately, the ratio of number of jobs to number of people must be constant. This is formulated as assumption.

C.1a. The job-people ratio is constant, or at least it is not so elastic upward that the increase in total employment results merely in a decrease in unemployment among the existing population. As the reader has probably noticed, this is almost tantamount to assuming a constant volume of unemployment.

Either assumption C.1 or C.1a is absolutely necessary in order to predict population by means of base analysis. However, it may be seen that certain other assumptions are implicit in the reasoning process. These implicit assumptions become obvious when one recalls that we are engaged in a problem of comparative statics, examining the relationship between basic employment and population in two different periods of time. But if population changes, as presumably it does according to base analysis, the reliability of *all* estimates is contingent upon the assumption that population changes do not affect the previous postulates, B.1 - B.5. In particular, we must assume that an increase in urban population by in-migration does not affect either the essential composition characteristics of the population or the attitudes of the residents. Formulating these assumptions more specifically, we have:

C.2. In-migration does not cause shifts in the community marginal propensity to consume, marginal propensity to import, or tastes.

C.3. In-migration does not result in a change in productive technology in either basic or residentiary activities. Such a change could be induced, for example, by the availability of human resources of a qualitatively different nature than before the immigration occurred.

C.4. The labor force-population ratio or the job-people ratio (depending upon whether C.1 or C.1a is relevant) is unchanged as a result of immigration.

The methodological validity of these latter assumptions, C.2-C.4, is very questionable. There is a wealth of sociological data which indicates that immigration and increased degree of urbanization tend to cause changes in the basic attitudes and reaction patterns of the urban inhabitants. Even in the special and not very credible case in which the immigrants are homogeneous with the previous residents in all respects, the mere fact of size increase tends to cause adjustment in attitudes and behavior. That is to say, in order to satisfy the *ceteris paribus* assumptions necessary for the prediction of population change by the economic base method, we are forced to hold constant certain elements that inevitably must change as a consequence of population change.[16] The proponents of base analysis are

---

[16] For a discussion and critique of similar mistakes in other economic models, cf. Buchanan, *op. cit.*

in the uncomfortable position of violating *ceteris paribus* method by using *ceteris paribus* reasoning! Consequently, we conclude that the prediction of population changes is less likely to be empirically successful than the prediction of income and employment.

IV.

DYNAMIC ANALYSIS OF INCOME, EMPLOYMENT AND POPULATION

Having previously discussed the form of the dynamic economic base hypothesis and the nature of the *ceteris paribus* assumptions incident to static analysis, we are now in a position to treat dynamic prediction rather summarily. Since the technique of prediction is unchanged, dynamic analysis merely involves correlation of the rate of change in residentiary employment with the present *level* of basic employment. The regression coefficient is a *dynamic* employment multiplier which is used for the prediction of employment, income, and population by the same *ceteris paribus* method as is utilized in static analysis.

The same elements must be impounded in *ceteris paribus*, but the validity of this action is, *a fortiori*, doubtful. Rather than repeat the detailed discussion of Section III with slight modifications, we will simply illustrate the necessary change in three of the *ceteris paribus* elements. Suppose that there is a dynamic increase in basic activity; accordingly, there is an increase in real community income.

In the first place, the increase in income will lead to a change in the marginal propensity to consume and probably in the marginal propensity to import. That is, the consumption function is *not* linear; there is neither theoretical nor empirical evidence to support the assumption that it is. Indeed, the notable failure of the post-war predictions of national employment provide evidence that the consumption function is non-linear. Hence a change in income leads to a change in the marginal propensity to consume; thus the income generated by the initial change in basic activity will not correspond to the change predicted by the least-squares regression method.

Secondly, by reference to innumerable sociological studies or by mere empiricism, there is a temporal change in taste and behavior patterns. Certainly urbanization and further urbanization contribute to such time changes. Under these circumstances, it is difficult to believe that the labor force-population ratio or the job-people ratio stands docilely unchanged while our predictions are made.

Finally, external economies or external diseconomies are almost certain to emerge during a period of industrial expansion. Either of these leads inevitably to a change in technology (the production function) in both basic and residentiary activities.

Consequently, for these reasons, as for others which it does not seem necessary to describe, we infer that prediction by means of the dynamic form of the economic base hypothesis is even less likely to be successful than prediction from the static model.

CONCLUSION

The predictive ability of the economic base hypothesis has been tested empirically and found to be negligible.[17] While it is not likely, the negative results of these tests could be attributable to change, for all statistical inferences are probability statements. It has been the purpose of this paper to show that there are methodological, as well as empirical, reasons to believe that base analysis predictions of employment, income, and population are not satisfactory. And, it should be noted, this is in addition to the palpable theoretical weakness of the economic base theory.

However, to be only critical is tantamount to substituting

---

[17] Cf. Pfouts, *op. cit.*, and R. W. Pfouts and Erle Curtis, "Limitations of the Economic Base Analysis," in *Social Forces*, Vol. 36 (1958), pp. 303-310.

nothing for *something* in a situation which demands action. Accordingly, in conclusion, at least a brief suggestion for a positive program is desirable. I believe that students of urban problems would be well advised to direct their research to new channels in the hope of finding a technique of analysis that is theoretically more satisfying and empirically more reliable than the economic base hypothesis. One such technique has already been suggested, namely the model of urban income determination developed by Pfouts. This model appears suitable for both explanation and prediction of income and employment; certainly it has the advantage of considering more than one economic variable as relevant in problems concerning urban development.

However, this model is not readily adaptable to explanation or estimates of population growth. As a matter of fact, I am not acquainted with any model that has been notably accurate in population forecasts. Nevertheless, I have elsewhere proposed an approach to the study of urban growth which recognizes the obvious mutual interdependence of several variables.[18] In this system, predictions are obtained by statistical estimation of the parameters of a set of simultaneous equations involving the population growth rate, the growth rate of retail sales, and the growth rate of urban wage payments as the dependent variables. I hope to complete the statistical analysis and report the results of this research within a reasonably short period of time.

In any event, models alternative to the economic base theory are available for researchers in the field of urban development. An overwhelming preponderance of evidence, both theoretical and empirical, indicates the desirability of utilizing these alternative approaches to problems related to urban income, employment, and population growth.

---

[18] "Urbanization and the Economic Base: A Preliminary Investigation of Interdependence," paper delivered at the 1957 meeting of the Southern Economic Association.

As the reader will have gathered by now, the theory that the dissident economists would substitute for the economic base theory centers around the multiplier, the expansions of income due to the flow of money, or of goods and services, through the economy. One of the few attempts to measure the multiplier for an urban area is presented in the paper that follows, which was written by Charles M. Tiebout. In considering Tiebout's numerical results, it should be kept in mind that he was working with a small suburban community, Winnetka, Illinois, and consequently the multiplier is smaller than it would be for a larger community or for a community of the same size that was not a satellite community.

Charles M. Tiebout—The Community Income Multiplier: A Case Study

The Community Income Multiplier: A Case Study*

Since World War II empirical research in the area of regional economic analysis, for the most part, has taken one of two forms: (1) The region is seen in the framework of an input-output matrix. (2) The region, usually the city, is cast in terms of its "economic base." Both uses will become apparent in the discussion that follows.

Missing from the analysis is an explicit attempt to view the community in terms of a Keynesian model. Whatever the limitations of such models at the national level, their contribution to aggregative analysis is important. This is especially true in explaining and predicting short-run income levels.

The purpose of this paper is to construct such a Keynesian model for a community and then to test it in order to see if it is operational. Note, we are only testing the operationality of the model. This is not the same, as will be shown, as showing the stability of the structural relations.

To this purpose, we shall: (1) build a simple model of a community; (2) show how the needed data was collected; and (3) give the results of our study.

A COMMUNITY ECONOMIC MODEL

One of the advantages of the Keynesian system and other systems as well, is that it allows us to say that certain variables are exogenous while other variables are endogenous. Given the structure and parameters of the system, if the exogenous variables are known, the endogenous variables may be determined. The simple, Income = Consumption + Investment, Investment = exogenous, and Consumption = f (Income); is a sufficient example.

If this sort of analytical framework is useful at the national level, there is no reason it cannot be used at the regional level.

* See Acknowledgements

The first step in the construction of such a model will be to see if the community can be divided into exogenous and endogenous sectors.

EXOGENOUS AND ENDOGENOUS SECTORS: GENERAL VIEW

Exogenous activities, as the term is used here, are taken to include all activities whose level is set by forces outside the economic system of the community under consideration. Note, this is not the same as identifying exogenous with things happening outside the community, but outside the economic system of the community. *Endogenous activities* implies those activities whose level is set by forces within the economic system of the community.

Clearly, these assumptions are polar extremes. Few activities are either one or the other, but contain a mixture of exogenous and endogenous elements. The issue is a matter of degree. If some activities are largely exogenous while others are largely endogenous, we shall assume them to be pure polar cases.

EXOGENOUS ACTIVITIES

The Role of Exports

The major exogenous item for a community is its exports. Even here, exports may or may not be exogenous, depending upon whether or not they are "true" exports. Examples will suffice to make this difference clear.

Exports of the City of Peoria, Illinois to the surrounding farmers in the form of retail sales are true exports. Exports of the City of Chicago to suburban communities may not be true exports. The difference comes in that the level of income in the suburbs is itself a function of the level of Chicago income. The level of income of the farmers surrounding Peoria, however, is set by forces exogenous to Peoria, i.e. the national demand for farm products. The same analysis holds true for larger regions. It is simply a question of the intensity of the foreign trade multiplier feedback—how closely communities are economically intertwined.

One point concerning exports should be noted. There is nothing magical in the ratio of export employment measured against total employment.[1] The ratio of exports to total activity is, in large part, a function of the regional boundaries drawn—the larger the boundaries, the lower the ratio. This shows an important point. The failure to recognize other variables as exogenous would leave a substantially closed economy, say, the United States, without exogenous variables.

Other Exogenous Activities

To stop here in listing exogenous activities would be a mistake. Other income creating activities in the community have their level set by forces outside the economic system of the community. Residential housing, business investment, and local government expenditures appear to be determined by forces outside the local economy. In so far as this is true, then they function as exogenous variables. While these may not be too important for small areas, the larger the community, the greater their importance.

LINKED ACTIVITIES

One sector of the local economy which is apt to cause some difficulty are the "linked industries." Linked industries are those whose function it is to provide goods and services directly to the export industries. For example, automobile parts manufacturers in Detroit would be classified as a linked industry. Conceptually, the way to find linked industries is to drop exports to zero, holding consumer demand constant. Those industries which suffer a decline in the level of activity are either export or export linked industries. Linked industries may also be shown through the use of an input-output matrix. The

---

[1] City planners seem to look for *the* ratio. See, Richard Andrews, "Mechanics of the Urban Economic Base," *Land Economics*, XXIX-XXXII (May, 1953-February, 1956).

interindustry demand derived from the export industries shows the linked industries.

ENDOGENOUS ACTIVITIES

The discussion of linked industries provides a transition to the discussion of endogenous activities. Activities whose level is set by forces within the economic system of the community, as noted above, are considered endogenous. Clearly such sectors as retail trade, local services, and so forth are endogenous. This simply recognizes that the income of the local department store is a function of the income of the local factory.

It would be possible to spend a good deal of time on just which industries are endogenous, or only partly so, as opposed to exogenous industries. This would not be useful discussion. In some cases, only actual field work can determine the nature of the industry.

STABILITY OF THE EXOGENOUS—ENDOGENOUS FUNCTION

In predicting short-run community income fluctuations, some knowledge of the stability of the function relating exogenous to endogenous activities is important. This is the community counterpart to the question of the stability of the consumption function. (Discussion of the shape of the function will be taken up after a brief look at earlier studies.)

On a priori grounds, it does seem that the ratio of exogenous to endogenous activities would tend to be more or less stable. This follows in part from the ease of entry into endogenous activities—communities do not suffer shortages of barber shops, shoe stores, and so on. Fortunately, there is a bit of empirical evidence which suggests that this function is stable, at least in the short-run.

Earlier Studies: The Economic Base Approach

Such evidence as is available on the stability of the exogenous-endogenous function arises out of previous community studies using, in the accepted terminology, the approach via "the eco-

346

nomic base." The model developed here may be viewed in a more meaningful manner if we take a brief look at this approach and some of its results.

The economic base approach is largely the work of city planners and has developed with little appreciation of the economic theory involved. Essentially it seeks to divide the sectors of the community into basic versus non-basic activities. Basic activities are the exports of the city, and non-basic activities *may be* defined as everything else. The model developed in this paper could be stated in terms of basic and non-basic activities instead of exogenous and endogenous activities. We have used our terms to avoid the notion that exports are the only basic activity.

Due to the shortage of data, all studies estimating the economic base have used employment figures. This study, in so far as it falls within the economic base approach, is the first to use income flows.

The whole concept of the economic base has been lovingly mulled over in a series of articles by Richard Andrews.[2] It is not worthwhile to try to summarize his statements. Instead, it is useful to turn to the works of others along this line.

Employment Multipliers

An unsung piece of work in the field of regional economics is the study of Hildebrand and Mace.[3] Their work is among the first to somewhat integrate the multiplier analysis of Keynes with regional economics.[4]

The method by which the authors determine the basic versus

---

[2] *Op. cit.*

[3] George Hildebrand and Arthur Mace, "The Employment Multiplier in an Expanding Industrial Market: Los Angeles County, 1940-47," *Review of Economics and Statistics*, XXXII (August, 1950), pp. 241-49.

[4] An earlier attempt at a regional multiplier may be found in, M. C. Daly, "An Approximation to a Geographic Multiplier," *Economic Journal*, L (June-September, 1940), pp. 248-58.

non-basic (export versus localized) employment is through a location quotient. This quotient merely takes a ratio of employment in industry i compared to total employment for all industries in the Los Angeles area, and divide this ratio by a ratio of national employment in i to total national employment.[5] If this ratio is greater than one, this industry exports part of its outputs. If it is less than one, then the product is not exported. Given the division between basic and non-basic employment for the years 1940 through 1947, a regression equation is determined. This equation has a correlation coefficient of .95 indicating the stability of the relationship. The ratio they arrive at is: for every 100 persons employed in basic activities, 125 are employed in non-basic activities; i.e. a ratio of 1 to 1.25. (Under our assumption this will give an employment multiplier of 2.2—as will be shown later.)

The Hildebrand and Mace study has one other interesting result—which will come into the discussion shortly. The linear regression equation has a y axis intercept, but this intercept is not far from the origin. That is to say, with non-basic employment plotted on the y axis, and basic employment or total employment plotted on the x axis; with the x value set equal to zero, the value of the non-basic employment is not large.

The Federal Reserve Bank of Kansas City tried to estimate the employment multiplier for Wichita, Kansas.[6] Their results were not very gratifying. Using approximately the same techniques as Hildebrand and Mace, their correlation appears to be low.[7] In part, this may reflect the extreme changes in the level of activity of the big bomber plant, located in Wichita, during the period under investigation. A closer correlation might have

---

[5] In an effort to trace out the Los Angeles market area, the authors used benchmarks other than the national economy. For present purposes, this is unimportant.

[6] "The Employment Multiplier in Wichita," *Monthly Review, Federal Reserve Bank of Kansas City,* XXXVII (September, 1952), pp. 1-7.

[7] No coefficient of correlation was given, just a scatter diagram.

been observed if incomes arising in each sector, not employment, were the variables investigated. It may well have been that increased *basic activity* merely reflected higher incomes for those already employed in *non-basic* activities without changing —to any marked degree—the number employed in the non-basic sector.

These two studies, to the writer's knowledge, are the only works which have investigated the stability of the exogenous-endogenous function. The study of Hildebrand and Mace seems to agree with out a priori statements. The shortcomings of the Wichita study may be explained on the institutional grounds noted above. Thus, earlier studies seem to support the logic of the exogenous-endogenous division and, further, indicates that such a function seems to be stable—granting the need for further empirical research in this area. Given the above analysis, we may explicitly construct a model of the community under consideration, Winnetka, Illinois.

A COMMUNITY MODEL: WINNETKA

The choice of Winnetka was not random. Winnetka, a small suburban community located some 20 miles north of Chicago's loop, is a relatively simple commuter's community in terms of its economic structure. Neither manufacturing nor apartment buildings are present—and this is convenient.

The activities assumed exogenous for purposes of this model are: all incomes earned outside Winnetka by Winnetkans, income earned within Winnetka as a result of sales to non-residents, and local and federal government expenditures. The major items in each of these categories are: commuters' incomes, retail exports, and educational expenditures.

The activities assumed to be endogenous are retail sales, service sales, and rental income. Clearly, these activities do not fluctuate only in response to income changes—even though this will be the assumption. For example, the opening of the new shopping center just outside of the village by Marshall

Field and Company, will change the level of retail sales in Winnetka.

Once the ratio of income originating in exogenous, to income originating in endogenous activities, is determined; it is assumed to hold for all levels of income. This assumes that Winnetkan's marginal propensity to consume Winnetka products is constant. Further, in the nature of our data which only gives an observation for one year, the average propensity to consume Winnetka products is assumed constant and equal to the marginal.

Thus, the exogenous-endogenous function reduces to a linear function coming out of the origin. Two comments are in order on this assumption: (1) If the use of this sort of study is to predict the effects of, say, new residents moving into the community, this assumption is fairly safe. Unless new residents have a different propensity to consume than established residents, their consumption patterns may well approximate those of older residents. This is to be contrasted with the case of increased community, *per capita income*. Here the marginal propensity to consume may well be falling and additional income may imply a smaller proportion is spent on goods and services.

(2) The study of Hildebrand and Mace indicated that our assumption, that the function comes out of the origin, may not be too far off. Their value of the y axis intercept was quite small —as noted above.

Given the above discussion, the Winnetka model becomes:

(W.1) $Y_w = Y_{ex} Y_{end}$

(W.2) $Y_{ex} =$ exogenous

(W.3) $Y_{end} = a bY_w$, where $a = O$.

Here, Y_w is the total income accruing to Winnetka residents. Y_{ex} is income originating in exogenous activities. Y_{end} is income originating in endogenous activities. The condition that $a = O$, satisfies the assumption that the marginal propensity to consume local goods = the average propensity to consume local products = a constant.

This is the model which will be shown to be operational. Note again, that we are not out to test the stability of the function. That would require repeated studies. This paper is only concerned with finding the value of b in equation W.3. If the value can be found for one year, then there is no reason it may not be determined for other years. It is, in large part, to the method of determining the value of b, that we now turn.

METHOD OF IMPLEMENTATION

The Winnetka model may be empirically implemented if incomes arising out of exogenous and endogenous activities are known. Thus, the first step is to construct a set of income and expenditure accounts which recognize this division.

INCOME AND EXPENDITURE ACCOUNTS

The income and expenditure accounts—as well as their estimated values—as set up for the Winnetka study are shown in Tables 1 and 2. Total income is shown as the sum of exogenous plus endogenous income.

Table 1 notes which activities are assumed to be exogenous or endogenous. It is constructed in such a manner that it will show the major sources in the accounts and, thereby, will give an internal check on the accuracy of the data. Put another way, if total incomes earned inside Winnetka by Winnetkans can be estimated from two independent sources, it will help in judging the accuracy of the results. Thus, income earned inside Winnetka by Winnetkans, item 1.2, should, conceptually, equal the sum of items: 1.5, 1.8, 1.11, and 1.14.

Table 2, the expenditure flows for Winnetka need not be discussed, since—as will be shown—it is not too important for this study.

Table 1 suggests that two of the key magnitudes to be determined are total income and income originating within Winnetka. This information is not available in published or unpublished form. The determination of these magnitudes becomes a major task of this study. It was necessary to make a

TABLE 1

WINNETKA INCOME: BY SOURCES*

	Income Source	Millions of Dollars	Exogenous**	Endogenous
	Total Income Accruing to Residents	65.1	x	x
1.1	Income earned outside Winnetka	60.9	x	
1.2	Income earned inside Winnetka	4.2	x	x
	Income Earned Inside Winnetka: by Sources	4.2	x	x
1.3	Local government (including schools)	0.7	x	
1.4	Federal government (post office)	0.1	x	
	Retail Sector			
1.5	Wages paid resident employees	0.8	x	x
1.6	Originating from sales to Winnetkans	0.6		x
1.7	Originating from sales to non-Winnetkans	0.2	x	
1.8	Income to resident owners	0.6	x	x
1.9	Originating from sales to Winnetkans	0.5		x
1.10	Originating from sales to non-Winnetkans	0.1	x	
1.11	Income from the sales of services	1.9	x	x
1.12	Income from the sales of services to Winnetkans	1.3		x
1.13	Income from the sales of services to non-Winnetkans	0.6	x	
1.14	Rental Income	0.1		x

*Sources of estimates are given in Appendix A.

**Sectors with both exogenous and endogenous checked contain both elements.

TABLE 2

WINNETKA EXPENDITURE FLOWS*

	Expenditures	Millions of Dollars	
	Purchases Outside the Village	22	
2.1	Selected items		10
2.2	Non-covered merchandise		3
2.3	Services		9
	Purchases Inside the Village	18	
2.4	Retail Goods		16
2.5	Services		2
	Taxes	14	
2.6	Federal and State		12
2.7	Local		2
2.8	Savings	11	
		65	

*Source of estimates given in Appendix A.

field survey in order to arrive at an estimate of these values.

FIELD SURVEYS

The estimates presented in Tables 1 and 2 are taken from a variety of sources. Items 1.1 and 1.2 are taken from a field survey of 139 spending units in Winnetka. The other estimates are derived from various sources; the major sources being: a survey of Winnetka businesses, and the 1954 *Census of Business*.

The methods by which items 1.3 through 1.14 were estimated is given in Appendix A. It is not necessary here to dwell on each item. Instead, it is useful to make a few general remarks about the estimates as a whole.

The field survey of Winnetka spending units was our most important source of data. A random sample of spending units was drawn and interviewed by paid interviewers. The income question, asked after other data not needed for this paper was asked of the respondents, was taken from the questionnaire of the Survey of Consumer Finances. The general construction of the questionnaire was "rapport building."

The response rate was not as high as desired. Outright refusals amounted to some 10 percent of these interviewed. Many respondents were not at home, even after several call backs. Of course, this introduces a possibility of error, but in which direction cannot be stated a priori.

THE WINNETKA INCOME MULTIPLIER:
EMPIRICAL RESULTS

The information given in Table 1 along with the assumptions presented above, are sufficient to determine the value of the Winnetka income multiplier.

Before presenting the value of the multiplier, one point, which could cause some confusion, should be cleared up immediately. As a simplified closed economy, the multiplier may be seen as 1/the propensity to save. If imports and taxes are introduced as a function of income, they may also be added. The multiplier is then seen as 1/leakages. Of course, this is the same value as 1/1—the propensity to consume.

Keeping these two methods of reaching the same figure in mind, suppose we turn to the Winnetka income multiplier. Instead of merely looking at it in terms of leakages and/or the propensity to consume, consider it in terms of rounds of spending. But in doing this, remember that our definition of income is "income accruing to residents of Winnetka."

Suppose a new family moves into Winnetka with 10,000 dollars of income. Further, suppose that the new family earns its income in Chicago, i.e. a commuter has moved to town. By definition, income is up 10,000 dollars. In the first round of spending some fraction of this income will be spent within Winnetka on goods and services. Let us call this the average propensity to consume local goods and services (*apcl*), which is assumed equal to the marginal propensity to consume local goods and services—both assumed constant. This spending within the community, however, will not create an equal amount of new income. Indeed, most of the dollars will flow right out of Winnetak to Chicago wholesalers, non-resident employees, and so forth. At the end of the first round only a fraction of the amount originally spent within Winnetka will remain to become income to residents.

Thus, the income accruing to Winnetka residents is a function of local sales. Local sales in turn, are a function of local income. Hence, we are back to equation W.3 where endogenous income is a function of total income. The parameter *b* may now be called the "income creating propensity to spend with Winnetka"—a descriptive, but clumsy term.

Notice that the b in W.3 is not the same as the apcl. It will be a much smaller figure than the *apcl*. This relation can now be shown concretely by giving the estimated value of the Winnetka income multiplier.

Table 1 gives the sum of items 1.5, 1.9, 1.12, and 1.14; as 2.5 million. Thus, equation W.3 takes on the values,

(W.3) $2.5 = b65.1$.

Here 2.5 is the total endogenous income, and 65.1 is the total income accruing to residents. The value of b = .0384 is the income creating propensity to spend in Winnetka. Given this value, the multiplier is easily determined.

$$(\text{W.4}) \quad k = \frac{1}{1 - b} = \frac{1}{1 - .0384} = 1.040 \;.$$

This, of course, means that if a family with 10,000 dollars income moved into the community, total income would rise by 10,400—after due time. This is the usual multiplier analysis.

Looked at in terms of the *apcl* and the income created in the first round, our figures (not shown) indicate that a new family will spend approximately .277 percent of its income locally, i.e. *apcl* = .277. In the first round, then, sales of goods and services will increase by 2,770 dollars. Our data (not shown) shows that for every dollar of sales of goods and services, 13.9 cents of local income is created. Applying this ratio, .139, to 2,770 dollars yields an increase in local income of 384 dollars at the end of the first round. Obviously, this figure could be estimated directly as b x 10,000 dollars or 384 dollars. We have introduced the step to show the flow of dollars.

Some of the 384 dollars of local income created at the end of the first round of spending will be spent again locally and create more endogenous income. This process will continue until income reaches, in the limit, 10,400—a multiplier of 1.040.

PROBABLE ERROR

It would be desirable in looking at the Winnetka income multiplier to give the figure 1.040 with a statistically founded standard error of the estimate. Unfortunately, this is not possible. It is, nevertheless, possible to make some inferences with respect to a probable range of error.

The standard error of the arithemetic mean of the spending units income is 800 dollars. At a 95 percent confidence interval average income for Winnetka falls between 19,200 and 17,600 dollars around the sample mean of 18,400 dollars. This is based on the reported income given by 125 spending units. In those cases where bracket figures were reported, the median figure was assumed. Where incomes over 15,000 were given as a bracket figure, the average of those reporting was used— 26,300 dollars. On this basis, the 95 percent confidence interval for total income accruing to Winnetka residents lies between 67 and 63 million dollars.

The survey also showed that 8 percent of the spending units earned their incomes inside Winnetka. At a 95 percent confidence interval, given the sample size as 125, the range is 15 to 4 percent working in Winnetka.[8] The survey estimate of incomes originating inside Winnetka, on this basis alone, ranges from 7.5 to 2.1 million around the estimated figure of 4.2 million.

The income earned locally, estimated from other sources, suggests that the 4.2 million figure may not be too far off. While some estimates were quite rough, the overall possible error seems small. As a suggestion, income earned inside Winnetka is probably no greater than 5.5 million nor less than, say, 3.3 million. These are merely bounds inferred by the above analysis.

Deducting from these suggested bounds, income earned in exogenous activities, leaves an endogenous range from 3.3 to 2.0.[9] Given the methods by which the income multiplier was calculated, and the assumption that 5.5 to 3.3 represents the true range of locally earned income; the multiplier limits are 1.054 to 1.032 around the estimated 1.040.

---

[8] Estimates from a chart given in, S. S. Wilks, *Elements of Statistical Analysis,* (Princeton: Princeton University Press, 1951), p. 201.

[9] Table 5 shows that the endogenous income amounts to 2.5 million of the total of 4.2 earned locally, i.e. 60 percent. 60 percent of 5.5 and 3.3 yields 3.3 and 2.0 respectively.

While these figures are rough, and do not allow for reporting errors, they do suggest that the statistical error may not be too large.

CONCLUSIONS

The study presented in this paper has set up a model of the local economy. The economic analysis and assumptions behind the model were given. The methods by which it was shown to be operational were set forth. Finally, the results were presented.

Although somewhat similar models have been suggested, this is the first time a Keynesian sort of model has been explicitly set forth for the local community. It is also the first time that income and expenditure flows have been presented for a community. Since this paper is a first on these two counts, there may well be some rough spots which future studies may be able to avoid.

In appraising the value of such a study, two questions may be raised: (1) Did the study really show what it set out to show? (2) Why bother with such a study in the first place? Even if it shows what it set out to show, is it worthwhile?

The answer to the first question is a matter of judgment. The fact that empirical results have been presented does not remove the question from the area of judgment.

Whether or not this sort of work is worthwhile is another question. Two arguments can be presented on the affirmative side: (1) the implications at the policy level; and (2) the implications at the level of pure economic research.

The local economy is beginning to come into its own in terms of economic importance. In part, this reflects the probability that the modern tools of monetary and fiscal policy have solved the problems of unemployment and inflation at the national level. But these tools were not designed to deal with regional or "pocket" problems. If local action, then, is the solution to local problems, it requires an understanding of the local economy.

Above and beyond this consideration, regional analysis is, or should be, of interest to economics in general. While much of the regional analysis presented in this paper is derived from its counterpart in national aggregative theory, there is no reason to assume that the flow of ideas need only be one way. Further research at the regional level may be expected to turn up interesting implications for general economic theory.

APPENDIX A
METHODS OF ESTIMATION: TABLE 1, ITEMS 1.3 - 1.14

Items 1.3 and 1.4 are direct figures gathered for us by the various local government agencies. They represent only payments to Winnetkans.

Item 1.5 is a bit complicated. Total wages paid retail employees amounted to 3.3 million dollars according to the 1954, *Census of Business*. A survey of Winnetka businesses indicated that 75 percent of the employees lived outside of Winnetka. Thus, only 25 percent of the 3.3 million accrued to Winnetkans as employees of retail trade—0.8 million. Further, not all of this income came from sales to Winnetkans, some 25 percent arising out of sales to non-residents. Hence, item 1.6 is 0.6 million and item 1.7 is 0.2 million.

Income to resident owners, item 1.8, is an exceedingly tentative figure. There were 135 merchants in Winnetka. The survey of Winnetka businesses showed that approximately 50 percent of the owners lived in Winnetka. On the basis of talks with the Chamber of Commerce Secretary, average income is estimated at 10,000 dollars per year. (Average income to persons living in Winnetka and working in Winnetka, from the spending unit survey ran around 8,000 dollars per year. Since this included employees as well as owners, the 10,000 estimate seems feasible. There is some reluctance to use this method to estimate income to resident owners, since we would like independent estimates for income originating within Winnetka.) Thus, if resident owners income is assumed to be 10,000 per year with 60 living within the village, item 1.8 has the value 0.6 million. Item 1.9 recognizes that not all this income came from sales to local residents, but only 75 percent of the total—0.5 million. Item 1.10 is merely 1.8 less 1.9.

Income from sales of services, item 1.11, assumes that the sales of services amounted to 2.7 million dollars. This figure simply, and arbitrarily, adds 1.0 million to the figure reported in the Census of Service. The Census of Service, 1954, does not include doctors, personal services, and so forth. Of this 2.7 million, 2.3 was assumed to be income—largely due to the high amount of personal services in Winnetka. Of the 2.3 millions of income from the sales of services, only 80 percent or 1.9 accrued to Winnetka residents—from the survey of Winnetka businesses.

Sales of services to Winnetkans, item 1.12 recognizes that only some 70 percent of the sales of services were to local residents. Item 1.13 is merely item 1.11 less 1.12.

Item 1.14 was estimated by two local realtors.

The estimates for Table 2 were derived as follows:

Item 2.1 represents those items covered by questions in the survey of spending units—largely durables and clothing. Item 2.1 is a residual taken from item 2.1 and 2.4 using an estimate based on national expenditures for durables. Item 2.3 was determined as a residual from item 2.5, and national estimates of the percent of income spent on services.

Item 2.4 was taken from a survey of Winnetka businesses and sales figures from the 1954, *Census of Business*. The same method was used for item 2.5.

2.6 is estimated on the basis of average income taxes with an allowance for state taxes. Item 2.7 is direct from local sources. 2.8 is a residual.

Note that all the items except 2.4 and 2.5 are leakages from the income stream. These estimates, which appear to be accurate, are the only important items for purposes of estimating the income multiplier. Hence, it was not worth too much effort to get accurate estimates of the other values.

III. AN ALTERNATIVE METHODOLOGY: THE INPUT-OUTPUT APPROACH.

A second group of economists have entered the field of urban studies in recent years. This second group has brought input-output or inter-industry methods into urban studies. They have not, up to this time, commented on the economic base theory discussions. In fact, it might be claimed that input-output methods are a methodology and not an economic theory, i.e., assuming they are valid, they are compatible with any valid economic theory and could be used to test some economic theories.

Essentially, the input-output methods define and measure an economic structure of the community. The methods clearly are well suited to comparative statics and can be adapted to dynamic problems.

In the next selection Walter Isard and Robert Kavesh, well-known economists who have specialized in spatial economics, demonstrate the fundamentals of the input-output methods and show how they can be used in urban economic studies.

Walter Isard and Robert Kavesh—Economic Structural Interrelations of Metropolitan Regions

Economic Structural Interrelations of
Metropolitan Regions*

ABSTRACT

A model for analyzing and projecting metropolitan community development by examing basic interindustrial and interregional relationships is presented. Various economic regions specializing in manufacturing and agriculture are integrated by use of an economic matrix. The serious limitations of the model arising from its abstraction of changes in behavioral patterns from the uncertainties of technological change, and from the inedaquacies of the data are examined. As a demonstration, the model is applied to Puerto Rico, a developing area.

The complex internal organization of any given metropolitan region is influenced by the delicately interwoven net of relationships that bind sets of city-regions into a unified whole. It is the purpose of this paper to study certain interurban connections. In setting forth hypotheses concerning spatial flows among metropolitan areas, we shall extend previously developed principals and illustrate with an abstract interdependence model.[2] In the first section a simplified model will be presented. In later sections this model will be qualified in an attempt to make it more realistic.

Assume a large area is meaningfully divided into three regions. Each of the first two has a major focal point at which social and economic activity center, which is a major industrial

---

* See Acknowledgements

[1] This study was done under the auspices of the Social Science Research Center, the University of Puerto Rico, and of the Center for Urban and Regional Studies, the Massachusetts Institute of Technology.

[2] Elsewhere, a model depicting some of the structural interrelationships *within* a given metropolitan region has been sketched (W. Isard, R. A. Kavesh, and R. E. Kuenne, "The Economic Base and Structure of the Urban Metropolitan Region," *American Sociological Review*, XVIII (June, 1953), 317-21). Clearly, however, self-sufficiency is not characteristic of large city-regions.

city. These two are designated Metropolitan Region I and Metropolitan Region II. The third region, specializing in agricultural and extractive pursuits, lacks a single clearcut focus and is designated Region III.

In addition to a delineation of regions, a classification of various economic and social activities is undertaken. Certain goods and services are marketed only in the region in which they are produced, in contrast, others are marketed not only in the region in which they are produced but also in the other regions, though to different degrees. The former are called "local" activities, the latter, "export."

To avoid cumbersome detail, the numerous economic functions are grouped into nine categories. These are recorded for each region in Table 1. The first for each regions represents the characteristic export industry (heavy manufacturing for Metropolitan Region I, light manufacturing for Metropolitan Region II, and agriculture and extractive activity for Region III). The next eight are identical for each region: namely, power and communications; transportation; trade; insurance and rental activities; business and personal services; educational and other basic services; construction; and households.[3] Each of these eight activities is for the moment assumed to be local in nature. None of their output is shipped outside the region in which it is produced. Thus by definition, it is through export activities alone that the simplified economies of the several regions are interrelated.

Classification of outputs represents only one phase of our problem. Another phase concerns input structures; more specifically, the inputs of each of several factors—raw materials, power, transportation, labor, equipment and other services—requires to produce a unit of output. In actuality, much of the output of many industries such as basic steel is absorbed by

---

[3] The output of households roughly corresponds to the value of the services of labor and of capital and land owned by them.

TABLE 1

HYPOTHETICAL INTERMETROPOLITAN TRANSACTIONS TABLE, 19—— CENTS WORTH OF INPUTS PER DOLLAR OF OUTPUT

Industry Purchasing (column key):

Metropolitan Region I: (1) Heavy Manufacturing · (2) Power and Communication · (3) Transportation · (4) Trade · (5) Insurance and Rental · (6) Business and Pers. Serv. · (7) Educational and Other Serv. · (8) Construction · (9) Households

Metropolitan Region II: (10) Light Manufacturing · (11) Power and Communication · (12) Transportation · (13) Trade · (14) Insurance and Rental · (15) Business and Pers. Serv. · (16) Educational and Other Serv. · (17) Construction · (18) Households

Region III: (19) Agriculture and Extraction · (20) Power and Communication · (21) Transportation · (22) Trade · (23) Insurance and Rental · (24) Business and Pers. Serv. · (25) Educational and Other Serv. · (26) Construction · (27) Households

Industry Producing	1	2	3	4	5	6	7	8	9	10	11	12	13	14	15	16	17	18	19	20	21	22	23	24	25	26	27
Metropolitan Region I:																											
1. Heavy manufacturing	33	1	3	1	2	9	1	18	3																		
2. Power and communication	1	58	2	2			2		1																		
3. Transportation	1	4	58	1		4	2	4	3																		
4. Trade	1	1	6	63	1	1	5	9	12																		
5. Insurance and rental activities	2	11	2		53	3	4	2	12																		
6. Business and personal services	1		5	5	1	46	2	3	10																		
7. Educational and other basic services	1	2	2	7	1	4	50																				
8. Construction	4				8		1	40	1																		
9. Households	6	5	4	1	10	14	15	18	20																		
Metropolitan Region II:																											
10. Light manufacturing										33	1	3	1	2	9	1	18	3									
11. Power and communication										1	58	2	2			2		1									
12. Transportation										1	4	58	1		4	2	4	3									
13. Trade										1	1	6	63	1	1	5	9	12									
14. Insurance and rental activities										2	11	2		53	3	4	2	12									
15. Business and personal services										1		5	5	1	46	2	3	10									
16. Educational and other basic services										1	2	2	7	1	4	50											
17. Construction										4				8		1	40	1									
18. Households										6	5	4	1	10	14	15	18	20									
Region III:																											
19. Agriculture and extraction																			28	1	3	1	2	9	1	18	3
20. Power and communication																			1	58	2	2			2		1
21. Transportation																			1	4	58	1		4	2	4	3
22. Trade																			1	1	6	63	1	1	5	9	12
23. Insurance and rental activities																			2	11	2		53	3	4	2	12
24. Business and personal services																			1		5	5	1	46	2	3	10
25. Educational and other basic services																			1	2	2	7	1	4	50		
26. Construction																			4				8		1	40	1
27. Households																			6	5	4	1	10	14	15	18	20

other industries as inputs rather than by households. Therefore, in order to understand the economic base of metropolitan
regions and to anticipate changes within them, it is necessary
to know the intermetropolitan input structures of industries.
This requires a table of intermetropolitan[4] interindustrial relations for a base year period, on the order of Table 1.[5]

---

[4] To avoid awkward phrases we use the term "intermetropolitan" as if Region
III were a metropolitan region.

[5] Most of the coefficients in Table 1 are based upon a consolidation of the
50 x 50 interindustry flow matrix developed by the Bureau of Labor Statistics
(W. D. Evans and M. Hoffenberg, "The Interindustry Relations Study for
1947," *Review of Economics and Statistics*, XXXIV (May, 1952), 97-142).
In reducing the B. L. S. 50 industry classification to our three export and eight
local industrial categories we crudely defined:

1. Heavy manufacturing as the aggregate of iron and steel, plumbing and
heating supplies, fabricated structural metal products, other fabricated metal
products, agricultural, mining and construction machinery, metalworking machinery, other machinery (except electric), motors and generators, radios, other
electrical machinery, motor vehicles, other transportation equipment, professional
and scientific equipment, miscellaneous manufacturing, and scrap and miscellaneous industries.

2. Light manufacturing as the aggregate of food and kindered products,
tobacco manufactures, textile mill products, apparel, furniture and fixtures,
paper and allied products, printing and publishing, chemicals, rubber products,
and leather and leather products.

3. Agriculture and extraction as the aggregate of agriculture and fisheries,
lumber and wood products, products of petroleum and coal, stone, clay, and
glass products, and nonferrous metal.

"Service Activities" were expressed in a less aggregative form in order to
present some detail on the internal structural processes of metropolitan regions
associated with these activities. The category, "Education and Other Basic
Services" consists of the services of medical, educational and non-profit institutions, amusement, and eating and drinking places.

Certain activities are omitted from the analysis because their levels of output
are not structurally related to the interindustrial matrix of coefficients. These
are: inventory change, foreign trade, government, capital formation, and unallocated. Households, generally included with this group, were introduced into
the structural matrix in order to catch the local multiplier effect of new basic
industry upon a community via the additional income generated.

The actual derivation of a coefficient involves the division of the total value
of inputs from a given sector into a second sector by the output of the second
sector. That is, if in 1947 the amount of chemicals used in steel production was
$99 million and the output of steel was $12.3 billion, the input coefficient representing the cents' worth of chemicals per dollar of steel would be 0.8049.

The data are rounded to the nearest whole figure. Inputs of less than one-
half cent per dollar output are not recorded.

In Table 1 any one column records the cents' worth of inputs of output of a given industrial category of a given region where both the given industrial category and the region are specified by the column heading. For example, reading down column 1 furnishes information on the cents' worth of various inputs from the several regions per dollar output of heavy manufacturing in Metropolitan Region I. Thirty-three cents' worth of heavy manufacturing in Metropolitan Region I is fed back as an input into the same activity in the same region for every dollar's worth of its output (such as Pittsburgh steel, which is fed back to Pittsburgh steelworks). Two cents of transporation services of Metropolitan Region I is absorbed per dollar's worth of heavy manufacturing of Metropolitan Region I. In addition to inputs from other service sectors and the household sector of Metropolitan Region I, the heavy manufacturers of Metropolitan Region I require inputs from the light-manufacturing industry of Metropolitan Region II and from agriculture and extractive activities of Region III. These latter, of course, entail interregional flows.

Consider another column, the fifteenth, which refers to "Business and Personal Services" in Metropolitan Region II. Per dollar of its output nine cents' worth of heavy-manufacturing products from Metropolitan Region I is required. None of the other sectors of Region I furnishes inputs, because these other sectors are defined as local and hence export nothing. Since the business and personal services sector of Metropolitan Region II does not consume any agricultural and extractive products, all its other inputs must come from Region II, as is depicted in Table 1.

Aside from their obvious descriptive value, of what significance are the data of Table 1? In general, input structures are not haphazard; rather they reflect to a large extent stable and meaningful relations. If the output of an efficient aluminum works is doubled, it is reasonable to expect that approximately twice as much power, alumina, carbon electrodes, and other inputs will be required. In short, subject to certain serious qualifications to be discussed later, the input of any service or good into a particular activity may be said within certain limits to vary approximately in direct proportion with the output of that particular activity.

To illustrate the usefulness of input structure information, suppose a resource development program calls for an increase of one million dollars in the output of heavy manufacturing in Region I. How will this affect the output of each activity in each region?

In column 1 of Table 1 are listed coefficients which indicate the cents' worth of various inputs required per dollar output of heavy manufacturing. Multiplying these coefficients by one million gives us the direct inputs required to produce one million dollars' worth of heavy manufactures. These are called the first-round input requirements and are listed in column 1 of Table 2.

But to produce the first-round requirement of $330,000 of heavy manufacturing (item 1 in column 1, Table 2) likewise requires a whole series of inputs. These can be obtained by multiplying column 1 of Table 1 by 330,000. And to produce the $20,000 of transportation (item 3, column 1, Table 2) requires inputs which can be obtained by multiplying column 3 of Table 1 by 20,000. Similarly, the inputs required to produce each of the other items listed in column 1 of Table 2 can be derived.

It should be noted that the $340,000 which is listed in the ninth cell of column 1, Table 2, represents an increment of income received by the households in Metropolitan Region I. This increment results in increases in effective demand for a series of products. On the arbitrary assumption that two-thirds of this new income is spent, these increases in effective demand can be obtained by multiplying column 9, Table 1 (which shows how a dollar spent by households is typically distributed among various products), by 226,667.

TABLE 2
INPUT REQUIREMENTS (HYPOTHETICAL), BY ROUND, FOR $1 MILLION OUTPUT OF HEAVY MANUFACTURING IN METROPOLITAN REGION I

Industry Grouping	First-Round Input Requirements (1)	Second-Round Input Requirements (2)	Third-Round Input Requirements (3)	Fourth-Round Input Requirements (4)	Fifth-Round Input Requirements (5)	Sixth-Round Input Requirements (6)	Seventh-Round Input Requirements (7)	Sum of Rounds (8)
Metropolitan Region I:								
1. Heavy manufacturing	$330,000	$118,810	$ 47,793	$ 23,417	$ 13,407	$ 8,559	$ 5,884	$ 550,870
2. Power and communication	10,000	8,670	7,763	4,614	2,858	1,667	994	36,566
3. Transportation	20,000	14,910	7,417	4,508	2,516	1,475	871	51,697
4. Trade	10,000	31,440	15,687	11,021	6,042	3,573	2,060	79,823
5. Insurance and rental activities	10,000	32,940	18,965	12,612	7,135	4,155	2,430	88,237
6. Business and personal services	10,000	11,810	8,159	4,860	2,906	1,664	983	40,382
7. Educational and other basic services	10,000	22,700	10,077	7,463	3,945	2,359	1,344	47,888
8. Construction		2,600	4,759	2,731	1,789	1,031	622	13,532
9. Households	340,000	148,070	110,102	57,920	34,886	19,773	10,805	721,556
Metropolitan Region II:								
10. Light manufacturing	40,000	75,600	60,601	47,894	34,849	25,264	18,115	302,323
11. Power and communication		400	971	1,182	1,190	1,056	856	5,655
12. Transportation		800	1,781	1,821	1,601	1,309	1,016	8,328
13. Trade		800	2,364	3,044	2,858	2,470	1,963	13,499
14. Insurance and rental activities		400	1,696	2,689	2,706	2,490	1,972	11,953
15. Business and personal services		800	1,825	1,954	1,772	1,479	1,159	8,989
16. Educational and other basic services			670	1,387	1,394	1,275	1,033	5,759
17. Construction			104	325	446	455	391	1,721
18. Households		10,000	20,747	20,643	18,918	15,744	12,381	98,433
Region III:								
19. Agriculture and extraction	60,000	60,220	50,741	39,365	29,244	21,250	15,387	276,207
20. Power and communication		600	1,122	1,402	1,386	1,229	1,019	6,758
21. Transportation		1,800	2,430	2,360	2,085	1,673	1,310	11,658
22. Trade		1,200	3,226	3,541	3,481	2,922	2,385	16,755
23. Insurance and rental activities		2,400	4,646	4,962	4,701	3,917	3,156	23,782
24. Business and personal services		600	1,256	1,490	1,463	1,260	1,032	7,101
25. Educational and other basic services			1,600	1,876	1,969	1,260	1,397	8,522
26. Construction			372	664	719	682	581	3,018
27. Households		24,000	27,936	28,508	25,037	20,595	16,189	142,265
Total	$830,000	$571,570	$414,810	$284,253	$211,303	$151,006	$107,335	$2,583,277

Adding together all these inputs (including the new effective demands of households) necessary for the production of the first round of requirements yields the second round of requirements which is recorded in column 2 of Table 2. In turn, the production of the second round of requirements necessitates a third round. This is computed in the same manner as was the second round. Furnishing a third round requires a fourth; a fourth round, a fifth; etc. Each of these rounds is recorded in Table 2. It should be noted that the totals of the rounds converge.[6] After a point it become feasible to stop the round-by-round computation and to extrapolate the remaining requirements. However, we have not carried through any extrapolation; as a refinement it implies a degree of accuracy and stability in the data, which, as we shall see in the following section, does not exist in fact.

Thus, we have developed a round-by-round description of how on impulse acting upone one sector of a metropolitan region is transmitted to every sector in the same region and every other region. To derive the total effect, it is merely necessary to sum the rounds horizontally. The totals are recorded in column 8 of Table 2. These totals, of course, can be compared with other sets of totals which reflect impacts of others types of impulses.[7]

II

The simplified model presented above may now be qualified

---

[6] The convergence of rounds results from the assumption that only two-thirds of the income received by households in any given round is expenditure in the succeeding round and from the omission of the nonstructurally related sectors of inventory change, foreign trade, government, capital formation and unallocated, as noted in n. 5.

[7] E.g., if instead of $1 million of new heavy manufacturing, an equivalent amount of new agricultural and extractive output is required, the impact will be more localized and confined to the region of initial expansion (Region III). For full details and other contrasts see R. Kavesh, *Interdependence and the Metropolitan Region,* (unpublished doctoral dissertation, Harvard University, 1953), chap. iii.

and fashioned somewhat more realistically.[8]

First, re-examine the problem of industrial classification. The categorization of an activity exclusively as local or export is, in many instances, unjustified. There is no provision for those industries, by far the majority, in which both local and export elements are coexistent. As an instance, most educational services are local in character; yet on the university level some are definitely national in that they perform services for persons whose permanent residences are in all parts of the country. As another example, the products of the cotton industry are for the most part export; yet the by-product cottonseed, which is typically considered as part of the cotton industry, is consumed almost entirely locally by various vegetable-oil mills.[9]

In theory a fine enough classification of industries could be adopted so as to circumvent this shortcoming. In practice, however, such an industrial grouping would be infeasible in terms of the tremendous number of computations to be performed. Hence, whatever the classification finally chosen, some imperfection will exist which in turn will restrict the validity of the analysis.

Examination of the classification of Table 1 immediately dis-

---

[8] Because of limitation of space, we shall discuss only briefly the several important points which are raised. Full discussion of these points is contained in W. Leontief et al., *Studies in the Structure of the American Economy, 1919-39* (New York: Oxford University Press, 1953); W. Isard, "Interregional and Regional Input-Output Analysis: a Model of a Space-Economy," *Review of Economics and Statistics,* XXXIII (November, 1951), 318-328; W. Isard, "Regional Commodity Balances and Interregional Commodity Flows," *American Economic Review,* XLIII (May, 1953), 167-80; W. Isard, "Location Theory and Trade Theory; Short-Run Analysis," *Quarterly Journal of Economics,* LXVIII (May, 1954), 305-20; and various papers on input-output analysis at the Conference on Research in Income and Wealth, November, 1952.

[9] The pattern of gasoline sales by metropolitan regions presents another intesting case of overlap. For the most part, gasoline is sold in neighborhood stations for local consumption. To this extent it is a local good. However, many service stations are situated along major intermetropolitan highways and sell gasoline for transient automobiles and trucks. In this sense, the consumption of gasoline takes place on a supraregional basis: thus there is a distortion of the local balance of production and consumption.

closes an oversimplification. In general, the exports of any metropolitan region do not fall into one category alone. Characteristically, exports consist of diverse outputs, ranging from agricultural and mining products to light and heavy manufactures. Therefore, the export sectors should be specified by component parts (subject to computational resources), particularly since disaggregation of any industrial category into finer parts is usually desirable where such is feasible.[10] On the other hand, one should not overlook the definite tendencies for metropolitan regions to assume definite specializations as implied by the oversimplified model.[11]

Second, reconsider the problem of the stability of input coefficients—the assumption that from round to round the cents' worth of any input per unit of a given output remains constant, or the equivalent, namely, that the amount of any input supplied an industry varies proportionally with the output of that industry. As the output of an industrial activity expands, new combinations of the various inputs and new technical processes may become economically feasible. These new combinations and processes would require different percentage increases in the various inputs into the production process; this would be inconsistent with the basic assumption. For many industries such changes might involve minor substitutions of one type of input for another and hence not significantly bias the results. In other industries there may be major substitution effects.[12] However, to the extent that these effects can be anticipated, they can be incorporated into the model by the appropriate alteration of coefficients in the relevant rounds.

---

[10] See M. Holzman, "Problems of Classification and Aggregation," in W. Leontief et al., op cit., chap. ix. However, see qualifications below.

[11] See, e.g., Colin Clark, "The Economic Functions of Cities in Relation to Size," *Econometrica*, XIII (April, 1954), 97-113; and G. M. Kneedler, "Functional Types of Cities," *Public Management*, XXVII (July, 1945), 197-203.

[12] See J. S. Duesenberry, "The Leontief Input-Output System" (Harvard Economic Research Project, Harvard University; Cambridge, Mass., 1950). (Mimeographed.)

Associated with the above shortcoming are the restraints which limited resources impose. For example, as the demand for coal rises, veins of an inferior quality may need to be exploited. This in turn would lead to greater consumption of coal per unit of output of a coal-consuming industry. At the extreme, where there are fixed limits to a given resource (including human labor services), entirely new production techniques and/or locations may be dictated to realize increments of output.[13]

Again, to the extent that resource limitations and associated changes in production techniques can be anticipated, to the same extent the coefficients for the several rounds can be altered to incorporate into the analysis relevant information on these factors.

Still more critical a qualification stems from changes in consumption patterns incident to income changes.[14] Simple cents' worth of inputs per dollar of income, which are listed in columns 9, 18, and 27 of Table 1, are misleading. Consumers'

---

[13] The data presented in the above tables are expressed in dollars and cents. Yet they can be easily translated into physical units. For example, consider the labor problem in a given market area (metropolitan region). It is possible to introduce new rows in Table 1, where each row corresponds to a particular type of labor (skilled, semiskilled, manual, etc.), the nature of the problem determining the particular breakdown of labor to be adopted. Reading down any column would denote the requirements of each type of labor (in terms of man-hours) to produce a unit of output corresponding to the industry and region listed at the head of the column. Thus, in studying the impact of any given resource development program, we can derive the additional requirements of various types of labor by regions; this in turn throws light not only on the short-run feasibility of a given resource development program but also upon the likely longrun interregional labor migrations (given information on reproduction rates and other population characteristics). In similar fashion, a conversion of the table into physical terms could supply insights on the adequacy of actual power facilities, housing, and transportation networks of various metropolitan regions.

[14] The socioeconomic data basic to Engel's law indicate this tendency. For discussion of this law see, among other, Carle C. Zimmerman, *Consumption and Standards of Living* (New York: D. Van Nostrand Co., 1936, and S. J. Paris, "Nonlinear Estimates of the Engel Curves," *Review of Economic Studies*, XX, No. 2 (1952-53), 87-104.

371

studies are required in which households are broken down by occupation, ethnic grouping, family size, rural-urban location, and other key indicators to reveal how expenditure patterns are related to changes in the level of income and associated occupational shifts. Once obtained, relevant information can be injected into the model to yield more valid results.

Another major set of qualifications is linked to the resource limitations already noted. As long as there is vacant housing in a metropolitan region, excess capacity in the transit and power systems, available space for expansion at the center, the calculated growth of the area can be effected. However, where vacant housing does not exist and where streets are congested and transit and power systems overloaded, additional capacity must be constructed to permit expansion in the various industries and service trades. Therefore, in addition to the inputs that are required to produce expanded outputs from existing and new facilities, a whole series of inputs is required to construct the new facilities.

Here, too, appropriate modification of the model can be made. For example, given a knowledge of the capacity of an existing housing complex (together with information on the doubling-up effect and other cultural adaptations to shortage known to be feasible, the nature of the demand for diverse types of housing, and the input structures of the several sectors of the housing industry), it is possible to allow for the phenomenon of housing expansion in our analytic framework. It should be borne in mind, however, that to the extent to which a particular resource in short supply is diverted from producing output on current account to building up plant equipment and other capacity to produce, then to a similar extent the expansion of the noncapacity building activities are curtailed.[15]

---

[15] For a treatment of the problem underlying these assumptions see: A. Grosse and J. S. Duesenberry, *Technological Change and Dynamic Models* (Conference on Research in Income and Wealth, November, 1952). To be published by the Princeton University Press, Princeton, N. J.

In effect, the initial, highly simplified linear model—linear in the sense that each input varies in direct proportion to the output—has been molded into a less hypothetical, nonlinear model which does recognize important nonproportionalities in interactivity relations.

III

In the previous section a number of considerations were introduced to lend more reality and validity to the simplified model of Section I. However, granted that data can be obtained to describe meaningfully nonlinear interrelations, to the extent that such a three-regional construct does not exist, the model remains hypothetical. Let us now re-examine this hypothetical characteristic.

It is a commonplace that social science has not yet reached the stage where it can explicitly consider every variable in a given problem. Those investigators who attempt to obtain results applicable to policy questions concentrate upon what they consider to be the relatively few important variables. Even though this procedure suffers from omission and oversimplification, it still may afford the most useful results for practice. This, too, must be our way of implementing the above model.

Let the problem be an attempt to project various economic magnitudes in the Greater San Juan Metropolitan Region, Puerto Rico. Immediately the problem of demarcating the boundaries of this region arises. Some sociologists might stress the rural-urban dichotomy and draw the line where the influences of the city proper become subordinate to those of the smaller settlements and rural communities. A strict economist might include only those contiguous areas trading extensively with San Juan. An ecologist might attempt to identify the dominant-subdominant-influent-subinfluent relationships of the core and the various sectors of the hinterlands.[16]

For our purposes, no single orientation suffices. If we imagine the Puerto Rican economy in 1975, we anticipate that improvements in transportation and communications will co-ordinate the entire island into one major region, with its focus at San Juan. This is not to deny that there will be major satellite cities such as Ponce and Mayaguez; but the bonds of these cities to the San Juan area will be so strong and connections so closely interwoven that it will be feasible to recognize the whole of Puerto Rico as one "Greater" metropolitan region. Such a metropolitan region would be akin to the Greater New York Metropolitan Region, which includes such major satellite cities as Bridgeport, New Brunswick, and Norwalk.[17]

Consider the external relations of this Greater San Juan Metropolitan Region. Currently the major ties are with the metropolitan construct embracing the Greater New York-Philadelphia-Baltimore urban-industrial region. A lesser economic connection is with the Gulf Coast. Recognizing the difficulties of establishing new ties, and that institutional resistances and entrepreneurial inertia are among several forces tending to keep incremental economic activities within the framework of existing transportation and communication channels, one is inclined to anticipate that these two regions of the United States will continue to dominate the external relations of the Greater San Juan Metropolitan Region.

There is a second ground for such belief. From a transpor-cost standpoint, Greater San Juan is closer to both the Gulf

---

[16] Among others, see Stuart A. Queen and David B. Carpenter, *The American City* (New York: McGraw-Hill Book Co., 1953), and Donald J. Bogue, *The Structure of the Metropolitan Community* (Ann Arbor: University of Michigan Press, 1949).

[17] The 3,423 square miles of the Greater San Juan Metropolitan Region (the entire island) contrast with the 4,853 square miles included in the Census Los Angeles Metropolitan Area and with the 6,914 square miles included in the Greater New York Metropolitan Region as currently defined by the New York Regional Plan Association.

Coast and New York-Philadelphia-Baltimore urban-industrial region than to any other region of the United States. Even though in terms of physical distance the South Atlantic region is nearest Perto Rico, at best the likelihood is small that a sufficient volume of commodity movement will be generated between the South Atlantic region and Puerto Rico to realize the economies of scale, both in handling costs and in use of transport facilities, which are achieved in the Gulf Coast and New York-Philadelphia-Baltimore trade. This signifies that from an economic standpoint the South Atlantic region is considerably more distant.

Moreover, Greater San Juan, as a growing economy, is likely to find that the sale of additional industrial output through displacing existing suppliers in a well-established market is more difficult than through capitalizing on new market demand. Because the Gulf Coast and the New York-Philadelphia-Baltimore areas will be among the most rapidly expanding regions of the United States, it does not appear unreasonable to expect that Puerto Rican businessmen will concentrate for the most part on these two regions for new sales outlets.

Hence, if the problem is to project the interrelations between Greater San Juan and the mainland and if we are given techniques of analysis which can treat only a relatively few variables, the Gulf Coast and New York-Philadelphia-Baltimore, urban-industrial complex may be considered the most significant external regions for our analysis. This lends a partial justification for our three-regional model.

The specific situation of Greater San Juan has still another point of contact with our model. As indicated above, in general no region specializes in one export product alone. Each usually produces a number of goods for export, although frequently with distinct specialization. For our particular problem, the Gulf Coast, with its extensive agricultural production as well as its emphasis on oil-refining, natural gas production, and other extractive industries, may be taken as Region III. This is specially relevant in the case of Puerto Rico, since her chief imports from the Gulf Coast are lumber, petroleum products, rice, wheat, flour, and mixed dairy and poultry feeds.[18]

Furthermore, the presence of heavy manufacturing in the Greater New York-Philadelphia-Baltimore complex, with the corresponding shipments of finished good to Puerto Rico, justifies treating this area as Metropolitan Region I. This judgment is reinforced by the major steel development program currently being undertaken in the Delaware River Valley. The heavy metal output of this area may by 1975 attain proportions comparable in magnitude to the present Pittsburgh complex.[19]

Finally, consider the human and natural endowment of Puerto Rico. Mineral and agricultural resourced are of a very low order.[20] In contrast, population is excessive, which, together with the expectation of continued high reproduction rates, suggest the continuance of relatively depressed wage rates. Those industries migrating to Puerto Rico tend, therefore, to be both labor-oriented and of such a nature that the assembly of required raw materials and shipment of product incur relatively low transport costs. Textiles are a good example. Therefore, Greater San Juan may be taken to conform with our light-manufacturing economy, Metropolitan Region II.

IV

We have now converted a simplified model into one which though still hypothetical is of more practical significance. The initial 9 industry classification takes on added meaning when it is disaggregated into a 50-industry or even a 192-industry classification. This operation is currently feasible. Too, the recent input-output study of Puerto Rico permits a similar meaningful

---

[18] S. E. Eastman and D. Mars, Jr., *Ships and Sugar: An Evaluation of Puerto Rican Offshore Shipping* (Rio Piedras: University of Puerto Rico Press, 1953).

[19] W. Isard and R. Kuenne, "The Impact of Steel upon the Greater New York-Philadelphia Urban-Industrial Region," *Review of Economics and Statistics,* XXXV (November, 1953), 289-301.

disaggregation for Metropolitan Region II (Greater San Juan).

At this point it is appropriate to re-examine the problem of substituting non-linearities for linearities and nonproportionalities for proportionalities, with special reference to the input structures of the existing and potential industrial activities of Puerto Rico.

Consider the input structure of any particular industry of Puerto Rico. Since the area is still relatively underdeveloped, the stability of coefficients can be seriously questioned. It is quite likely that, as plants take root in Puerto Rico, new techniques will be used, especially since incipient industrialization has a significant effect on the attitudes of the working force, which in turn is reflected in labor productivity.[21] As a result, it is necessary to secure for such new plants the set of inputs which prospective management may expect to be required for current operation and/or to approximate from social science research studies for current operation and/or to approximate from social science research studies the effects of the introduction of new industry upon labor productivity and in turn upon the set of inputs and techniques utilized. Obviously, where no adequate information is available, it becomes necessary to rely heavily upon individual judgment. Another set of nonlinearities is introduced when we consider the problem of effective demand in underdeveloped countries such as Puerto Rico. In many cases the justification for erecting a plant in a given industry is lacking because the potential market is inadequate to absorb the output of a plant of a minimum technically feasible size. However, as development proceeds and effective demand mounts, a stage may be reached where demand does become adequate for a particular market-oriented operation, such as

---

[20] H. S. Perloff, *Puerto Rico's Economic Future* (Chicago: University of Chicago Press, 1950), chap. iv.

[21] See, e.g., W. E. Moore, *Industrialization and Labor* (Ithaca: Cornell University Press, 1951).

cement production. When effective demand does reach such a level, it becomes necessary to alter the entire set of technical coefficients relating the input of the given commodity, say, cement, from any given metropolitan region into each industrial activity of every metropolitan region. This and similar alterations can be effected in round-by-round computations if, beforehand, information relating to such potential shifts is available.

As indicated, another extremely important set of non-linearities arises in attempting to anticipate consumption habits. Data are relatively sparse on how industrialization, increasing urbanization, rising incomes, and intensified contact with the mainland will influence cultural patterns of the island. Additionally, more research is required on how such institutional factors such as entrepreneurial vigor and savings schedules will be modified. Obviously in any attempt at a determination of the extensive ramifications of new industrial expansion, reliance upon the considered judgment of social scientists as well as local residents for pertinent information is necessary, the more so when relevant data are sharply limited.

V

To conclude, a model has been developed, which, it is hoped, will have some validity for purposes of projection, either in its present or in a less comprehensive form. The model has many shortcomings. Since they are fully discussed elsewhere, we have treated them here only cursorily. Further, there are serious problems arising from the inadequacies of the data, the unpredictability of changes in behavioral patterns and culture, and the uncertain direction and magnitude of technological development. Nevertheless, we feel that where decisions on metropolitan community development and regional welfare must be made *now* for planning for the future, this procedure is useful, especially as a complement to our existing set of analytical tools and techniques.

In the essay that follows, Abe Gottlieb, a City
Planner with the New York City Department of
Planning, shows how input-output techniques may
provide a useful basis for certain planning problems.
Gottlieb's work is a pioneering attempt and he does
not deal with specific planning problems in as much
detail as planners might wish. But he does deal
with the fundamentals of metropolitan input-output
analysis, and he says enough about specific planning
problems to indicate some of the possible uses of
input-output techniques in planning.

Abe Gottlieb—Planning Elements of an Inter-Industry Analysis: A Metropolitan Area Approach

Planning Elements of an Inter-Industry Analysis—A Metropolitan Approach*

In recent issues of the AIP Journal, a lively discussion has developed around the concept of an area or regional economic frame of reference. Dr. Hans Bluemenfeld introduced the question:[1] Can the application of basic-nonbasic industrial relationships to an urban area be expected to clarify its economic structure and meaning? Can such relationships be used for population forecasting? These he answered in the negative and effectively demolished a number of Mercantilist postulates that are inherent in the basic-nonbasic formulations. In a subsequent article by James Gilles and William Grigsby,[2] some of the mechanics of the "base ratio" were carefully scrutinized and generally found inadequate for area economic analyses.

At a time when the regional organization of American life is assuming transcendent importance, it is somewhat ironic to contemplate the loss of a theory of its economic framework. There is no valid reason why such "poverty" need exist in this field nor can the clearing away of the basic-nonbasic fetters that have shackled economic and planning studies be an excuse for such lack. The continual sharpening of existing tools and techniques of economic analysis and, what is more important, the lively concern with untried hypotheses and theories of spatial economics enhance the possibilities that a formulation of the important elements governing regional growth and development can be attained.

In recent years, the study of input-output relationships among industries (also referred to as inter-industry analyses) has made it possible to examine the fabric of national or regional eco-

* See Acknowledgements

[1] H. Blumenfeld, "Economic Base of the Metropolis," *AIP Journal,* Fall 1955, pp. 114-132.

[2] Gillies and Grigsby, "Classification Errors in Base-Ratio Analysis," *AIP Journal,* Winter 1956, pp. 17-23.

nomies with considerable more detail than heretofore. The central core of this body of analysis is ideally a table showing what every industry supplies to each of its customers and, conversely, what every industry purchases from each of its suppliers. (These relationships are expressed in dollar value of sales and purchases.) Since this double entry accounting system would be extremely cumbersome to present if shown on a single industry basis, they are generally grouped into major industrial and commercial categories embracing all segments of the economy.

This table or "grid" is essentially a graphic device to show the structural dependence of one industry on all the others. It then becomes possible to isolate the significant relationships among all the industrial, commercial and consuming sectors of the economy and to estimate the effect of important changes in the output of a single industry on all the others in the area under study. In many respects, we are witnessing a process akin to an operating mechanism such as the functioning of the human circulatory system. In the latter analogy, a constriction at a single point or a change in the rate of heart pumping action or in the volume of oxygen intake will have a determinable effect on the manner in which the entire system will operate. For the first time, this kind of germ's-eye view (or X-ray picture, if preferable) becomes possible for the economy of a region or area.

THE INPUT-OUTPUT GRID

In order to understand some of the detail of an input-output grid, we have prepared an abbreviated version of one developed by the Bureau of Business and Economic Research of the University of Maryland. The Bureau, in September 1954, examined the inter-industry relationships in the State of Maryland and showed the movement of capital among 32 industrial groups. However, for our purpose, we have condensed the original table into a much smaller version.

The grid has two basic components. The first (Items 1-24) delineates the intermediate sectors of the economy such as sales and purchases of production, fabricating, transportation and service industries, while the second group (Items 25-32) comprises industries and sectors that are generally considered capital formation activities as well as households (i.e., consumers). Included in this "final demand" category are exports, and imports, plus Federal, local government and construction sales and purchases in the area under consideration. In this manner, it is possible to follow the expenditures and inputs of a single industry to and from all intermediate users and then to final consumers.

For example, when read horizontally, the following table shows the sales of each of the 32 industries to every one of the others. Reading in columns down the page, we obtain the purchases of each of the 32 from all the others. Thus, the fabricated metals industry in the State of Maryland sold about 13 million dollars of its output to food processing plants and less than one million dollars to the aircraft industry. Continuing along this row, about 50 million dollars worth of fabricated metal products were shipped to the construction industry, 5.2 millions were exported out of the country and 9.5 sent to the rest of the nation. The total output or sales of this industry amounted to 148.5 million dollars.

Reading down column 4, we see that Maryland's chemical industry purchases 222.3 million dollars worth of goods and services from all others both in the state and elsewhere. About 7 millions is bought from all branches of agriculture and 10 million from the Federal government. The 56 million dollars recorded against "Households" indicates that the chemical industry purchases "labor" i.e., pays wages and salaries in that magnitude.

Some additional observations should be made about the "Final Demand" rows and columns (items 25-32). The sum of all imports and the additions of all exports measure the relative dependence of an area under study upon trade with the rest of the nation and the world. In the case of Maryland, this is

Maryland Inter-Industry Relationships—1947
(In Millions of Dollars)

		Industry Purchases									
		2	4	7	18	21	25	27	28	32	
		Food Prod.	Chemicals	Aircraft	Machinery	Services	Construction	Federal Govt.	Foreign Exp.	Households	Gross Md. Output
1	Agriculture	247.0	6.8	...	...	8.0	1.4	2.4	11.8	153.8	506.5
5	Steel	...	3.3	1.6	13.5	...	13.8	.2	15.7	a	256.9
10	Apparel	2.2	1.3	...	a	1.4	.6	2.1	6.7	156.1	214.1
12	Paper	9.9	10.0	.3	.6	7.7	2.6	.5	1.8	5.7	96.2
17	Fabricated Metals	13.5	2.0	.9	6.5	1.8	47.8	.5	5.2	14.8	148.5
25	Construction	1.3	.4	.1	.8	6.9	.1	21.7	...	2.4	419.5
27	Fed. Govt.	15.0	10.4	.5	16.6	79.2	5.6	22.7	6.3	417.6	711.1.
28	For. Imports	36.6	11.5	a	.4	.9	...	55.6	...	12.1	208.7
32	Households	110.0	56.0	11.9	138.5	697.8	153.9	349.9	11.4	48.9	2,887.5
	Gross Maryland Outlays	616.1	222.3	24.5	235.1	1,285.9	415.6	547.3	530.3	2,779.7	11,293.5

a—Under $50,000

not inconsiderable with a "balance of trade" achieved at approximately one billion dollars. Moreover, the import-export detail by industry makes it possible to evaluate what effect the expansion or contraction of specific out-of-Maryland activities may have on the economy of that State. At the same time, the dollar value of foreign and coastwise imports and exports highlights the significance of the Port of Baltimore to Maryland's business potential.

Our sample grid treats Households (Row and Column 32) as though they are an industry like all the others since they purchase goods and services from most industries and sell their labor, management and technical services in the form of wages and other income payments. Column 32 indicates that Maryland families purchased 153.8 million dollars of food and other agricultural products and expended 156.1 millions for apparel in 1947. Actually, households, (i.e., families or consumers) purchase a very significant part of the output of most industries and "sell" equally important labor services to each industry. The final row (Gross Maryland Outlays) shows the sum of all the purchases of goods and services by each of the 32 industries while the last column (Gross Maryland Output) is an industry summary of total sales. By definition, each of these should equal the "gross area product" and is akin to the concept of the gross national product derived from national income accounts.

INTER-INDUSTRY FLOWS AND THE PLANNING PROCESS

The ability to qualify industrial outputs and purchases and to organize them in such a way that they can be followed from producer to consumer throughout the economy introduces a new element in regional and area economic analysis. Our existing tools of measurement such as employment trends, productivity and output, retail sales, expenditures for public and private construction, etc., are essentially geared to time concepts and, of course, also measure relative magnitudes in urban areas. An input-output analysis makes no claim to replace these essential concepts but rather to supplement them with a working hypothesis concerning the degree of dependence of one industry upon another in a given geographic area and the flow of goods and services into and out of the area.

Obviously, the dollar value of purchases and sales of one industry vis-a-vis any other is not fixed or immutable. Shifts in consumer preferences, new technological processes and demand for new consumer goods and services, changing price and wage levels, degree of product substitution and major locational shifts of raw materials and industrial plants will tend to affect the extent to which industrial activities are related to each other in a "buyer-seller" nexus. These factors, however, are not generally subject to rapid changes so that the industrial relationships expressed in a grid are essentially valid for a considerable period of time.

Perhaps the most important contribution of an input-output analysis to area planning is the element of forecasting that it brings to bear on this process. For if total output of a particular industry is distributed among all other sectors of the economy (including consumers and export) in a known proportion, it should be possible to calculate a "table of coefficients" which would show the effects of a given increase of output of one industry on the purchases of all others. Leaving aside, for the moment, the frame of reference imposed by community size and complexity, the relocation of a new plant into an area or the major expansion of an existing one will undoubtedly have a direct and indirect effect on the number of employees, scale of operation, volume of output and other characteristics of related industries. Under certain circumstances, such additions may stimulate other industrial in-migrations, i.e., a new steel producing plant would be likely to increase the need for fabricating metal factories and other auxiliary producers. It would certainly increase the pace of retail and service activities in that community. There is, indeed, the kind of effect obtained by throwing a pebble into a pond and observing ever-widening circles spread out from the center.

This kind of definable relationship or "chain reaction" spelled out in an input-output grid can be exceedingly useful to the city planner. With this information, he is in a better position to assess the need for additional land and floor space for industry, the nature of this new demand and the stresses that will be placed on the movement of people and goods by an impending change in a community's industrial and commercial structure. Ultimately (in the sense that the initial action or change sets other economic and demographic processes into motion), the size and character of the area's population, labor force, income level and output can be more intelligently gauged by observing the "grid" effect on specific segments of the economy.

Obviously, a sense of proportion and realism is necessary in the evaluation of relationships shown in an input-output analysis. For example, it is much more likely that industrial changes in a smaller community or one dominated by a single industry will have a sharper and more direct effect on the arear's economy than in a more diversified or larger urban unit. Nor will an input-output grid reveal at what precise point and in what manner an increase in sales and purchases of a given industry will result in such physical changes as new plants or establishments, additional transit lines, terminals and arterial highways. While an input-output grid can indicate the industrial possibilities that may bring these into existence, there can be no substitute for an intimate knowledge and understanding of an area's economy for the timing, location and scope of such improvements. Indeed, an inter-industry table is a coldly impersonal instrument, giving no indication of what is economically desirable for a community. As the London *Economist* has aptly expressed it:

"Anatomy is not healing and radar is not navigation. Elaborate input-output of an economic choice by individuals or local governments but they will not insure that this choice will be made at all or made wisely."

A REGIONAL APPLICATION OF INPUT-OUTPUT

A pioneer in input-output analyses, Professor W. W. Leontieff of Harvard published the first national table before World War II. This showed the interactions of 19 industries and was based principally on the U. S. Census of Manufacturers of 1939. However, before long, and in collaboration with the Bureau of Labor Statistics, an expanded analysis of 50 industries was prepared and by 1947, the purchases and sales of as many as 200 industry groups were developed. British economists have followed suit and are now in the process of constructing a 450 industry input-output table reflecting the current flow of goods and services in the British economy.

Most input-output tables thus far constructed have dealth with the entire national economy, i.e., the U. S. was treated as a single geographic unit. However, very important advances have been made recently by the Federal Reserve Bank of St. Louis which applied these techniques to an inter-industry analysis of the St. Louis District, making it possible to examine not only the functional relations among the major segments of St. Louis' industries but to ascertain the implications of that area's trade with the rest of the country. A very similar "localization" of input-output techniques was published in September 1954 by the Bureau of Business and Economic Research of the University of Maryland. (An abbreviated version of their input-output grid was presented in our earlier analysis.) The Maryland study treated that state as an economic area and its internal flow of goods and services as well as imports and exports (primarily through the Port of Baltimore) were traced.

These applications of input-output relationships to smaller geographic areas merit the closest attention of regional scientists and city planners. An imaginative regional framework for an inter-industry study was suggested recently by Professor Walter Isard of the Massachusetts Institute of Technology. Dividing the entire country into four segments (North, East, South and West), Professor Isard constructed a hypothetical table that showed the nature of industrial flows both within each area and from each to every other section.

Even more significant would be a metropolitan area analysis of industry relationships using the central city, the outer counties and the entire metropolitan area as a separate geographic units. The metropolitan organization of America is primarily a consequence of the concentration of economic processes in and around large cities. In 1950, almost 85 million people or a little more than 56 percent of our national population resided in 170 metropolitan areas. About 56 billion dollars were added to the value of manufacturers in metropolitan areas in 1947 and retail sales of approximately 83 billions were transacted in these urban agglomerations. Obviously, an enormous volume of goods and services are produced and consumed within the standard metropolitan areas of the United States. Equally apparent is the fact that a vast exchange of material wealth continuously takes place among the 170 areas and from these centers to the rest of the nation and the world.

Yet, aside from formal descriptive characteristizations of such areas as developed by the U. S. Census Bureau for data gathering purposes, very meagre literature exists on the economic organization of a standard metropolitan area, its internal dynamics and the relationship of its central city and outlying counties with each other and with the rest of the country. The construction of a metropolitan "input-output" table showing trade flows within such an area could provide an exceedingly useful picture of the economic relationships between segments of a metropolis in terms of both specific industrial categories and of the mutual impact of their total economies. With the continuing economic specialization of central cities and suburban areas, their political, social and economic ties become a matter of paramount concern.

If we were to consider the New York-northeastern New Jersey Metropolitan Area for examples of central city-suburban county relationships, we would be most likely to "recognize" the five boroughs of New York City as a single entity and the remaining 12 suburban counties as another grouping. This kind of automatic compartmentilization may run counter to more precise of functional delineations but it will serve as a starting point. Again, we could marshal a considerable array of data for this (and any other Standard Metropolitan Area) to show the economic magnitudes of the entire area in relation to the country and the position of the city or suburban areas in relation to the whole metropolitan area. For example, New York City now has about 58 percent of this area's population against 42 percent for the remaining counties with the trend in favor of the latter sector. Wage and salary employment distributes in the following manner: 3.55 million in New York City and 1.81 million in the rest of the metropolitan area. Relative proportions can easily be derived for a great number of similar economic indices such as retail and wholesale receipts, value of building construction, level of manufacturing activity, etc., but beyond indicating that New York City is a center of concentration for some of the major economic functions that take place in the area, little else can be deduced from these figures. Even if we consider the fact that a complex network of highways, tunnels, bridges, water lines and air routes connect the city with its suburbs, that between 350 and 400 thousand non-New Yorkers commute daily to work and that perhaps 150,000 City residents work elsewhere in the area, we still have only the barest indications of intrametropolitan relationships.

The truth of the matter is that the above "measurements" are gross quantities reflecting a rich and complex interplay of social and economic forces that operate between central city and suburban or outlying sectors. When we direct our attention towards the industrial and commercial structure of the New York-New Jersey Metropolitan Area, we can begin to get insights into the economic role and nature of New York City vis-a-vis the suburbs.

An input-output analysis of this area can be developed by constructing a grid along the same principles used in our previous illustration. When read horizontally, the dollar value of sales among industries are shown and in the vertical columns, purchases are indicated. Here, however, we have divided our table into nine segments so that industrial and commercial flows among New York City, the remainder of the counties in the area and the rest of the nation and the world can be delineated. The framework of such a table is presented and even a cursory examination will indicate that it reveals economic relationships entirely germane to basic metropolitan analyses.

At this point, it may be appropriate to examine the sources and nature of the data that would have to be assembled for the preparation of a metropolitan input-output grid. Two alternatives are possible. The first would be an examination of a sample of bills of lading of railroad freight lines and all other transportation companies that operate between the area and the rest of the country to determine a—nature of product, b—place and industry of origin and c—place and industry of destination. The application of such a sample to the value of total sales by industry in the New York-New Jersey Metropolitan Area could provide most of the requisite information for a metropolitan grid. However, complexities in this method of data collection and, even more important, the fact that a considerable volume of business and other services (not measurable in physical terms) is involved in our consideration make it highly desirable to assemble this data directly from the individual company, which is both a purchaser and seller. Here, however, it would be necessary to select a sample of firms in the metropolitan area (stratified by industry group) and tabulate separately the industrial and geographic origins and destinations of products or services entering and leaving the establishment. The dollar value of output or sales of firms in this area is then distributed by industry and area in accordance with the sample returns.

As shown on page 391 our nine-section grid is organized in such a manner that it shows industrial relationships among the city, the surrounding area and the rest of the U. S. and the world. Reading across the page, Sections 1, 2 and 3 indicate the sales volume of New York City's industries within the City itself, to the remaining 12 counties of the metropolitan area and to the rest of the U. S. and overseas. Sections 4, 5 and 6 show the same destinations for goods and services produced in the rapidly growing economies of the eight nearby Jersey counties and of Nassau, Suffolk, Westchester and Rockland in New York State while 7, 8 and 9 apportion the sales of goods and services that originate out of the metropolitan area to purchasers within its boundaries. The same geographic and industrial relationships can be traced when the grid is read vertically except, of course, purchases rather than sales are recorded.

This kind of table can become physically large and cumbersome and even our example is an abbreviated version of one that would contain 75 items on both its horizontal and vertical axis. Nevertheless, this grid makes it clear that there are varying degrees of economic dependence existing between industries in New York City and the other counties in the area. It is very likely, for example, that the output of the printing and publish-

Model for a Metropolitan Area Input-Output Grid

	New York City (Industry Purchases)						Remainder of Metropolitan Area 12 Counties (Industry Purchases)						Rest of U.S. and World (Industry Purchases)					
	1 Food Products	5 Apparel	10 Chemicals	17 Exports	20 Government	25 Households	1 Food Products	5 Apparel	10 Chemicals	17 Exports	20 Government	25 Households	1 Food Products	5 Apparel	10 Chemicals	17 Exports	20 Government	25 Households
New York City (Industry Sales) 1 Food Products / 5 Apparel / 10 Chemicals / 17 Imports / 20 Government / 25 Households			**1**						**2**						**3**			
Remainder of Metropolitan Area — 12 Counties (Industry Sales) 1 Food Products / 5 Apparel / 10 Chemicals / 17 Imports / 20 Government / 25 Households			**4**						**5**						**6**			
Rest of U.S. and World (Industry Sales) 1 Food Products / 5 Apparel / 10 Chemicals / 17 Imports / 20 Government / 25 Households			**7**						**8**						**9**			

ing industry, located principally in Manhattan below 60 St., finds a wide market in the suburban countries as well as in New York City. On the other hand, apparel contracting and the assembling and fabricating of other semi-finished products may flow in the opposite direction, i.e., from New Jersey, Long Island or Westchester to the five borough. It should be remembered that industry sales (except when made to wholesalers, retailers or directly to consumers) are usually transfers of raw or semi-processed materials and that there may be several such intermediate steps before a product can enter the channels of distribution. An input-ouptut grid makes it possible to examine not only the flow of such products between New York

City and its "suburbs" (which include such important industrial centers as Newark and Jersey City) but to express these relationships in terms of measurable magnitudes, i,e., dollar sales and purchases.

Secondly, the regional or metropolitan planner must be sensitive to the movement of establishments from the central city to the rest of the area or vice versa and should be in a position to evaluate the motives as well as the economic consequences of such moves. He should critically examine any trends towards central city or suburban area specialization and, in a larger frame of reference, should relate the economic structure of the entire metropolitan area to the economy of the nation. The type of grid suggested in this analysis should indicate to the planner or economist to what extent such moves and specializations affect the industrial and commercial patterns of the area and its segments. In a real sense, the beginning of an industrial location theory for the New York-northeastern New Jersey Metropolitan Area can emerge from an input-output analysis and it can be expected that such a theory will point the way to a program designed to encourage optimum industrial and commercial distributions within the area and its constituent parts.

Retail sales in New York City, for example, are made largely to residents of the five boroughs as Section 1 of our metropolitan grid will undoubtedly indicate. However, Sections 2 and 4 present an "interchange" phenomenon, i.e., the former will show the dollar volume of sales in New York City to suburban residents while the latter will contain an estimate of suburban retail sales to New Yorkers. This is likely to be not inconsiderable in terms of both aggregate money transactions and city-suburban boundary crossings. Actually, the "pull" of modern and conveniently located million dollar shopping centers in Westchester, Nassau and Bergen Counties is strongly felt by New Yorkers living in nearby northern Bronx, eastern Queens and elsewhere in the city. On the other hand, suburban shoppers in New York City account for a substantial volume of retail purchases both as commuters to the major downtown stores and as workers in New York City who shop during lunch periods and after work. The implications of this kind of an analysis to Central Business District department stores and to existing and planned shopping centers on both sides of the city's boundaries are immediate and far-reaching.

Carrying our analysis one step further, a grid will enable us to isolate those industries where inter-change of goods or services between city, suburbs and the rest of the country are heaviest so that they can be studied in considerable detail. Apparel, wholesale trade and finance are examples of broad industry groups that sell a substantial volume of their goods or services in markets beyond the city's borders. On the other hand, New York City is practically the only center for such industries as toy manufacturing and other special lines. By examining those activities that are heavily dependent on the economy of the rest of the area and the entire country (both as purchasers as well as sellers), we not only establish the transportation pattern that this relationship calls into being but can evaluate the degree of economic dependence of the city with external markets. The same relationships can, of course, be obtained for the suburban counties with New York and the nation.

The structure of a metropolitan area's economy is complex but it lends itself to an inter-industry analysis. More than that, it is difficult to see how effective regional or area planning for industrial location, and future labor and economic facilities requirements can be accomplished without a framework of relationships that are spelled out in an input-output grid.

In this final essay, the ubiquitous Charles M. Tiebout turns up again, this time in the role of critic of interregional input-output models which, by implication, includes intermetropolitan input-output models. His criticisms are stated moderately and are well-reasoned. No answer to them has been published as yet.

Charles M. Tiebout—Regional and Interregional Input-Output Models: An Appraisal

Regional and Interregional Input-Output Models:
An Appraisal*

It is not too much of an overstatement to say that post World War II regional research has been almost completely dominated by regional applications of input-output models. Whatever the form of the variations, the basic input-output theme is present. While users of, and writers on, input-output techniques are quite honest in admitting its limitations, one does sense a feeling that this approach is clearly preferable to other frameworks in attacking regional problems. Indeed, one leading writer in the field of regional analysis notes that, "too many of (the economists) tools represent transfers of concepts and methods traditionally used by the national-international type of economist."[1] It is not the function of this paper to put forth the case for the Keyensian-style "national-international" framework in regional analysis as an alternative form of or supplement to input-output. This has been done elsewhere.[2] Rather it is the purpose of this paper to review the various operational uses of regional input-output analysis. Such a review will not only give the reader some idea of the current uses of input-output in regional analysis, but will also enable him to more adequately judge its possibilities and limitations.

NATIONAL AND REGIONAL INPUT-OUTPUT MODELS: SUMMARY VIEW

The conceptual framework of an open, static input-output

---

* See Acknowledgements

[1] Walter Isard, "The Value of the Regional Approach to Some Basic Economic Problems," *Regional Income, Studies in Income and Wealth*, XXI, (Princeton: Princeton University Press, 1957), p. 78.

[2] See M. C. Daly, "An Approximation to a Geographic Multiplier," *Economic Journal*, June-September 1940, L, pp. 248-58. George Hildebrand and Arthur Mace, "The Employment Multiplier in an Expanding Industrial Market: Los Angeles County, 1940-47," *Review of Economics and Statistics*, August 1950, XXXII, pp. 241-49. Charles M. Tiebout, "Exports and Regional Economic Growth," *Journal of Political Economy*, April 1956, LXIV, pp. 160-165.

model is given by Leontief.[3] The accounting balance equation is given as:

$$(1.1) \qquad X_i - \sum_{k=1}^{m} x_{ik} = Y_i.$$

Here X_i represents the total output of industry i. x_{ik} gives the amount of i products absorbed by industry k. Given the number of industries $1, 2 \ldots, m$; equation (1.1) yields the amount of i products going to final demand, that is to Y_i.

The structural equations are given by the production coefficients for each industry,

$$(1.2) \qquad x_{ik} = a_{ik}X_k \qquad\qquad i = 1, 2, \cdots, m. \qquad k = 1, 2, \cdots, m.$$

where, a_{ik} is the production coefficient indicating the amount of i needed to produce a unit of k. Substituting (1.2) in (1.1) yields:

$$(1.3) \qquad X_i - \sum_{k=1}^{m} a_{ik}X_k = Y_i.$$

This system of linear equations may be solved for X_i if a bill of final demands, $Y_1, Y_2 \ldots, Y_m$, is known.

Regional models have the effect of adding another dimension to national models, namely the regions are identified. X_i become $_rX_i$, which represents the total output X, of industry i, in *region* r. Here $_{rs}x_{ij}$ represents the flow from industry i in region r to industry j in region s. If the number of regions r, $s = 1, 2 \ldots, n$ is known, the interregional model takes the form,

$$(2.1) \qquad _rX_i - \sum_{s=1}^{n} \sum_{j=1}^{m} _{rs}x_{ij} = {_rY_i} \qquad\qquad j = 1, 2, \cdots, m.$$

In this equation $_rY_i$ represents the final demand for the products of industry i in region r.

Production coefficients are given as,

$$(2.2) \qquad \frac{_{rs}x_{ij}}{_rX_i} = {_{rs}a_{ij}}.$$

[3] Wassily Leontief, "Structural Change," in Wassily Leontief, *et al.*, *Studies in the Structure of the American Economy* (New York: Oxford University Press, 1953), p. 18.

(2.2) states that the inputs from industry i in region r to industry j in region s are some proportion of the total production, X, of good j in region s. (Note that the production coefficient now has a spatial as well as technical component.)

Total output for the whole system of regions and industries may be determined by substituting (2.2) in (2.1) and solving for $_rX_i$. This is the same process as used in equations (1.1), (1.2), and (1.3). Four further considerations apply to regional models.

(1) Not all of the sub-boxes come into interregional trade, i.e., possibly, $_{rs}x_{ik} = 0$. Such industries as barber shops do not enter interregional trade.

(2) Regional models, like their national counterpart, may be open or closed. Here, however, a greater variety of alternatives exist. Models may be open regionally; for example, households within the region may be part of final demand. Models may also be closed regionally, e.g., households are endogenous. Either of these two possibilities may be combined within a national model which, in turn, may be either open or closed.

(3) Another characteristic of regional models is that they may or may not assume technological equivalence. That is to say, the production coefficients, equation (2.2), may be assumed the same throughout the nation or they may vary from region to region.

(4) The final point concerning regional models is that the balance of regional payments equilibrium, may be considered. Not all models are concerned with this condition.

Yet the major item to note is that equations (2.1) and (2.2) merely add a spatial component to national models. This is important. National models have limitations of their own which have been discussed elsewhere.[4] Any limitations placed on national models also apply with equal force to regional models. Above and beyond these limitations, regional models have limitations of their own.

INPUT-OUTPUT MODELS IN REGIONAL ANALYSIS

In general there are three frameworks in which the input-output techniques may be used in regional analysis: (1) *local impact studies*: (2) *regional balance of payments studies*; and (3) *interregional flows studies*. Other uses may exist, but they will not be discussed here.

Regional impact analysis poses the following question: if a new industry were to be located in an area, what would be the *total* change in the level of economic activity?[5] One method of studying the total impact is through the interrelations of an input-output matrix. Using steel as an example, not only is the expansion due to a new steel plant taken into account, but secondary effects are considered as well. Other industries will expand in response to the increase in steel output. Some of these industries will agglomerate at the site of the new steel plant while other inputs will come from outside the region under consideration. Those which do agglomerate, however, are part of the increased activity of the region. Just which industries will agglomerate around the new steel plant can only be decided on the basis of location theory. Of course, the in-

---

[4] Robert Dorfman, "The Nature and Significance of Input-Output," *Review of Economics and Statistics,* May 1954, XXXVI, pp. 121-33. Carl Christ, "A Review of Input-Output Analysis," *Input-Output Analysis: An Appraisal, Studies in Income and Wealth* (Princeton: Princeton University Press 1955), pp. 137-69. Wassily Leontief, "Some Basic Problems of Empirical Input-Output Analysis," *ibid.,* pp. 9-22.

[5] Walter Isard and Robert Kuenne, "The Impact of Steel Upon the Greater New York-Philadelphia Urban-Industrial Region," *Review of Economics and Statistics,* November 1953, XXXV, pp. 289-301. Walter Isard and Vincent Whitney, "Atomic Power and Regional Development," *Bulletin of Atomic Scientists,* April 1952, III, pp. 119-24. Walter Isard, Robert Kavesh, and Robert Kuenne, "The Economic Base and Structure of the Urban Metropolitan Region," *American Sociological Review,* June 1953, XVII, pp. 317-21.

dustries which do agglomerate will have input requirements of their own which may be analyzed.

Regional balance of payments studies have been carried out using input-output techniques.[6] Essentially, these studies seek to show, in a quantified way, the relation of a region to the rest of the nation. Thus, for example, an autonomous change in the level of exports can be shown to have certain implications for the regional economy.

One of the more interesting applications of this technique is the work of Moore and Petersen.[7] Strictly speaking, their study is not merely a balance of payments study, since it contains elements of interregional analysis. The Moore-Petersen model used regional production coefficients wherever possible. Also, they close the model somewhat at the regional level by placing households within the bill of goods. National figures, however, were used to estimate the consumption aspects of the multiplier.

Their techniques in estimating the balance of trade is similar to that used by Isard.[8] Total production of the ith commodity in the region was measured against total consumption in both the industrial and household sectors. The difference, by assumption, represents the net imports or exports.

Interregional flows studies attempt to show, again in a quantifiable manner, the structural relationships between regions. The effects of an autonomous shock may be traced to, and through, the n regions under consideration.

The only empirical study of interregional flows is the splen-

[6] Walter Isard, "Regional Commodity Balances and Interregional Commodity Flows," *American Economic Review, Supplement*, May 1953, XLIII, pp. 167-80. Frederick Moore and James Petersen, "Regional Analysis: An Interindustry Model of Utah," *Review of Economics and Statistics*, November 1955, XXXVII, pp. 368-80.

[7] *Op. cit.*

[8] "Regional Commodity . . . ," *op. cit.*

did work of Leon Moses.[9] Moses uses the conceptual framework discussed earlier for a three region eleven matrix. Solving this system he shows, for the first time, the interregional flows within the United States. The assumptions of the Moses model, as well as greater details concerning the assumptions of the other models, will be discussed next when we turn to the limitations of regional input-output techniques.

LIMITATIONS OF REGIONAL INPUT-OUTPUT MODELS

Two choices are open to us in reviewing these regional uses of input-output techniques. (1) We may take up each type of study in turn; or (2) we may take up the assumptions common to all or most of the studies, and then see what implications this has for the various areas under review. While neither method is completely satisfactory, the second method seems to provide the simplest exposition.

Regional Production Coefficients

The criticism of regional input-output analysis may well start with the whole issue of production coefficients. If their use at the national level is at all dubious, even more is left to be desired at the regional level. This will be apparent in the discussion of three aspects of regional production coefficients: (1) the use of national coefficients at the regional level; (2) the use of "average" coefficients; and (3) the implications of the spatial component of the production coefficient.

As an operational necessity, all models discussed (Moore and Petersen excepted) have used national coefficients as regional coefficients. That is to say the production functions for various industries are assumed to be uniform throughout the whole country. Yet a mere examination of Northern versus Southern fuel bills is enough to indicate that this is not the case. Obviously, other instances could be cited.

---

[9] "Interregional Input-Output Analysis," *American Economic Review*, December 1955, XLV, pp. 803-32.

Production coefficients may be divided into three categories: (1) average coefficients as determined, operationally, by the last Census of Manufacturers; (2) best coefficients which represent the coefficients of the newest of "planning board" plants in the industry; and (3) the worst coefficients which represent the coefficients of the marginal firm. Which coefficient one chooses depends on the assumed capacity of the industry and which firms bear the impact of demand changes. If demand is assumed to increase, best coefficients will apply if the industry was previously operating at capacity; added production will have to come from new plants. If the industry is assumed to be operating at less than capacity, worst coefficients could be the ones to use. Further, with a decrease in demand, worst coefficients will come into play, it is the older marginal firm which is assumed to drop out.

In regional studies, it is important to use the correct coefficients. In regional impact studies, for example, best coefficients are the ones to use. They are not used, however, since they are not known or can only be ascertained at great expense. In balance of payments and in interregional flows studies the difference between best, worst, and average coefficients is important. The best coefficients are associated with newer or more efficient producers in the industry. Insofar as newer producers are more efficient than older firms, a drop in demand may have relatively less effect on the producers using best coefficients. For example, a general drop in textile demand may have a greater impact on older New England mills than mills in the South. If average production coefficients are used throughout, this result will not be shown in the model.

Regional coefficients have still another serious pitfall. They not only specify the amount of needed inputs per unit of output, but they also specify the regional source. This source is assumed to be a constant proportion of total output, i.e., trading patterns are assumed to be stable. Thus if region h imports half of its coal from region i and the other half from region j, this trade pattern is assumed to told for *all* levels of output.

Now there is no logical reason to expect trading patterns to exhibit stability. Moses, aware of this, attempts to investigate the stability of trade coefficients for the years 1947, 1948, and 1949, using I.C.C. Waybill data.[10] His hesitant conclusion is that "the author believes that they have exhibited sufficient stability to warrant their being subjected to further statistical evaluation on various levels of regional and commodity aggregation."[11] Such instability as exists in the data given by Moses *may* be correlated with changes in the demand of the sectors under consideration.[12] The real test which trade coefficients must withstand is stability in the face of changes in final demand.

The case for stable trading coefficients presents an interesting paradox. Moses is quite explicit that "the assumption of stable trade coefficients is the crucial issue."[13] Even for short run predictions, "the following conditions should be satisfied: (1) There is excess capacity in the transport network between every pair of regions. (2) Each industry in each region has excess capacity. (3) There is a pool of unemployed labor for each region."[14] These assumptions are necessary to justify constant costs. Constant costs, Moses feels, are needed to justify stable trade patterns.

---

[10] *Op. cit.*

[11] *Op. cit.*, p. 826.

[12] Variations in total shipments were checked against the stability of Moses' coefficients. A weighted average of percent changes in trade coefficient (Moses, *op. cit.*, p. 824) with percent changes in I.C.C. Waybill total tonnage for each of the five commodity classes. [Interstate Commerce Commission, *Statistics of Railways in the United States*: 1947, (Washington: U. S. Government Printing Office, 1949), p. 43., and the 1948 and 1949 editions.] Changes in the coefficients and total tonnage were compared for the years 1947-48 and 1948-49. The coefficient of linear correlation $= .61$. With a standard error of 1.83, this correlation could happen by chance about 6.5 percent of the time. This is certainly not conclusive evidence, but may offer a clue for further testing.

[13] *Op. cit.*, p. 810.

[14] *Op. cit.*, p. 812. While it will not alter the analysis that follows, Moses may be too severe on this point. If various costs *rise proportionately*, trade patterns will be stable.

Now let us go back to the operational method, not that of Moses, by which net imports or exports were determined. In every case it is the residual of regional production measured against regional consumption. Thus it is possible for a region to produce a commodity and import it as well. Indeed, the Moses model contains many examples of such flows. But this is inconsistent, (except when spatial extent is considered—a region may import a commodity at one border and export it at another border.) Surely, if local producers have excess capacity and constant costs, the region cannot import that commodity. Local producers with lower transport costs would be able to undersell their more distant rivals. Neither the assumption of stable trade patterns nor that of importing and exporting the same commodity makes too much sense alone—granting a case can be made for the latter. Together they clash head on.

Product Mix

The residuals method of determining export balances is not only inconsistent with the assumptions of constant cost and excess capacity, but may not measure imports and exports in any meaningful manner at all. This is an extreme statement; but if excess capacity is assumed for industry i in region r, any imports of i into r may be more indicative of product mix, the degree of heterogeneity of products in an industrial classification, than of an import balance.[15]

---

[15] This point arises an interesting side issue. The usual method by which the various industrial sectors are classified runs in terms of similarity of input requirements. A supplementary method might be to divide the economy into m regions. For any arbitrary interindustry classification, the degree of product mix is indicated to the extent to which regions import and export the same commodity. That classification which minimizes this simultaneous flow may be considered as containing the least product mix. In some cases the export-import flows are not known. Where excess capacity exists and is known, product mix may be assumed if the same commodity is imported—for reasons shown above. Again, to the extent that this inconsistency is minimized, the product mix is cut. The possibility of simultaneous imports and exports due to spatial extent, as discussed above, is no problem since all we are seeking is a minimum, not a zero.

The failure to handle product mix adequately can lead to some ridiculous results in determining net exports and imports. In Wisconsin, for example, where the internal production of automobiles just about equals consumption, there would be no imports of automobiles. This implies, in turn, that Wisconsin residents drive only the local product, a Nash or Hudson. Clearly, this is one area where no further research is needed to see if Wisconsinites do actually drive only Nash or Hudson cars. Yet, even a more homogeneous product such as premium beer, a major Wisconsin industry, does not eliminate imports. Budweiser from St. Louis and Hamms from St. Paul are large sellers in Wisconsin.

A moments reflection will point out the general inadequacy of the residuals method of determining the volume of net exports and imports. In an economy where the degree of product variation is as high and the ratio of transport cost to total cost is as low, one might expect a great deal of product mix, even in a 200 industry matrix. The residuals assumption is not a very safe one. Those concerned with export-import balances might do well to try alternative approaches.[16]

The final problem relating to product mix and net exports and imports, comes in determining the regional multipliers. Moore and Petersen have calculated a series of Utah income multipliers which average, unweighted, 3.9. This multiplier should not be confused with the simple Keynesian consumption function multiplier. The Utah multiplier has two components: (1) the intraregional interindustry effect of a change in export demand, and (2) the consumption function multiplier effect via changes in household income. Moore and Petersen note that, "the multiplier would be different if gross figures (for exports and imports) had been used."[17] In other words, in

---

[16]Alternative approaches includes: the use of I.C.C. Waybill data, unfortunately given in weights and not values; direct estimates from local producers; and money flow analysis from the Federal Reserve Districts.

[17] Op. cit., p. 379.

measuring the imports and exports as net figures instead of gross flows, the sum of the import leakages is understated. It is impossible with the data now available to estimate this error, but it may be substantial.

Regional Impact Studies and Agglomeration

The final operational criticism of input-output models deals with agglomeration considerations in regional impact studies. It is argued that once the new industry is established in a region other industries will agglomerate and they, in turn, will need inputs. Just which industries will agglomerate, it is argued, can be decided on the basis of location theory. This is a bit too glib. It may be stated, without trepidation, that, except for a limited number of industries, location theory is not in a condition to predict at the fine margin this analysis requires.[18] At best, all that can be hoped for is a rough approximation. Moreover, any failure in predicting the production coefficients of the impact industry (steel in our example) will appear in the estimates of agglomeration. Beyond this, nonappearance of an industry which is expected to agglomerate will break the link in the interindustry effect. Alternatively, any industry which unexpectedly does agglomerate will have just the opposite effect.[19]

---

[18] The shortcomings in location predictions stems in part from the shortcomings in location theory. At present, partial equilibrium analysis in location theory can do no more than specify the conditions for spatial equilibrium. This is not the same as specifying the conditions and showing the operational well behaved conditions of calculus by which this optimum may be reached. This is what Losch had in mind when he stated, quite bluntly, that, "there is no scientific solution for the location of the individual firm, but only the practical one: the test of trial and error." [August Losch, *The Economics of Location,* trans. William Woglom with the assistance of Wolfgang Stolper (New Haven: Yale University Press, 1954), p. 29.]

[19] Isard, Kavesh and Kuenne feel that input-output techniques are useful in describing the "economic base" of a city. (Isard, Kavesh, and Kuenne, *op. cit.*) Again using the steel plant as an example, they construct a city around such a plant. Evidently they assume a closed regional model, since "households which receive wages, salaries, and other income in the first round . . . also behave like industries" (*op. cit.,* p. 318). Adding to the total of steel and

Regional and Interregional Input-Output Models: Summary

The past discussion of input-output techniques as applied to regional analysis has been wholly one-sided. Only the operational limitations have been discussed.[20] No doubt this may appear to be unfair, but for purposes of review and appraisal it was necessary. The empirical results of regional input-output analysis present us with a set of data which is supposed to describe reality. Unfortunately, there is no alternative set of data with which the researchers' results may be compared. Hence, it is vital to scrutinize the method and assumptions to see such limitations as may exist.

It seems fair to state that most operational regional studies have produced only the most tentative results. Basically this stems from two considerations: (1) the lack of adequate data; and (2) the necessity to make certain operational assumptions which depart, in varying degrees, from what we usually assume about reality. It may be that further work in this area will eliminate some of the problems raised above. Note, however, that this is not necessarily a call for further research in this area. Such a call for further research, certainly a common expression in academic circles, implies a judgment as to the allocation of scarce research resources. Before such a call is put forth in behalf of regional input-output research, alternative methods of attacking similar issues should be appraised.

---

agglomerating export industries the total of local activities, "yields a meaningful net of economic interrelations which may be viewed as the economic base of the city" (*op. cit.*, p. 319).

Ordinarily the "economic base" of a community consists of the exogenous activities which, when known, determine the level of income for the whole city. Yet this use of the term implies that the economic base of the city is all of the economic activities within the community. If this is what the authors mean, it isn't very useful. If it is not what they mean, they would do well to create an exogenous and endogenous sector. Under their current usage, all activity is export or export linked which, in terms of the usual base analysis, means the whole economy is exogenous.

[20] At the *conceptual* level input-output analysis offers many advantages. The reader is reminded that this is not the issue at hand.

EDITOR'S EPILOGUE

The papers offered in this book present at least three different and conflicting viewpoints. How can a decision be made as to the correct viewpoint?

At the present time, no conclusive decision is possible; one can argue and refine a theoretical viewpoint, but a theory can be proved finally only on the basis of its empirical validity. Consequently, it is only from experience and from empirical studies that we can discriminate between what is sound and what is unsound in the various theoretical constructions. Indeed it is possible that none of the viewpoints advanced are correct and a new theory based on empirical evidence and quite different from existing theories will emerge.

It should be made clear exactly what type of empirical work is needed. The need is not for more economic base studies or more measurement of community multipliers or more estimates of input-output coefficients. The need is for empirical evidence that tests the validity of each theory. If one makes an economic base study of a community, that does nothing in and of itself to prove or disprove the base theory. It is only if a study shows that inferences drawn from the base theory are consistent with observed data that a validation of the theory is made. In other words, the ultimate test of a theory is its power to predict actual events. Furthermore, the theory must be capable of repeated prediction so we may find that its predictive success is not fortuitous. These thoughts apply to any theory, of course, and not merely to the economic base theory.

Careful theoretical reasoning is always welcome, but there is an urgent need for empirical studies of the predictive powers of the various approaches to the problems of urban economic development.

ACKNOWLEDGEMENTS

We are indebted to the following persons or organizations for the permission to include their articles in this book:

URBAN LAND INSTITUTE

Richard B. Andrews, "Mechanics of the Urban Economic Base: Historical Development of the Base Concept," *Land Economics,* May, 1953, pp. 161-167;
"The Problem of Terminology,"
Land Economics, Aug., 1953, pp. 263-268;
"A Classification of Base Types,"
Land Economics, Nov., 1953, pp. 343-349;
"The Problem of Base Measurement,"
Land Economics, Feb., 1954, pp. 52-60;
"General Problems of Base Identification,"
Land Economics, May, 1954, pp. 164-172;
"Special Problems of Base Identification,"
Land Economics, Aug., 1954, pp. 260-269;
"The Problem of Base Area Delimitation,"
Land Economics, Nov., 1954, pp. 309-319;
"The Concept of Base Ratios,"
Land Economics, Feb., 1955, pp. 47-53;
"The Base Concept and the Planning Process,"
Land Economics, Feb., 1956, pp. 69-84.
Charles M. Tiebout, "The Urban Economic Base Reconsidered," *Land Economics,* Feb., 1956, pp. 95-99.

AMERICAN INSTITUTE OF PLANNERS

James Gillies and William Grigsby, "Classification Errors in the Base-Ratio Analysis," *Journal of the American Institute of Planners,* Vol. 22, Winter, 1956, pp. 17-23.
Hans Blumenfeld, "The Economic Base of the Metropolis," *Journal of the American Institute of Planners,* Vol. 21, Fall, 1955, pp. 114-132.
Ralph W. Pfouts, "An Empirical Testing of the Economic Base Theory," *Journal of the American Institute of Planners,* Vol. 23, Spring, 1957, pp. 64-69, (A corrected version).
Abe Gottlieb, "Planning Elements of An Inter-Industry Analysis: A Metropolitan Area Approach," *Journal of the American Institute of Planners,* Vol. 22, Fall, 1956, pp. 230-236.

ROLAND PRESS COMPANY

Arthur M. Weiner and Homer Hoyt, "Economic Base Analysis," Chapter 18, *Principles of Real Estate*, 3rd ed., Roland Press Co., New York, 1954, pp. 343-358.

CLARK UNIVERSITY

John W. Alexander, "The Basic-Nonbasic Concept of Economic Functions," *Land Economics*, Feb., 1956, pp. 69-84.

SOUTHERN ECONOMIC ASSOCIATION AND THE UNIVERSITY OF NORTH CAROLINA

Charles M. Tiebout, "Interregional Input-Output Models: An Appraisal," *Southern Economic Journal*, Vol. 24, Oct., 1957, pp. 140-147.

Ralph W. Pfouts and Erle T. Curtis, "Limitations of the Economic Base Analysis," *Social Forces*, Vol. 36, No. 4, May, 1958, pp. 303-310.

THE AMERICAN JOURNAL OF SOCIOLOGY

Walter Isard and Robert Kaveth, "Economic Structural Interrelationships of Metropolitan Regions," *The American Journal of Sociology*, Vol. LX, No. 2, Sept., 1954, pp. 152-162.

CHARLES E. FERGUSON, "Statics, Dynamics and Economic Base."

CHARLES M. TIEBOUT, "Community Income Multiplier: A Case Study." This paper was presented before the Joint Conference of the Econometric Society and The American Statistical Association, Detroit, September, 1956.